Anti-Theory in Ethics
and
Moral Conservatism

SUNY Series in Ethical Theory

Robert B. Louden, Editor

Anti-Theory in Ethics
and
Moral Conservatism

Edited by
STANLEY G. CLARKE
EVAN SIMPSON

State University of New York Press

Published by
State University of New York Press, Albany

For information, address State University of New York
Press, State University Plaza, Albany, N.Y., 12246

Library of Congress Cataloging-in-Publication Data

Anti-theory in ethics and moral conservatism / edited by Stanley G.
   Clarke and Evan Simpson.
      p.   cm.
   Includes index.
   ISBN 0-88706-912-6.   ISBN 0-88706-913-4 (pbk.)
   1. Ethics.   2. Practice (Philosophy)   I. Clarke, Stanley G.,
   1939–   . II. Simpson, Evan, 1940–   .
   BJ1031.A57 1989
   171'.7—dc19   88-12660
                                                                  CIP

10   9   8   7   6   5   4   3   2   1

For Ted Marshall and Thel Simpson

Contents

Acknowledgments

Annette Baier, "Doing Without Moral Theory?" previously appeared in her *Postures of the Mind: Essays on Mind and Morals* (London: Methuen, 1985), 228–245.

Cheryl N. Noble, "Normative Ethical Theories," is reprinted from *The Monist*, 62 (1979), 496–509.

Bernard Williams, "The Scientific and the Ethical," is taken from *Objectivity and Cultural Divergence*, ed. S.C. Brown, Copyright © 1984 The Royal Institute of Philosophy is reprinted with the permission of Cambridge University Press.

John McDowell, "Virtue and Reason," was initially published in *The Monist*, 62 (1979), 331–350.

Martha Craven Nussbaum, " 'Finely Aware and Richly Responsible': Literature and the Moral Imagination," originally appeared in *The Journal of Philosophy*, 82 (1985), 516–529; however, in this volume, a revised version is reprinted from *Literature and the Question of Philosophy*, ed. Anthony J. Cascardi (Baltimore: The Johns Hopkins Press, 1987), 169–191.

Stuart Hampshire, "Morality and Conflict," is Chapter 7 of *Morality and Conflict* (Oxford: Basil Blackwell, 1983, and Cambridge, Massachusetts: Harvard University Press, 1983).

Richard Rorty, "Solidarity or Objectivity?", is from *Post-Analytic Philosophy*, eds. John Rajchman and Cornell West (New York: Columbia University Press, 1985), 3–19.

Michael Oakeshott, "The Tower of Babel," is the third essay in his *Rationalism in Politics and Other Essays* (London: Methuen, 1962), 59–79.

Roger Scruton, "Freedom and Custom," *Of Liberty*, A. Phillips Griffiths, ed., Copyright 1983 The Royal Institute of Philosophy is reprinted with the permission of Cambridge University Press.

Charles Taylor, "The Diversity of Goods," *Utilitarianism and Beyond,* Amartya Sen and Bernard Williams, eds., Copyright © 1982 *Maison des Sciences de l'Homme* and Cambridge University Press is reprinted with permission.

Alasdair MacIntyre, "Epistemological Crises, Dramatic Narrative and the Philosophy of Science," originally appeared in *The Monist,* 60 (1977), 453–472.

Sabina Lovibond, "Realism and Imagination in Ethics," consists (with some omissions) of sections 41–44, 46, and 48 of her book so-titled (Oxford: Basil Blackwell, 1983, and Minneapolis: The University of Minnesota Press, 1983).

The editors are grateful to the Dean of Arts of Carleton University and the McMaster University Arts Research Board for their support of this volume.

Introduction:
The Primacy of Moral Practice

Most modern moral philosophers have pursued a common project in ethics: the search for a theory providing universal principles that apply systematically to particular cases. Only recently has this approach to ethics become enlivened by a challenge to normative theory and by the articulation of forms of moral conservatism that regard local moral practices as primary in moral reasoning. The writings collected here represent important aspects of this contemporary development in philosophy. In contrast to the preoccupation with justifying principles, which has dominated moral inquiry for most of this century, these dozen recent pieces define a nascent movement from abstract principle to common practice.

The contributors to the volume are Annette Baier, Cheryl Noble, Bernard Williams, John McDowell, Martha Nussbaum, Stuart Hampshire, Richard Rorty, Michael Oakeshott, Roger Scruton, Charles Taylor, Alasdair MacIntyre, and Sabina Lovibond. To them could be added Cora Diamond, Iris Murdoch, Michael Sandel, Jeffrey Stout, Michael Walzer, and a number of others who might be surprised to find themselves associated in this way. The philosophers whose work appears here are at least as inclined to explore the differences among their views as to celebrate the likenesses.

The differences are many. Some critics of normative ethical theory are moral realists, believing in the possibility of moral knowledge; others are non-cognitivists whose doubts about ethical theory rest upon the opposite conviction. Anti-theorists appeal to very different philosophical traditions, including those associated with Plato, Aristotle, Hume, and Wittgenstein. Some are political conservatives, others are liberals or socialists. Given these disagreements, they could hardly be expected to promulgate a common doctrine in any deliberate way.

Although original thinkers never share identical doctrines, even the most opposed may belong to currents of intellectual opinion that reinforce rather than interfere with one another. It is the pattern of reinforcement which determines the purpose of bringing these writings together. They define an intellectual tendency to which we want to call attention and, in large measure, to support. In order to do so, we try, in this introductory essay, to isolate and outline the principal features of the movement, describe the most significant issues it addresses, and indicate how the outstanding problems may be pursued in directions which are sometimes as surprising as they are important.

When expressions of this point of view are set beside those of theory builders, agreements become obvious and impressive. Among these many theorists one might include Richard Brandt, David Gauthier, Alan Gewirth, R. M. Hare, Thomas Nagel, and (with qualifications outlined in a concluding bibliographical essay) John Rawls and Ronald Dworkin. They seek to articulate normative theories that can guide our behavior by systematizing and extending our moral judgments. These judgments, they think, can be thought of as consequences of applying abstract principles to moral problems in an almost computational way, giving a procedure for deducing the morally correct answer in any given circumstances. The dominant conception of morality that they represent requires it to identify universally binding principles which govern all rational persons. It is rejection of this form of rationalism that unites our authors. As Baier puts it, they no longer find it "hard to see how there could be any such thing as moral philosophy if there were no such thing as 'the moral law' " (36).[1]

This is not to doubt the underlying rationale for seeking principles—it is surely the desire to have good reasons for what one does—but only to question the identification of these reasons. To reject the adequacy of abstract principles in dealing with practical problems is not necessarily to be skeptical about the rationality of moral thinking as long as other conceptions of moral reasoning are available. In this respect the anti-theoretical viewpoint differs markedly from that of ethical skeptics, like J.L. Mackie, who also reject rationalism but understand morality in the same way as theorists. These negative theorists see the task of ethics as providing a general test for ethical beliefs and maintain that there can be no such test.

The existence of alternative conceptions of morality is evident in the two groups of writings that follow. The first, headed *Antitheory in Ethics*, presents various types of argument against normative theory and associated forms of skepticism. The expression "antitheory" emphasizes opposition to any assertion (whether in the form of a substantive moral principle or a meta-ethical theory about the nature of moral claims) that morality is rational only insofar as it can be formulated in, or grounded on, a system of universal principles. It also denies that the intellectual virtues of theorizing, such as universality, explicitness, consistency, and completeness, are essential to the moral life. The second group of writings, *Moral Conservatism*, offers positive accounts of morality in terms of custom and practice. These accounts are basically descriptive, characterizing moral rationality in terms of critical reflection which seeks no support from first principles of any kind.

On the positive side, anti-theorists describe two features of morality that stand in direct contrast to the dominant rationalist paradigm. One is a contextualism that favors specific rationales for particular cases and stresses the ways in which the practices of a community determine the meaning and appropriateness of deliberation and appraisal. Morality does not require an application of universally valid principles on this view. The other distinctive feature is a pluralism that derives from the way in which practices determine conceptions of goods. Different communities will have differing conceptions, and even within one community there will be a plurality of practices each containing its own ends. The lesson is that goods are diverse rather than reducible to any single good, such as utility. Such pluralism about goods does not entail, although it may permit, the acceptance of principles that are neutral between competing conceptions of the good.

The authors grouped here represent a spectrum of opinion about the relationship of rational principles to social practices. Some hold that while there are universal principles that are "superior" to the contingencies of particular ways of life, morality also includes custom and convention that cannot be justified by the considered moral judgments of the participants. Still others allow principles to have only a heuristic role as summaries of patterns of approved behavior. Nowhere on this spectrum, however, is there a place for the homogenizing tendencies of rationalistic moral philosophy. Each point is dominated by the notion that morality is primarily concerned with the particular virtues of particular cultures—traits of behavior whose sanction has nothing to do with universal principles.

CONCEPTIONS OF MORAL THEORY

Anti-theorists reject normative theory as unnecessary, undesirable, or impossible, and usually for all three reasons. The success of their criticisms depends upon how much is built into the notion of theory. The literature generates confusion around this essential point. Anti-theorists often write as if their arguments were refutations of any set of claims that could sensibly be said to constitute a "theory," but the use of this word varies widely.

Two primary conceptions of normative theory have been exhibited by moral philosophers. One is a rationalistic formulation. It requires a set of normative principles governing all rational beings and providing a dependable procedure for reaching definite moral judgments and decisions. This understanding of theory is exemplified by both contractualist and utilitarian accounts. For contractualists right action is determined by a system of rules that any rational person would accept. Utilitarians regard moral assessments as measures of the capacity of actions or institutions to promote the single rationally acceptable value—individual welfare. The status of principles in this form of theory is foundational; they justify moral judgments but are not themselves justified by such judgments.

The second conception of moral theory is expressed by the method of reflective equilibrium. This method construes ethical inquiry as a matter of reflective testing of ethical beliefs against others or against particular ethical conceptions presented for exploration. Such an inquiry begins with people who have already had a moral education, usually informal, and arrives at a harmonious adjustment or readjustment of their considered moral judgments, moral principles, and other relevant beliefs. This is a broadly coherentist conception of theory. The theories it accommodates are not necessarily applicable to all rational beings, and they need not require a unique set of normative principles providing a decision procedure. In addition, the structure of a coherentist theory is not foundationalist. Though principles are given a systematizing and justifying role with respect to considered judgments, the latter also function to justify the principles.

Anti-theorists who eschew moral theory in any sense may nevertheless give positive accounts of moral rationality in terms of reflective practices. For Baier, these practices constitute dialectical processes of turning natural responses, sentiments and self-interest upon themselves, resulting in adjustments and corrections. For Williams, they aim at using everything available to critical reflection for purposes of making our ethical lives transparent and free of self-deceptions. Although these accounts display commitment to certain values, they do not promote any sort of normative theory from which we could infer what we ought to do. They ascribe no inherent logic to reflective practices, in contrast to the requirement of coherence in the method of reflective equilibrium.

BASIC ARGUMENTS AGAINST RATIONALIST MORAL THEORY

Any theory is formulated to fulfill certain goals, such as the explanation of behavior or the justification of judgments. Insofar as a purported theory includes requirements that prevent it from fulfilling its goals, it fails to satisfy one of the minimal requirements of being a theory. The purpose of normative theory is to systematize the justification of moral actions and practices. Three main arguments tend to show that rationalist moral theory cannot reach this goal because of its own theoretical requirements. In this sense, rationalist attempts to provide a normative theory do not even succeed in producing a theory.

1. *The semantic features required of principles by rationalist theory are incompatible with those of norms as they function in moral practices.* One requirement of a principle is to function as the premise in a deductive argument. The concept of a norm includes no such requirement. Norms are socially constructed standards which function to guide behavior and may be given a verbal formulation. Principles must be definite in meaning in order for them to play their role in the deduction of particular moral judgments. However the norms of actual moral practices must be vague in order to have any practical content. Baier makes the point effectively in noting that even simple moral injunctions—"Don't Kill," Don't steal," "Don't break promises"—have to be imbedded in a network of cultural assumptions if they are not to be purely abstract requirements that do not yet prohibit anything. Their determinate interpretation is provided by the rules of background institutions and ways of life that cannot be formally and precisely spelled out. This conventional background cannot be definitely fixed, but it is essential for the practical understanding of moral imperatives.

The vast semantic distance between principles and norms creates a serious problem for normative theory. This distance shows that principles are useless in their purported justifying role. A possible reply is that our appeal to vague norms that are interpreted through a web of cultural relations is only a convenience—a practical device which in normal cases leads to correct conclusions more easily than deriving answers from a theory. This implies that the theory itself is capable of generating correct answers independently of appeal to such norms. Unfortunately for the rationalist's claim, this is what the semantic distance between abstract principles and concrete ways of life prevents. Without the interpretive background of cultural institutions and moral practices, principles yield no definite conclusions.

A different possible reply is to acknowledge the semantic distance and maintain that normative principles are not intended to justify particular moral judgments directly. They justify the norms of moral practices and thereby provide indirect justification for the moral judgments conforming to these norms. However the background institutions and cultural expectations that help determine the content of norms will not be justified by appeal to those principles. Furthermore, attempts to justify the background interpretations by appeal to other explicit principles will be faced with the need to justify still other background interpretations for these principles, and so on. The gap remains between what might be justified by appeal to explicit principles and what is added to norms by the interpretive context.

Thus, a rationalist formulation of normative principles cannot function to fully justify the norms of moral practice.

One final possible reply is to deny the semantic difference between principles and norms by requiring that norms also be precise. In this case, though, norms as well as principles will be too abstract to be capable of appropriate application. They will be unable to serve in deductive justifications because they will lack reference to the background institutions and ways of life which give them determinate meaning. Again rationalist normative theory will be incapable of fulfilling its goals.

The features that rationalists require of principles make them unable to justify moral practices, and in this sense rationalist normative theory is not theoretically possible. Conventional practices arise from social history and agreement; no other sanction is needed and none is imaginable.

2. *A rationalist theory requires an account of the virtues which is incompatible with the features they actually exhibit.* Any adequate account of moral practices will include reference to the dispositions to promote socially approved actions which are called "virtues." Any rationalist theory must describe virtues as dispositions to behavior whose desirability is explained by their relationship to independently justified moral principles. Our moral approval of honesty and justice, for example, derives from the moral quality of principles like the categorical imperative.

This account is plausible as long as our attention is restricted to those virtues that appear to be linked to accepted principles. It would be natural for rationalists to adopt a strategy of diminishing virtues which lack connection with universal principles—humility, for example—as being culturally specific and morally irrelevant. In a variation on the distinction between morality and convention, one could follow Hare in identifying morality with the use of "right" and "ought," which can be parsed in principled and universalistic terms. On this view, virtues that resist such expression belong to cultural anthropology rather than to ethics.

This strategy is effectively criticized by pointing out that the rationalist account of moral language implies a narrow and distorted account of moral practices. To suppose that "kind," "generous," and "gentle" are not terms of moral assessment is to express a severely truncated view of morality. In many actual moralities, including our own, such terms of character assessment are central in expressions of moral concern. The virtues make the same kind of unavoidable claim on us that "oughts" seem to, and they cannot reasonably be dismissed simply because they fail to fit a preconceived notion of morality. The fact that judgments about "ought" and "right" are less prominent in common use than words for virtues should alert us to the excessive attention given them in recent moral philosophy.

If gentleness, humility, generosity, and kindness are considered moral qualities, then the rationalist account faces a more serious objection than that of narrowness and incompleteness. These and many other virtues not only function independently of principles but are also inhospitable to them. Consider gentleness. In her *Postures of the Mind* Baier notes it can be a response to others in conditions of risk. The other may exploit one's friendly response, but part of the friendly response is non-suspiciousness—a setting aside of a possible return of evil for good. It may turn out that the object of one's gentleness was not worthy of it in virtue of responding cruelly or manipulatively, but no principles govern when to approach another person gently. To be intelligently gentle includes attending to the details of a situation and being sensitive to the other's response so that one can retreat from gentleness in the face of threat. Being gentle is thus like taking an experimental stance in order to see what it will bring rather than applying principles known in advance.

If these reflections are correct, there are virtuous practices which are not explicable in terms of principles. Since it can be sufficient in the case of these practices to justify action by appealing to the virtues they express, this form of non-principled moral judgment cannot be accommodated by rationalist requirements. Rationalist normative theory cannot, therefore, provide a complete theory of the

virtues without arbitrarily ruling out certain types of virtues as irrelevant to rational moral behavior and deliberation. This is arbitrary
not only because gentleness and other traits of character are morally
praiseworthy in spite of lacking connection with principles, but also
because such virtues are norms which are essentially imprecise and
unorderable in any hierarchy. To exclude such norms by fiat is simply
to take the requirements of rationalism for granted. They are, in fact,
far from obvious.

3. *Moral practices exhibit irremovable conflicts and dilemmas that
confound rationalist theories.* Conflicts arise because practices include
norms that can generate mutually incompatible obligations. The struggle between Creon and Antigone, the dilemma of Isabel in *Measure
for Measure*, and the impossible choice of Sartre's freedom fighter all
exemplify the opposition of norms inevitable within any way of life.
This is a natural consequence of the above problems. Once we begin
to think of morality in terms of practices and virtues rather than
calculation and deduction from principles, there is no reason to expect
reconcilability to be built into moral thought in advance.

Examples alone cannot prove conflicts are inherent possibilities
within moral practices. They do not refute the rationalist's claim that
moral dilemmas, problems, conflicts, are always resolvable in principle. The contradictions that arise within natural languages can be
obviated through a variety of rational stratagems; why should the
contradictions arising in moral reasoning not be as well?

One answer is phenomenological. If we examine our experience
of moral matters, it confounds rationalist confidence in the resolution
of conflict. We justifiably feel regret for having failed to fulfill one
of two conflicting obligations, but we should not have this feeling
if we could reflectively identify one obligation as the right one to
act on. However this evidence is inconclusive. The rationalist does
not have to maintain that we can know our overriding obligation in
every 'case, only that it is possible in principle to do so. When
limitations of time, information, or intelligence preclude certainty,
we can feel justifiable regret that we may have done the wrong
thing.

The rationalist's position is weakened by lack of proof, but the
anti-theorist's case is no better, unless it can provide support for the
claim that there are unresolvable moral conflicts. Hampshire provides
this support in linking conflict to the conventional status of much
of morality. Although he supposes some moral principles, such as
the requirements of justice and benevolence, may be partially grounded
in universal features of human nature, he sees clearly there are also

norms that derive from historically specific ways of understanding human needs and capacities. These norms are conventional embellishments of natural humanity. We are carriers of genes, but we order our sexuality through customs of family and kinship which have no ideal rational arrangement. Together with other conventional arrangements sexual norms are always liable to make incompatible demands.

The plurality of conventions in any society means the possibility of conflict that cannot be resolved by rational principles. Attending to responsibilities towards one's family may conflict with a perceived obligation to fulfill one's special talents—to be a great artist, for example. It is not obvious that justice and utility can find satisfactory purchase here, and they may in other cases be dislodged by local norms. It is far from clear that there is a correct resolution to every conflict between loyalty to a friend and the obligations of justice.

The rationalist may respond by distinguishing the requirements of convention from those of morality. Because customs are not shaped by reason, agreement among them and between them and rational principles of justice and utility is not to be expected. However this is an arbitrary move. In actual societies there are norms understood by their adherents to be moral, yet they have no significant basis in abstract moral principles. Sexual norms invoke moral sanctions even in a society that recognizes their significance has more to do with discarded religious doctrines than justice or utility. They remain important ways of organizing behavior and are firmly attached to attitudes of respect and guilt which it would be strange to say are not moral ones.

Although it is often difficult to distinguish ultimate from apparent moral conflicts, descriptions of the conventional side of morality give reason to believe that moralities will include unresolvable moral conflicts. Here again rationalist normative theory makes demands of moralities which cannot be satisfied.

To sum up, these arguments show that rationalist normative theory is incompatible with familiar moral practices in three important ways. The theory misrepresents the semantic features of moral norms, cannot accommodate properties of virtues having no connection with rational principles, and wrongly denies existence of unresolvable moral conflicts.

These conclusions in no way entail irrationalism. It is perfectly possible to describe the rationality of moral practices without reference to universal principles. A holistic or coherentist description of these practices better accommodates the facts.

THE HOLISTIC ALTERNATIVE TO THEORY

The origins of many doubts about moral theory can be located outside of ethics in a critique of the positivistic conception of scientific theory. Anti-theoretically oriented discussions often refer to "Quineian" views. Willard Quine repudiates the reductionist "dogma of empiricism," which holds that any meaningful statement can be translated into a statement about immediate experience or at least that there is a unique range of possible sensory events whose occurrence would tend to confirm any given statement. He denies that statements can admit of confirmation at all when taken in isolation from others, proposing that "our statements about the external world face the tribunal of sense experience not individually but as a corporate body." The totality of beliefs is a synthetic fabric that impinges on experience only along the edges, where a conflict with experience requires revision elsewhere in the whole cloth. There is enormous latitude about where these adjustments are made, however, and no statement is immune to revision. What is crucial is the integrity of the whole.

An important moral application of Quine's holism is the use of "reflective equilibrium" in justification. As outlined above, this method seeks to produce coherence among a person's moral beliefs, judgments, principles, knowledge of general laws of nature and human nature. No part of such a coherent group has privileged status. An item in one set can be rejected in favor of items in one or more of the others. Considered judgments can overturn principles and vice versa. Moral beliefs do not require specification in terms of necessary or sufficient conditions, nor need they follow deductively from facts and principles. There is no demand that all morality be subsumed under a single theory. Coherence is not a hierarchical relationship.

Nothing in the method of reflective equilibrium makes it susceptible to the problems for rationalistic moral theory discussed above. The vagueness of norms is entirely consistent with a holistic understanding of moral justification; the possibility of unresolvable moral conflicts within a particular society is consistent with the fact that coherent beliefs and principles of different practices may be incompatible. And the existence of non-principled virtues, with their essential imprecision and lack of hierarchy, is perfectly coincident with the holistic approach, which does not require every practice to be rationalized through principles.

In one respect, the holistic approach is a theoretical one. It spells out a conception of morality and ethical life in a systematic way and allows principles to have a justificatory role. However it does not provide the clearly defined procedures for moral thinking sought by rationalistic moral theory, and it does not promise a universal test for the correctness of basic ethical beliefs and principles. In spite of these qualifications, it has been easy for anti-theorists to reject reflective equilibrium. This is because reflective equilibrium has usually been combined with contractualism and its universalist goals. It is important to realize that these goals are separable from reflective equilibrium and not even appropriately combined with it.

In the primary formulations of reflective equilibrium, it occurs within the judgments, principles, and theories of a single person. Broadening the base of this equilibrium to include other peoples' convictions can present problems. To gain coherence within this broader set of considered judgments, the judgments must be comparable: a set of judgments that includes claims formulated in different, incommensurable moral languages would not generate the required coherence. This situation will arise if we include the considered judgments of all people in our set, since we then have judgments formulated in terms of sin, taboo, tribal solidarity, formal obligation, and so on. Though it may not be possible to tell in advance which moral languages will be so incomparable as to prevent coherence, it is obvious there will be sufficient incommensurability between such different languages as those of taboo and formalistic ethics to prevent any reflective equilibrium from including all people from all times.

Reflective equilibrium can thus apply only to judgments that might be expressed in a single moral practice. For that reason it does not generate norms that are universal in the sense of binding everyone. Norms justified by appeal to one set of considered judgments have not been justified for those whose considered judgments have been excluded. Although we may use the norms justified for us in determining how we should treat those outside of our moral practices, reflective equilibrium does not show that our norms should be binding on them. In this sense the justifications provided by reflective equilibrium are ethnocentric. It does not follow that universally binding norms are an inappropriate goal, but only that the goal cannot be achieved through theory or reflection alone. The threats of universal destruction posed by the present world may be conducive to the formulation of such norms; but it is evident that norms of this sort are responses to practical problems and they would be globally, not timelessly, universal.

The reason many anti-theorists reject coherentist forms of moral inquiry is acceptance of the paradigm of scientific knowledge from which Quine's holism begins. According to this paradigm, the successes of scientific theory are best explained by a correspondence between theory and reality. In addition, it can, in principle, explain how its perceptual base operates. From such a perspective, the possibility of moral knowledge must seem largely illusory because neither moral realities nor moral perceptions appear to have any explanatory role.

No such restrictions are present in a form of holism most strongly associated with Wittgenstein. While similar to Quine's in many respects, Wittgenstein's holism lacks a scientistic bias. In Quine's conception there is no place in inquiry for distinctively philosophical theory; philosophy, insofar as it is worth doing, is continuous with science. For Wittgenstein, too, philosophy does not have its own theories; it describes our practices. Since these practices are literary, religious, mathematical, and political as well as scientific, philosophy should be continuous with all human discussion. Since skepticism about knowledge is a philosophical theory, it has no part in these descriptions. The restriction of knowledge to science is unwarranted, and a form of moral realism may be perfectly tenable. Lovibond constructs such an account on the basis of an "expressivist theory of language" in which thought is necessarily embodied in language and language is necessarily embedded in social life.

THE "EPISTEMOLOGIES" OF ANTI-THEORY

The writings of Quine and Wittgenstein raise difficult questions about the role of theory in philosophy. However, even for advocates of reflective equilibrium it is desirable that there be some account of the nature and origin of the moral judgments and decisions from which efforts to reach equilibrium begin. The same demand is freely accepted by those who allow no appeal to normative theory at all.

In their accounts of moral judgment, the issue of realism divides anti-theorists. Baier, Noble, and Williams reject any access to interesting moral knowledge. Lovibond and McDowell see these judgments as expressing perceptions of moral realities and suspect that doubts about moral knowledge rest upon a lingering idealization of science. This difference masks an important similarity, however. These writers frequently allude to moral judgments as expressions of emotion, and emotion has a central role in the psychology of the moral life. The accounts they give of emotion also differ, but they converge on a denial of any sharp contrast between emotion and reason. With this convergence they provide a framework from which to reject cognitivist theories of emotion that give only an artificial account of the rationality of emotions. This rejection is another blow against rationalist theories that tend to invoke a moral psychology emphasizing the Kantian dichotomy between reason and emotion.

Cognitivist theories retain this dichotomy in viewing emotions as composites of judgment and feeling. By requiring judgments as necessary conditions for emotions, they identify a place for good reasons, but there is persuasive evidence against such an analysis. The cognitivist account is seriously compromised by the many instances in which emotional experiences conflict blatantly with what one knows. Fear of flying in an aircraft, which is obviously safe by any reasonable standard, is a clear example. While such cases can be accommodated by skillfully formulated rationalizations, the plausibility of cognitivist accounts is further undermined by salient psychological facts. Animals and infants exhibit fear in spite of our unwillingness to ascribe value judgments to them, and even if cognitivist claims are confined to adult emotions there is abundant evidence that affective responses can occur without prior cognitive discriminations.

In place of the cognitivist account anti-theorists make two competing suggestions about the cognitive status to be ascribed to nonjudgmental aspects of emotion. Baier follows Hume's account, which insists that an emotion "contains not any representative quality that renders it a copy of any other existence or modification." Taylor, Nussbaum, and others suggest that emotion is best viewed as affective perception in which feelings appear to have something like a representational role.

As different as these positions appear to be, they coincide in blunting the contrast between reason and emotion. Baier's Humean account of moral sentiments construes them as being long-sighted and concerned with system, harmony, and consistency. Such corrected emotions gain this validity as a result of social interaction. The capacity to adopt the moral point of view, to be a moral judge, depends upon one's willingness to be corrected, to make the mutual adjustments needed for a stable point of view to be possible; and the virtues found in moral judges are abilities to function in company with others. In short, inherent features of emotion satisfy typical demands of reason and respond to recognized canons of social reasonableness.

A view of emotion as affective perception is conveyed in Nussbaum's approval of Henry James's suggestion that "moral knowledge is not simply intellectual grasp of particular facts; it is perception. It is seeing a complex concrete reality in a highly lucid and richly responsive way: it is taking in what is there, with imagination and feeling" (116). Elsewhere she characterizes this view of "passional reaction . . . as itself a piece of practical recognition or perception."

To speak of perception here is to imply that emotions are capable of attending to particular events, convey information in a manner comparable to sense perception, and can be formulated in judgments just as perceptions can. Expressing the similarity more analytically, it might be said that, just as sense perception involves sensations and perceptual judgments, emotion involves feelings and evaluative judgments. Sensations are information units and, although not sufficiently complex to have propositional form, are essential to the meaning and justifiability of perceptual judgments. Feelings, likewise, are units of information that are insufficiently complex to constitute judgments, but essential to the meaningfulness and corrigibility of claims about affective qualities such as danger, misfortune, wrongdoing, etc.

The notion of affective perception undermines the contrast between reason and emotion by tying the meaning of affective judgments to feelings. When the role of public discourse in the correction and interpretation of these judgments is also considered, this rationality without cognitivism exhibits significant analogies to the Humean view. The similarity is evident in Baier's remark that the correction of sentiments "can be done by sentiment and custom, and is not the prerogative of a purely intellectual 'reason' " (40). The account implies that arguments about affective judgments may be difficult to resolve if the disputants bring very different sets of norms and expectations to the discussion. Disagreements may be impossible to resolve if one of the parties has not had the feelings necessary for full understanding of the judgments in question. Yet there is also ample room for the objectivity of moral judgments within this account.

The psychology of the emotions enables us to refer to general facts of human nature in support of certain universals of emotional judgment. The object of fear is danger, the object of indignation is injustice. The universality of these claims provides one ground for gaining objective agreement. The claims, however, are abstract. The identification of danger and injustice is strongly dependent upon social criteria which develop from the experience of particular groups, and the appropriateness of fear and indignation is tied to particular sets of norms and expectations. Because such normative criteria exist, however, concrete emotional and specifically moral judgments can be publicly assessed. Objectivity in this second sense is attainable because agreements can be reached that are not merely coincidences of emotional responses and opinion but expressions of prevailing normative standards of judgment.

These senses of objectivity are far from the notion of a reality external to the life in which we are immersed. The tempting idea that scientific theories work because they faithfully represent a world existing independently of human beings seems easily distinguished from the subject-related descriptions that define the world of the human sciences. It is not clear, though, that the idea of such an underlying order represents a metaphysically interesting reality rather than a regulative ideal of physics. If arguments for or against moral theory are to be convincing, they must hinge on more than the issue of realism.

MORALITY WITHOUT THEORY

If there are no theoretical criteria adequate for assessing social practices, if moral principles can only express an internal point of view, then loyalties, conventions, traditions, and historical explanations cannot be eliminated from moral thought about the conduct of life and individual character. In this case, the common values of a group are the appropriate criteria of critical inquiry within it. Moral and political norms, therefore, cannot be rejected on the basis of critical standards contrary to the fundamental values and practices of the community. An appropriate expression for this cluster of "communitarian" ideas is "moral conservatism," although some care is required in order to differentiate a number of its forms. Contrary to a usage adopted by Lovibond, the notion need not be restricted to the attitude that approves strict conformity to the ethical life of the community, or to the unreflective way of life which Williams describes as "hypertraditional."

This view does include an attack on philosophical liberalism, but only as part of a criticism of philosophical politics in general; i.e., of attempts to give philosophical grounds for political convictions and programs. The attack on moral theory is thus politically neutral. While the traditions and institutions of modern democracies cannot be justified by rational principles independent of these social forms, we may be unable to describe better social arrangements.

The central features of the moral conservatism that gives priority to a community's practices parallel criticisms of theorism made above. 1. This conservatism is pluralistic and particularistic, recognizing the diversity of human groups and the internality and flexibility of the rules which define the practices in each. 2. It is pessimistic about utopian ideas of progress but sanguine about the apparent permanence of conflict among ways of life and conceptions of well-being. 3. It opposes the adequacy of any abstract or computational morality of principles. To elaborate:

1. The contributions to the latter half of this volume convey a strongly particularist view of practical requirements and possibilities. In gaining our personal identities largely in relationship to existing institutions, we are governed by the specific local attachments and specific historical associations that permeate our desires and purposes and define a multitude of moral obligations. The diversity of customs and conventions, and rivalries among them, also entail a plurality of values, a diversity of goods.

2. If this diversity is a primary feature of human nature then conflict is an inevitable part of life in any form of social arrangements. Moral claims collide and cannot be resolved by any accepted method of reasoning or through any imaginable sort of social revolution. Perfectionist and utopian aspirations do not figure in modern moral conservatism.

3. Nor do rationalist aspirations. Oakeshott depicts the rationalist as standing for freedom from obligation to any authority except the authority of "reason," as the enemy of prejudice, the merely traditional, customary, habitual. Of two forms of the moral life, the rationalist rejects one which is "a habit of affection and behaviour" in favor of the "reflective application of a moral criterion." However no general requirements of fairness and utility can guide the complex morality of the family, friendship, sexual relationships, and other institutional forms of behavior.

None of these characteristics support Burkeian theorists who would counterpose tradition and reason. Nor do they support those moral conservatives who believe that deontological and utilitarian theories express universal principles of moral rationality, but principles that are not sufficient to resolve all conflicts between customs and practices. The boundaries between tradition and reason effectively disappear if Taylor, Rorty, and MacIntyre are right to warn against identifying any supposedly foundational principles. Doing that simply privileges standards of ethical reasoning that do not come into dispute in our civilization. The anti-theoretical assertion of the primacy of moral practices lends itself to a view of reasoning as a traditional practice that takes various forms. Rational behavior is behavior that conforms appropriately to the behavior of other people in one's community. "Rationality" is a quality ascribed to people who are deemed capable of taking part in the family of practices known as reasoned argument, following their diverse rules of inference. Moves we expect people to make are not logically compulsory in virtue of criteria that are independent of such expectations.

Justification, on this view, always occurs within social traditions, which, as MacIntyre notes, are the bearers of reason. What counts as appropriate reasoning is determined by agreements about acceptable argument, but these agreements are inherently incomplete. They can not govern all novel and future cases and therefore leave open what is to count as appropriate evidence and decisive proof. Nor can they preclude the reinterpretation and contestation to which moral ideas are inherently subject. Traditions are characterized by conflicting views of what they mean and require. In any vital tradition, therefore, there will be a constant tendency for interpretations to diverge.

Further disagreements surround this point. Given the apparent convergence in results of scientific research, it is a plausible claim that the successes of this activity, in contrast to moral inquiry, come as a result of correspondence to realities which constitute a second, non-conventional set of constraints upon justification. On the related question of moral realism many moral conservatives appear to hold conventionalist opinions, viewing moral objectives and prohibitions as "human creations" that distinguish the world from the totality of barren facts. For others it is the job of philosophy to seek a higher authority, but they generally acknowledge that no such authority can be shown to exist and hold only that it is desirable for people to believe there is a reality that sustains the social order. Thus, while the issue of moral and scientific realism pervades conservative literature, it is not central to this conception of morality.

Moral conservatives come together in stressing that moral ideas are subject to assessment. Goods are objective in that there is a difference between desire and desirability. It is not true as individualists maintain that the satisfaction of any desire is desirable in itself and can be judged only by its relationship to other desires.

The objectivism of moral conservatism is the belief in a common moral order which specifies the satisfaction of some desires as inherently undesirable and, thereby, places constraints upon the individualist's appeal to autonomy and independence. Of course, to make judgments on the basis of the customs and morality of one's community does not permit applying the prescriptions to all people. Moral judgments are not universalizable in this sense, and the objectivity of moral claims stands in contrast to that of scientific assertions. The latter appear universalizable in encompassing classes of things that are similar in all perceivable respects. This characterization of the reality of science is not adequate for qualities whose identity resides partly in social understandings. Here we are limited to an "internal realism" that recognizes moral goods and requirements are identified only as integral to particular social practices.

Moral conservatives are thus in agreement about the priority of a first-person or internal perspective on human life, in contrast to the absolute conception of reality often ascribed to science and the form of philosophical thought that proceeds in abstraction from familiar ways of life. Contrary to the view of the self as standing above social affairs and making practical judgments from an abstract and universal point of view, our personal identity and moral starting point is an inheritance from family, city, tribe, and nation. In no strong sense are human beings autonomous agents who construct their personal view of the good. Nonetheless, the diverse interpretations to which moral concepts are subject create conflicts which cannot be rationally resolved.

Once this hermeneutical sensitivity arises in moral philosophy, it becomes clear there is no logic of interpretation that embodies a general procedure for deciding moral questions. Nor is there any possibility of resolving such differences by invoking a social theory, such as orthodox Marxism. For theory to have a place, there must be underlying features of social organization that explain human action in ways agents may not themselves be able to do, and moral conservatism denies to such hidden features any basic role in moral thinking. The reality of social action cannot be located completely outside the motives of social agents. Social structures distinct from human beliefs and sentiments enter into moral assessment only in the terms that contentious and competing human actors understand them.

While this point can be expressed positively as a condition of social vitality, the anti-utopian implications are important. Unlike revolutionaries who imagine a society freed from tradition and opposition, moral conservatives do not envisage an end to the conflict of moralities and moral ideals. The differences between moral ways of life is a difference between moral languages, and, like the peoples at the Tower of Babel, individuals and communities that practice different ways of life cannot expect reconciliation and mutual understanding. The picture of societies whose traditions are alive to argument amid the agreements which constitute settled habits of behavior is the happiest one foreseeable.

Do such communities exist today? MacIntyre's *After Virtue* develops an argument that they do not, the acids of modernity having dissolved the conventions that enable human beings to thrive and to converse seriously with one another. He sees the resolution of the resulting moral crisis in a return to communities more like the Greek polis than the nation-state. Only in such small and unified societies can there be rational agreement on a conception of the good.

Rorty expresses a different perspective in suggesting that the loss of their foundations makes liberal society and morality more defensible rather than less. Once false support for one's beliefs and practices is given up, loyalty to one's social institutions is morality enough. If in our way of life individual freedom and independence are important goods, then we have ample reason to defend the institutions that enshrine them. These are not philosophical reasons of the kind that express a liberal way of life as resting on a set of supposedly universal moral requirements. They express the practice of liberalism as it is understood in the North Atlantic democracies. The universalistic way of life it prizes is no less parochial than any other, but as a still successful manner of existing it has much to recommend to those who share it. We have not yet determined that the freedom and independence celebrated in our secular culture, together with the tacit assumptions on which we also agree, impair solidarity with a deep and rich set of traditions that we should be concerned to defend rather than to renounce.

The most pungent reason for a contrary view is moral anxiety at giving up theoretical foundations for moral belief. Without foundations we seem in danger of going off the rails, and we have no intellectual weapons against cultures which have, in our view, already done so. The moral conservative has surrendered any possibility of claiming rational grounds other than social consensus for preferring one way of life to another. Undemonstrable metaphysical notions like "human rights" and "our common humanity" are useless. The only remaining grounds of preference are the agreements of one's own society, together with whatever identifiable facts of human biology and psychology may establish an empirical standard of well-being.

These points might also be expressed by saying that fear of going off the rails is not a reason for continuing the practice of theory-building. It is the failure of theorism that shows there is no Archimedean point from which to assess moral claims. However this leaves a disagreement among anti-theorists largely unaddressed. Even if one urges preserving liberal institutions without appeal to philosophy rather than abandoning them as presupposing a discredited philosophy, the defense of liberal society is an ambiguous project. The good of freedom, like any other, is subject to interpretation. The objective of democratic institutions, as of any other institutions, is open to debate, and if these institutions are living they will be subject to a variety of reformist pressures. While moral conservatives like Oakeshott spurn undue public reflection on a society's ideals, even the kind of radical reformism advocated by critics of liberal society seems consistent with acknowledging the priority of practice over theory.

Freedom may be interpreted to mean that the point of democratic institutions is to enable people collectively to determine their community's policies and developments. If our institutions were to change in such a way as to permit this, would it be right to say that our current institutions had been abandoned or right to say that they had been preserved? Either story could be told. If pressures for change included the claim that important human needs are not satisfied in bourgeois society, on what grounds could it be objected that this assertion rests upon a theory of human nature and society that clings speciously to philosophy? Even if the reputed deficiencies of our society cannot be demonstrated by metaphysical appeals, they can be articulated through possible reinterpretation of freedom and other goods that contend for acceptance against unreflective solidarity with the existing way of life.

More needs to be said about the relationship between reflection and practice if these questions are to receive comprehensible answers. In particular, the depth of the conservatism typical of communitarian views needs to be sounded. The pressures arising within communities to assess and move beyond parochial conceptions mean that widely accepted norms and practices cannot be shielded against criticism. Even if there is a limit beyond which criticism is not intelligible, we do not know how closely the limit may be approached. In examining aspects of this problem, it is possible to gain a clearer sense of what moral philosophy can be without normative theory.

REFLECTIVE PRACTICES

The political conservatives who contrast reason and tradition, tradition and revolution, minimize one aspect of philosophy's traditional vocation. The form of the moral life which is founded in practice is undermined by the form which requires individuals to be moral philosophers. The unreflective form of the moral life is capable of change, but as Oakeshott sees it such internal movement "does not spring from reflection upon moral principles." It "represents only an unself-conscious exploitation of the genius of the tradition of moral conduct" (190) and contrasts with what Lovibond calls "the (reasoned) pursuit of change [which] demands that we intervene, from time to time, in the practice which constitutes the approved use of certain sensitive terms" (284).

Though Williams has few political agreements with Oakeshott, he provides Oakeshott's views with an epistemological complement when he addresses the question of understanding the relations between practice and reflection and concludes that "in ethics, reflection can destroy knowledge" (79). Williams allows that there is knowledge before reflection in so far as people apply moral concepts to the right things according to *sittlich* and static criteria. However reflection upon basic moral concepts in modern circumstances has left these concepts "essentially contested" and "uncodifiable." They have no accepted criteria of application and therefore permit no knowledge of moral matters.

It would seem to follow that the only possible conservative policy is one that discourages contestation, approving the letter of every existing consensus on the interpretation of moral concepts, and viewing deviant attitudes as tantamount to blindness or insanity. Yet Oakeshott finds it possible to honor eccentricity as an exercise of freedom and inventiveness which is sensitive to a tradition and remains faithful to it. Here imagination gives expression to the possibilities of behavior consistent with a practice or institution. This form of innovation is a condition of the contestation that animates MacIntyre's living institutions. It is a very different thing from the activity described by Hampshire in asking whether we should "subject every institution around us, and every loyalty thereby engendered, to constant rational scrutiny and criticism" (160). To this form of criticism the moral conservative's answer must clearly be no, but there are many possibilities for reflective inquiry between incessant skepticism of everything artificial and the unself-conscious modifications to behavior endorsed by traditional conservatives. The conservative viewpoint would seem, for example, to approve habits of criticism that seek to sustain a reflective equilibrium. Neither all habit nor all reflection, an appropriately mixed form of the moral life might, in Oakeshott's words once again, combine "the confidence in action which belongs to the well-nurtured customary moral life" yet also "enjoy the advantages that spring from a reflective morality," including "the power to propagate itself beyond the range of the custom of a society" (195).

Progressive possibilities for moral conservatism are evident here. Corresponding to the holistic alternative to rationalistic moral philosophy, they are faithful to the longer tradition of philosophical thought and help to clarify the relationship between reflection and practice. This art of critical inquiry contains Lovibond's interest in escaping "empirical parochialism" through critical reflection that pushes the boundaries of our conceptual scheme to their "transcendental limit." These related oxymora—progressive conservatism, transcendental parochialism—promise resolution of the contradiction between Lovibond's "struggle for the cultural unification of the human race" (285) and Rorty's refusal to "ask about the relation between the practices of the chosen community and something outside that community"[2].

In the abstract it is easy to agree both that reflection can lead from comfortable parochialism to disillusionment with many existing institutions and also that even the most relentless criticism will fail to achieve a prior-to-society perspective on human reality. It is possible to question any existing practice or institution; it is not possible to repudiate the place of these customary authorities en bloc or to offer compelling reasons to reject an existing way of life in its entirety. It is not at all clear, though, what equilibrium points exist between these opposite tendencies.

One central opposition occurs between the kind of objective knowledge representing "cultural unification" as freedom from fallacious ideologies and the local knowledge of particular communities. In its ideal resolution all bodies of local knowledge find harmonious expression within an illusionless worldview. This ideal supposes that philosophical reflection may dissolve fallacious ideologies while leaving locally valid moral conceptions intact. It implies that the traditional worldviews justifying particular forms of social organization—the myths of superiority and necessity that legitimatize the dominance of certain classes or interests—are vulnerable to contradiction in the manner described by Williams, but that conceptions of virtues, purposes, and obligations are subject only to reinterpretation, not refutation.

Philosophical theory, not philosophical reflection, confounds local knowledge. In viewing people impartially, modern moral theory raises the skeptical question why we should feel the obligations of children, husbands, employers, and other special social relationships. While these moral practices are permitted from this moral point of view, they are not required; and by regarding personal attachments as objects of moral preference the rationalistic perspective helps to weaken filial and analogous moralities. Conservative theory may have similar effects. Rather than denigrating moral conceptions along with moral ideologies, it tends to regard myths of domination and moral practices alike as necessary to the integrity of communities. Since this anti-rationalism is vulnerable to reflection, it lends support to the view that no coherent moral practices remain and that human beings are starved for moral meanings.

If philosophical theories are given up as mistaken, they cease to impair active engagement in existing moral practices while ideological reflection remains a potent critical instrument. Practical difficulties continue, but they lie in the conflicts to which any practice is liable in a complex culture and in the doubts to which reflective human beings are always subject. Sartre's freedom fighter is Everyone in having to decide on a course of action which will impair other possible courses of life. The absence of rational solution to such conflicts is a problem because they are painful, not because they pose a problem of philosophical understanding. From the anti-theoretical vantage point, moral conflicts are no more fatal for a body of belief than the paradoxical statements that can be formulated in any language are fatal to it. If languages were relevantly like logical systems, the possibility of formulating propositions like "this statement is false" would render them useless. In fact, the effects of such statements do not spread throughout language and make it incoherent. Nor do the effects of moral paradox which are intolerable to moral theory create incoherence in actual bodies of moral belief.

Some disputes are felt so deeply that silence or force replaces attempts at reasonable resolution. No satisfactory outcome exists when people view one another as absolutely wrong. This anti-rationalistic point acknowledges the tendency to regard those we cannot understand as mad. It must be paired, however, with the way in which the conservatism of anti-theory rules out absolutes. Because moral concepts are subject to a variety of practical interpretations, moral judgments are expressed in concepts that cannot properly claim indubitability. We must live with dilemmas that show morality is not a seamless fabric. If it were seamless, the failure of any part would mean the failure of the whole. Because it is not, the conflicting and overlapping dispositions, practices, and principles that make up a culture's moral outlook can each provide a partial and tentative perspective for the criticism of the others and encourage interest in developing new institutions. In its political neutrality, moral conservatism accommodates a wide spectrum of opinion about social policy and government and provides the locus for some of the most interesting disagreements among contemporary intellectuals.

Moral conservatives have not yet seriously explored the possibility of a society whose course of development is determined democratically rather than resulting from countless private decisions and acts of executive intervention. One reason for this diffidence is the apparent opposition between the totalistic vision of a society governed by consensus and the pluralism of the conservative argument. Another reason is that the radical critique of society may appear to permit only negative outcomes. It is possible to characterize consensual societies that agree on their collective purposes, but they are ones whose stable traditions provide a practical guide that resists change. To criticize these relatively unreflective forms of life is not to describe an alternative to the dominance of markets and bureaucracies in complex social organizations.

There is nothing inherently mysterious, however, about democratic forms of moral reflection. There is a first-person plural view as well as a first-person singular one, and it makes sense to speak of reflective societies in which fundamental alternatives are actively explored, debated and decided upon. Collectively generated expectations about the future would then replace rule by special interests. This is the outline of a communitarian sense of politics and defines the kind of consensual society envisaged by radicals as replacing political cultures. If forms of social reflection and discourse were the normal mode of making major social choices, we would have progressed beyond both dependence upon the traditional standards that retard reflection and the bourgeois tolerance that retards reform. The essential place of traditional norms would be filled, in part, by a tradition of open decision, entrenching norms of argument which fulfill a conservative function.

This is, like any conservative account, an anti-rationalistic one. People bring to a common exploration of social possibilities only the abstract purposes typical of the emotions that create a shared form of moral life. Important abstract goods—security, provision for the needy, knowledge, and the like—motivate social debate about shelter, welfare, education, etc., and argument alone cannot resolve conflicting views of these goods. Nothing will do but a decision of the kind that regularly faces any corporate body in which a variety of alternative possibilities vie for acceptance. To decide public policy in such matters is to fix interpretations of abstract goods for a time: minimum standards of housing will determine expectations in terms of which security is understood; welfare policies define notions of when suffering is not to be tolerated. In arriving at a policy, a contestable abstract good is thus given a particular interpretation which settles its public meaning in much the way that traditional patterns of housing and provision settle such meanings in unreflective societies.

These suggestions are consistent with the anti-utopianism of moral conservatism. They do not describe how such a reflective community might be brought about or establish any likelihood that one might arise. Philosophical speculation is able only to suggest possibilities which partisans of a point of view can use in trying to persuade others to perceive things their way. In such intellectual contests there is no preordained victor. The form of deliberation imagined here expresses one interpretation of a free society. It has no preferred place over alternative interpretations but defines a sense of freedom which can be compelling only if consensual modes of decision become normal.

The eventuality may appear impossibly remote. This conception of communicative practices seems too abstract to function in a manner analogous to established customs. The possible objects of human desire seem too various for conflict between moral ways of life to be stilled. Moral languages will sometimes prove incommensurable, so that no significant discussion can occur. But such doubts should take account of the constraints established by natural agreements. Given the common conceptual framework established by human psychology, it is possible to envisage the creation of common points of view even within pluralistic civilizations.

The passions and social institutions form the center of the conservative intellectual tradition. By interpreting them in terms of moral beliefs and progressive institutions, the resources of this view of the moral life can be seen to extend further than present statements of them. Together with the new vigor of the anti-theoretical view, they commend attention to the discussions that follow and exploration beyond.

NOTES

1. Page references to work in this collection are given in brackets. Details about other relevant writings are included in the bibliographical essay at the end of the book.

2. Rorty, Richard, "Postmodernist Bourgeois Liberalism," Journal of Philosophy, 80 (1983), 583.

Part I

Anti-Theory in Ethics

Chapter 1

Doing Without Moral Theory?

ANNETTE BAIER

When one turns from Aristotle's or Hume's moral philosophy to
contemporary moral philosophy, several differences are bound to
strike one. First is the fact that neither of these two (nor most who
come between them) anticipate much disagreement among their
readers about the actual moral judgments they endorse in their
philosophy—neither Aristotle nor Hume expect any serious dissent
from the list of virtues they endorse. (Hume, it must be admitted,
is sometimes disingenuous here—he knows that there will be those
who refuse to transfer celibacy, fasting, silence, humility, and the
rest of the monkish characteristics to the column of vices, but he at
least writes as if there is a consensus among all persons of good
sense in seeing them in the way he saw them.) They do expect some
disagreement on *philosophical* issues—Hume refers to the contemporary controversy over whether moral judgments are based on
reason or sentiment, and Aristotle argues against the hedonists, but
such disagreements at the philosophical level are not expected to
alter the assumed rough consensus at the moral level. By contrast,
we today often see moral disagreement as a datum, almost an
indispensable prerequisite for the very possibility of moral philosophy.
Stevenson, for example, begins with this datum. I think that this
presumption of a plurality of conflicting moral outlooks in the audience for whom a book of moral philosophy is intended dates back
to Bentham and J. S. Mill, who certainly expected some of their
audience to have to be persuaded of some of their moral conclusions.
Mill was not merely a moral theorist but a moral reformer—he
wanted to change people's views about the rights of women, about
sexual freedom, about suicide, and other topics. He created or at
least fomented moral controversy. Now earlier philosophers, such as
Kant, Hume, Locke, Hobbes, or even Aquinas, had certainly taken

"Doing without Moral Theory?" incorporates "Some Thoughts on the Way We Moral
Philosophers Live Now," *The Monist* 67, no. 4 (October 1984), and material from a
talk given at New York University, December 1981.

stands on some controversial social and political issues, but it is one thing to be a political reformer, making moral criticisms of social and political institutions, another to be a moral reformer, criticizing currently held moral beliefs. Mill was both, and his moral theory was used by him to try to change both moral and political attitudes. From Mill on, I suggest, philosophers writing on ethics no longer supposed that there was a moral consensus, a body of agreed moral judgments one could appeal to in support of a controversial political or social cause, or in support of one's particular philosophical theory about moral judgments. Apart from a few sheltered enclaves such as Oxford, where those like Ross, Pritchard, and Ryle still spoke as if there were a consensus, at least among all right-thinking Oxonians who had learned to tell right from wrong at their nannies' knees, and had learned of a few more elaborate and tempting wrongs at their public schools, serious moral philosophers took serious moral disagreement as part of their data. Among such serious thinkers I include Bradley, Bosanquet, Bergson, Moore, Stevenson, Ayer, Schlick, and Frankena.

What is striking about this shift from presumption of moral consensus to presumption of its absence is that the philosophers at the beginning of the transition saw themselves as working for some disputed moral cause, saw themselves as members of the nonagreeing community of moral judges, while more recent moral theorists mostly see themselves as above the moral fray, outside the everyday disputes about what is to be tolerated. Hare, for example, said in *Freedom and Reason:*

> Thus ethics, the study of the logical properties of moral words, remains morally neutral (its conclusions neither are substantial moral judgments, nor entail them, even in conjunction with factual premisses).[1]

Of course, present-day moral philosophers may take stands on disputed moral issues such as abortion, but there are very few contemporary Anglo-American moral theorists to whom one would naturally apply the term "moral reformer." (One such rare practicer of what he preaches in his philosophy is Peter Singer.) Rawls, the best-known moral theorist in this country, does not aim to enter the moral fray on particular issues—he quite explicitly limits the goal he sets himself to that of constructing a theory to accommodate his own considered judgments. He takes these to be typical of Americans, or of some Americans, but says, in *A Theory of Justice:*

I shall not even ask if the principles which characterize one person's considered judgments are the same as those that characterize another's . . . so, for the purposes of this book, the views of the reader and the author are the only ones that count. The opinions of others are used only to clear our heads.[2]

This is an interesting, and extreme, reaction to cultural pluralism. Rawls, as much as Stevenson or Harman, takes for granted that there *are* a plurality of possibly conflicting moral views, or "opinions," as he calls them. But he does not aim even to defend his own against contrary opinions—merely to construct the best possible theory on his own opinions, tested only by their confrontation with a variety of possible constructions. Rawls defends his contractarianism against intuitionism and utilitarianism (as if they exhaust the field of other alternatives) but this defense at the philosophical level is a defense against those with the *same* base of moral opinions, at least on most matters, and who differ only in their philosophical opinions on what theory that base best supports. This turns academic moral philosophy into the intellectual construction business—one attempts to outbid one's competitor constructors in erecting a theory that rationalizes the moral opinion of some group within which there is approximation to moral consensus. In the limiting case, the extreme limit of individualism and pluralism, the group is oneself. This, I suggest, makes moral philosophy into either ideology or into play-ideology. Like most of us, I welcome good ideology for a cause I espouse—I admire J. S. Mill for his cultural crusades and for his effort to use intellectual instruments along with any others he could get. What I am less happy with is professional play-ideology, and with unacknowledged ideology, ideology parading as detachment.

MacIntyre, in *After Virtue*,[3] says that our contemporary style as moral beings is indignation, protest, and unmasking. All that is left for us to do, after the breakdown of a religious moral consensus and the failure of the enlightenment attempt to provide a secular basis for a shared morality, is to react negatively to the contradictions present everywhere in our present moral situation—conflicts between slogans about rights and practices that ignore such rights, between the moral "fictions" to which we give lip service and the brute facts of the exercise of superior power. While I admire MacIntyre's illuminating version of how we got where we now are, as far as concerns morality, moral philosophy, and their perceived relation to one another, I do not agree with his very gloomy estimate of the prospects of a secular culture, and I shall claim that at least one version of the enlightenment project has not yet been given a fair enough trial for us to know whether it will or will not fail—I mean Hume's attempt to give morality a secure basis, not in moral theory but in human active capacities for cooperation. But I have, in my negative prolegomenon to that claim, exemplified MacIntyre's version of the typical contemporary moralizer—although I may keep my indignation under control, and although my form of protest is harmlessly academic. I have been indulging in that favorite twentieth century sport of unmasking—I have been presenting our twentieth century moral theorists as ideologists in fairly transparent disguise.

As MacIntyre points out, this game of unmasking can be played interminably. Just as I can ask why today's moral theorists like to present themselves, not as parties to moral disagreements but as either detached adjudicators or as solitary thinkers, in retreat from public dispute, as builders of systems for their own private satisfaction, so you can ask why I like to present myself as a critic of the current moral theory and applied theory industry, as if I can stand apart from it, see its self-delusions and its unacknowledged ideological functions, while myself keeping free from these forms of false consciousness. It is as easy to unmask me as a parasite on the moral philosophy I criticize as it is easy for me to criticize moral theorists. Unmasking is a game that has become boring due to the laxness of its rules. When Marx did it, it had some force. When Nietzsche did it, it had more force than most could tolerate—we wrote him off as mad. When Freud did it, and generalized the scope of the charge, then masks became an interesting cultural product, something to cultivate and on which to spend, in analysis fees, considerable sums so that one might understand and appreciate one's mask. To be civilized and to be masked became more or less identical, and the new art was to wear one's carefully studied and even carefully crafted mask with panache, rather than hiding behind it, or refusing to distinguish oneself from it. Once masks became fashionable, the game of unmasking began to lose its point. The sort of unmasking that still survives as a popular form of moral action is not the charge of hypocrisy—that was the form unmasking took when Strachey wrote about the Victorians, but rather the more general charge that, in MacIntyre's words, "behind the masks of morality [lie] what are in fact the preferences of arbitrary will."[4] The will that the wearing of the moral mask advances need not be one's own—or even one of which one is aware. Powerful wills in our era know how to manipulate others to do their will, and to do it unaware of the manipulation and of whose will they are doing. So today's form of "unmasking" is simply showing what cause is in fact furthered by particular moral posturings—and there need be no charge whatever that those taking up those postures are insincere, are *merely* posturers. The charge today is not of insincerity or hypocrisy, but of false consciousness. This is a charge so hard to rebut that it is easy to turn it on anyone and everyone. I therefore take it for granted that I, like the next person, am *not* fully aware of the forces that make me say what I say, nor aware of whose cause I may be furthering by the saying of it. False consciousness can now be taken as the successor concept to "original sin"—of course one is liable to it. That which distinguishes any sheep from the large herd of the goats will be not their escaping it, but their awareness of it and their attempt to find some method of "redemption" from its evils.

A second difference between Aristotle and Hume and most contemporary philosophers is that the latter have normative theories, and I think we find nothing analogous to these in Aristotle or Hume (although we do in Aquinas and Kant). By a normative theory I mean a system of moral principles in which the less general are derived from the more general. I want to attack the whole idea of a moral "theory" which systematizes and extends a body of moral judgments, and attack in particular the idea that the theorist might accept a theory with controversial implications, without thereby becoming a moral reformer, one dedicated to having those implications accepted and acted upon. It is perhaps appropriate that I should exhibit, in my moral philosophy, MacIntyre's mode of moral action—if I am right that there is no room for moral theory as something which is more philosophical and less committed than moral deliberation, and which is not simply an account of our customs and styles of justification, criticism, protest, revolt, conversion, and resolution, then any moral philosophy which is not such descriptive anthropology will tend to merge with moral action. To quote MacIntyre again, "There ought not to be two histories, one of political and moral action and one of political and moral theorizing, because there were not two pasts, one populated only by actions, the other only by theories. Every action is the bearer and expression of more or less theory-laden beliefs and concepts, every piece of theorizing is a political and moral action."[5]

I shall now briefly diagnose[6] what I think is the background error of the moral theorists, then I shall explore a different way of being a moral philosopher. Where do we have genuine and useful theories? Primarily in science—but there we find a plurality of them primarily over time, rather than at a time. We certainly do not find some engineers building bridges or spaceships by application of one theory, while others at the same time are applying another different theory. In practical fields, like engineering or cooking, we do not find *theories* of how to do what such practitioners do, merely schools to train people to do it. There may perhaps be theories of nutrition, or of taste, which a cook might consult, and there certainly are recipe books, but it would be a very odd enterprise to try to find the "principles" applied in such recipes, or to unify the rules of cooking into a grand system, from which we might deduce some new recipes, or menus for new occasions. Theories tell us what the world is like, and we need to know that if we are to act successfully in it, either to maintain something in it, or to change it. Engineers need theories of physics and chemistry; cooks need knowledge about what is edible, what is digestible, what tastes will result from certain combinations of ingredients and processes such as grinding, fermenting, baking, freezing. Moral agents also need theories, or rather the reliable facts good theories produce—facts about the way people react, about the costs and consequences of particular ways of life, on those who adopt them and on their fellow persons. We need psychological theories and social theories, and, if we are intent on political change, theories about political power and its working, and about economics. But do we need *normative* theories, theories to tell us what to do, in addition to theories that present to us the world in which we are to try to do it?

Why might we have thought that we do need, and that we can get, such theories? We certainly need some way of deciding what to do, especially in cases we find difficult; and the oldest way, in our culture, was by accepting the guidance of some religious teaching. Here a theory about the way the world is and a set of practical guides were closely interconnected, and it may be nostalgia for this theory-linked practical guidance that prompts philosophers today to construct moral theories, fairly elaborate systems of norms with the less general linked to more general principles. We have accepted, from Moore, the claim that we cannot base our moral precepts on any metaphysical theory, so instead we have tried to let the precepts themselves constitute a theory. The religious thinkers were the ones who really *did* have a theory, in the strict sense—a representation of God's creation. A theory, strictly, is the outcome of contemplating some unified structured world—in the first place a world manifesting the unity of the divine perfections, and so showing the coherence and structure to be expected in such a divine self-display. It is dubious if even scientific accounts of the way the world is can count as theories in this sense. But scientists seem eternally optimistic that there is some order there to be discerned and contemplated, that such an order-seeking being as a human being must be part of a universe exhibiting the order for which it yearns. It is like the dog's confidence that there are good smells out there—and probably about as well grounded. (That is to say, it is fairly well grounded. To paraphrase Hume,[7] how else would the order-seeking beings have survived unless they, with their needs, *did* fit at least into *some* niche in the world as it really is?) So those religious thinkers, like Aquinas, who outline a whole world-account, and one which entitled that world to the name *nature*, because of what it revealed about its divine creator, could indeed go on and read off a "natural law" which informed us how to pursue our true end. For a religious outlook, moral guidelines can be extracted from the total theory, that is from the contemplation of world-and-God.

But we secular moralists have no such total picture. We have a world view which is expected to reveal a "naturalized" version of some approximation to that order which originally was seen as a displaying divine unity-in-variety. We may also have an optional private religious view, worshipping the free-enterprise deity, the God of our fabrication, or the consumer deity, the God of our choice. Such religious views may impose religious duties upon us, but for our dealings with our fellow persons who have exercised their religious freedom differently, we need some less elite moral guide. Religion no longer either ties or reties us to many of our fellows. In place of the once-shared common morality of a community with a more-or-less shared religion, we have a great void in which a few moral memories echo forlornly. This void is of course a temptation to the moral philosopher, who constructs utilitarianism or contractarianism to fill the free space, and not merely to supplement a given moral guide, so as to get decisions in difficult cases. But what *really* would fill that space would be a moral force that was felt at the time when moral codes get accepted and paradigm moral ties get forged—namely in childhood. Until there are utilitarian and contractarian Sunday schools and pulpits, and until such moral outlooks are learned at the parent's knee, the void will not be filled by such philosophical enterprises. We philosophers are very squeamish about pulpits and knees—we cultivate a cool distant style, and like to think of our influence on culture as safely indirect and long-term. Yet the influence of our introductory classes in ethics may be fairly direct and immediate—exposure to a variety of moral theories, and the varieties of conflicting advice they generate when "applied" to business or medical decisions, is a very effective way to produce a moral skeptic. Our pluralist culture prepares a young person for moral skepticism, and a course or two in comparative moral theory (and application) is the perfect finishing school for such skepticism.

The belief that there was room for normative theory, for a systematic body of moral precepts, dates from Bentham's substitute for natural law, and from the continuity he saw between morals and legislation. In the old view, human morality was continuous with human law, itself continuous with natural and divine law. Even when human law is severed from this theological root, it clearly still was amenable to systematization. So it is a fairly natural move to suppose that, since there is no problem in stating the content of the human law of a particular community as a complexly organized and hier- archically arranged set of principles and precepts, the same might be done for the morality by reference to which these laws get made and changed. A natural move but, I think, a bad move.[8] The laws by which courts and judges arrive at verdicts *must* be expressed, must be general and perhaps hierarchically ordered, and must be sanction backed. *Need* moral beliefs be verbally expressed, to be beliefs? *Must* they take the form of universal pronouncements perhaps derivable from supreme principles? *Is* there a moral sanction? Af- firmative answers to these three questions are usually assumed— since Kant we seem to have found it hard to see how there could be any such thing as moral philosophy if there were no such thing as "the moral law" or "the moral rules." Alan Donagan's opening chapter in his book *The Theory of Morality* shows this prejudice in its full force. "The Theory of Morality," he says "is a theory of a system of laws or precepts binding upon rational creatures as such, the content of which is ascertainable by human reason."[9] Thinkers as diverse as Alan Gewirth[10] and Richard Brandt[11] also take the concept of "moral law" for granted—Gewirth's search for a rationally justified first principle, Brandt's attempt to formulate an ideal moral code, both assume that morality consists in a set of general principles or rules or laws. Today's moral theorists are all Kantians in their prejudice in favor of formulated general rules. Even if some, like Brandt, see inclination as much as reason as the *source* of those precepts, they all see reason as providing both the form and the tests that make them moral precepts. And those, like David Gau- thier,[12] who look to the market rather than to the law for moral inspiration, are still Kantian in making *reason*, in the form of rational self-interest in a social context, authoritative for their morality for bargainers. I find all these three assumptions to be mere Kantian prejudices, whose self-evidence does not survive self-consciousness. They might turn out in the end to be justified claims, but it is time that those who think they are justified produce the justification. Until they do, it remains mere prejudice to demand explicitness, universality, and coercive backing, in any moral guide. For any such guide to be passed on it must be learnable, but one can learn from example. For any such guide to be of general use, its precepts must apply fairly generally, but generality is not universality. For any such guide to be accepted *as* a guide, there must be some motive to accept it. But the motive need not be avoidance of sanctions.

On my diagnosis, where we now stand in moral philosophy is among an array of rationalistic systems, all of them aiming at universality, even if sometimes at degenerate versions of it, at personal "rational" moral utopias that are not expected to be shared, even by other utopia-fanciers, or rationality-admirers. The retreat of the theorists from moral problems in the real world to the construction of private fantasy moral worlds is, as it were, compensated for by the advance of a new breed of professionals, namely all those who assemble all the available theories, then "apply" them to suit their clients' needs. Can we approve of a division of labor in which the theorists keep their hands clean of real-world applications, and the ones who advise the decision-makers, those who do "applied ethics" are like a consumer reports service, pointing out the variety of available theories and what costs and benefits each has for a serious user of it? Does the profession of moral philosophy now display that degeneration of a Kantian moral outlook that Hegel portrays, where there are beautiful souls doing their theoretical thing and averting their eyes from what is happening in the real world, even from what is happening in the way of "application" of their own theories, and there are those who are paid to be the "conscience" of the medical, business, or legal profession, what Hegel calls the moral *valets*, the professional moral judges?[13]

The villain, as I see it, is the rationalist, law-fixated tradition in moral philosophy, which, given freedom from its religious base, breeds multiple and in the end frivolous systems and their less frivolous, more dangerous applications. MacIntyre sees the roots of the present mess to be the failure of Kantian and post-Kantian moral philosophies to defend a secular *rationalist* moral philosophy from Hume's attack on rationalism, a defense to which there seemed no option, on his account, given the failure of Hume's attempt to provide an alternative basis. I dispute that diagnosis, and that estimate of Hume's contribution.[14] As I see it, it is not so much that Hume failed as that his successors failed to continue his project. In the nature of that project, it could not be completed, once for all, by Hume himself, and I see no fatal weaknesses in the project as he launched it. I think that his preferred version of secular morality and his version of philosophical reflection on morality have not really been tried for long enough and so it is too soon to say if they are or are not viable and acceptable to sensible people. For present purposes, the important aspects of the latter are its nonrationalism, and its version of the relation between moral philosophy and the actual human practices in which appeals to moral judgments are made and in which morality makes a difference to what is done, thought, and felt.

I contrasted Hume's approach to ethics with the post-Kantian and post-Benthamite moral philosophy that went in for theory construction. Hume's way involves no normative theory—it involves a psychological theory, of course, and it also involves a political-economic theory, about the actual workings of human right-determining institutions. But no *normative* theory. The psychological theory, the account of human passions and their potentialities for self-regulation, is empirically testable, and so is the political theory. Hume indeed tested and refined it by his historical researches. What the Humean moral philosopher does is take well-based accounts of human nature, its malleability, its current condition, and equally well-based accounts of the workings of institutions, and of the interrelations between the two—the way institutions express and encourage some passions, the way some passions, or frustrations of them, lead to changes in institutions. Given this factual base, the moral philosopher's special interest will be in the workings of all the *reflective* sentiments, those reacting to other sentiments, and in particular to those that claim to be moral reflections, that is, to be reflections from a steady and general viewpoint. All of this will be "mental geography," as Hume called it,[15] *descriptive* moral and social philosophy, understanding the modes of individual and social moral reflection as they actually exist now rather than an "airy science"[16] that "opens up a world of its own,"[17] be it that of Kantian noumena or any of those full compliance human utopias favored by normative theorists. For such mental geography to be accurate and to yield reliable maps, the philosopher may have to leave her armchair, or have associates who do so.

In the conclusion to Book One of the *Treatise* Hume said that any philosopher whose "system or set of opinions" will prove "satisfactory to the human mind" will have to have "a share of the gross earthy mixture" of the nonphilosophers who do the world's more worldly work. "Of such as these I pretend not to make philosophers, nor do I expect them to be either associates in these researches or auditors of these discoveries . . . Instead of refining them into philosophers, I wish we could communicate to our founders of systems a share of this gross earthy mixture. . . ."[18] Hume has no wish to make nonphilosophers into philosophers, or even to tell them his philosophical discoveries. On the contrary, those philosophers who will have anything worth the telling must first acquire some of the solid virtues of the honest nonphilosophers. Later, in the first *Enquiry*, Hume describes the way he thinks that sound philosophy will affect these honest nonphilosophers, with or without their becoming the philosophers' auditors. "And though a philosopher may live remote from business, the genius of philosophy, if carefully cultivated by several, must gradually diffuse itself throughout the whole society and bestow a similar correctness on every art and calling. The politician will acquire greater foresight and subtlety, in the subdividing and balancing of power, the lawyer more method and finer principles in his reasoning; and the general more regularity in his discipline and more caution in his plans and operations."[19] This sounds as if it might be a manifesto for applied philosophy, a proclamation of the value of philosophical and moral valets to other professionals. But this puff for the public benefits of philosophy is carefully limited to philosophy as carefully cultivated, and Hume does not go back on his earlier claim that the philosopher must acquire something of the nonphilosopher to do the philosophical job properly, must become less of an ivory tower intellectual and spinner of airy systems. The Hume who wrote the *Treatise* knew a little law and had sampled the life of a businessman. By the time he wrote the second *Enquiry* he had a more varied experience of the world's affairs, and he went on to be a secretary to a general, a diplomat, and a historian. By the time he made the final revisions to the second *Enquiry*, he was well acquainted with several branches of the common life whose procedures and practices the Humean philosophy was to methodize and sometimes correct.

The brief for "applied" moral philosophy which we get from Hume, then, is one that directs the philosopher to learn from the nonphilosophers before presuming to advise them. Such willingness to learn, to become less of an intellectual judge and more of an apprentice participant, is to be found among contemporary moral philosophers less in the theorists than in those who *have* become associates of the nonphilosophers, in other professions. They are more or less forced to acquire some of the gross earthy mixture

Hume prescribed for the philosopher, forced to see what are the procedures they are hired to methodize and correct. If anyone is likely to be doing their philosophy "carefully" in the sense Hume meant, it will be this new breed of moral valets. They are in a position to enact a Hegelian master-slave reversal.

The "careful" moral philosophy Hume practiced was a mental geography of our powers of reflection, and of our reflective practices. His bold methodological claim was that the correction of motives, sentiments, and habits catering to them, can be done by sentiment and custom, and is not the prerogative of a purely intellectual "reason." His sort of moral reflection is empirically informed, that is to say, informed by psychological, political, and historical knowledge, and it is also practical, a reflective version of real motives in real-world conditions. The unfinished task Hume launched, in his bold antirationalist moral philosophy, was to find a better way of being a moral philosopher, a way which avoided unworldly intellectualism, which was as willing to correct its own methods as to criticize the customs of others. Hume's manifesto is a call for a self-critical, nonintellectualist, and socially responsible moral philosophy. His own practice of it was with the pen. Although the member of the republic of letters need not be an intellectualist, the pen or word processor of the Humean philosopher ought not to be her only tool (or weapon). If we are to carry on what Hume began, we should be looking for new and better ways both of designing our own role, and of conducting our reflection on and examination of the moral practices of our time.

Moral philosophers might be expected to be especially self-conscious about their own social role but, apart from Marxists, who like the true Wittgensteinians have tended to transmute their philosophy into more direct ways of acting on the world, they have not recently been very conspicuous for their sense of social answerability. In the analytic tradition particularly, moral philosophers (once tenured) have tended to take their own social niche for granted, and to turn their socially critical eye, and any modest proposals for reform, only on practices in which they are not themselves professionally involved (I exclude, of course, participation in internal university affairs, those local reorganizations that do not change the relation of academic philosophers to the rest of society). But should we not, at least occasionally, consider why the rest of society should not merely tolerate but subsidize our activity, given what we do and how many there are of us who do it? Is the large proportional increase of professional philosophers and moral philosophers a good thing, morally speaking? Even if it scarcely amounts to a plague of gadflies, it may amount to a nuisance of owls.

The fairly recent expansion of the socially tolerated role of salaried moral philosophers beyond colleges into hospitals and into the workplaces of other professions should encourage in us a sensitivity to our own place in the social division of labor. If we are to "do" applied ethics and professional ethics, we should not exclude our own profession from our attention. Is it in accordance with the moral principles we endorse in our philosophy that we should advise other professions before we have examined our own? Our own professional activities, until recently, have been restricted to teaching and writing. Just as most of us teach without having been trained in the art of teaching, learning, if at all, from sorry experience, so those who consult and advise other professionals are learning by trial and error, not usually by any study or expert training in the new areas. I suppose that it is no worse for philosophers to think that, simply by being philosophers, they can make a contribution in a hospital, than to assume, as most of us do, that merely by philosophizing aloud in front of our students we thereby contribute constructively to their education. We have not been notable for our efforts to check and see if this assumption is correct. Even our recent, usually externally demanded, attention to our performance as teachers has limited itself to trying to measure our success in converting nonphilosophers into beginning philosophers. We stop short of asking whether this conversion serves some good wider educational or cultural purpose. Our sacred ability to be critical and questioning seems to have as its limit a refusal to question the value of becoming, in our sense, philosophical and critical.

That any society ought to have philosophers in its midst seems to us an axiom of any possible social philosophy. Probably any society *will* have some reflective people in it, some Socrates or Mandeville or Wollstonecraft to ask awkward questions, but even if this is to be welcomed, it does not follow that any society should have *professional* philosophers in its midst, nor, if it does have them, that their activities should take the form ours assume. The very professionalization of philosophy makes the likelihood more remote that those awkward questions, necessary for a healthy social consciousness, should come from its philosophers. It may make for better philosophy and a better society if they come from a social misfit like Diogenes, or from an anathematized lense-grinder like Spinoza, or from a man of affairs, an unsuccessful aspirant to two chairs of philosophy, like Hume. (Even more conventionally acceptable moral philosophers like Aquinas and Butler earned their living as clerics, not as philosophers.)

The questions we need occasionally to ask are, first, why anyone should be a philosopher (in our sense); second, why anyone else should pay one to be a philosopher; third, how many should be paid philosophers; and fourth, what exact form the professional activity of paid philosophers should take, and in particular what sort of examination of moral practices the moral philosopher should conduct. These questions are, of course, connected—the answers to the third and fourth are obviously interdependent. The answers need not be true for all conditions. It is not *a priori* impossible that we today can put to good use a vastly higher proportion of philosophy professors in our population than did Hume's Europe. Social conditions have recently changed enough to make philosophers welcome in hospitals, playing there a role once played, approximately, by chaplains. Are we the new priesthood? Could good Humeans possibly become that?

As teachers, our activities have usually been anything but pastoral. Although generalizations are risky, I think most teachers of moral philosophy have prided themselves on their success in disturbing the complacent beliefs of their students. We have set out to produce in our students a willingness to challenge old beliefs, to pursue the implications of principles further than they naturally would, and to look at alternative beliefs. We like playing devil's advocate. Does this systematic assault on inherited and conventional moral beliefs corrupt the young? I do not think we know, and some of us can give no sense to the question. How, we would ask, can initiation into rational criticism *corrupt*—surely that can only cure the corruption of dogmatism, not itself corrupt. But most of us do know, by casual observation or by sessions with distressed students, that it can unsettle and upset, and it can also produce moral skeptics and even cynics. Part of our own faith, it seems, is that anything, even a moral skeptic, is better than an unconscious moral dogmatist. Better for whom? For the new skeptic and his fellows? For his children? An introductory course in moral philosophy ought perhaps to include J. S. Mill's *Autobiography*, so that the critical examination of beliefs will include an examination of the faith in reason alone, and the effects of trying to live by such a faith. If Socrates is our martyr in the cause of critical rationality, the young Mill stands as countervictim, reminding us of the incompleteness of critical rationality as a human goal. The examined life may be a sustainable goal, but only if the mode of examination does not destroy the life.

Not only are we dogmatic about the value of critical examination, of challenge to dogmas, but we are also fairly dogmatic in our beliefs about the best form of examination. We examine by lawyers' methods—by challenge, counterchallenge, argument. We give verdicts and pass judgments. For some moral philosophers this aping of legal procedures is self-conscious and deliberate; for others it is more automatic, the result of their analytic training. Among less analytic moral philosophers other styles exist, equally imitative but imitating other models. There is the meditation, the examination of conscience, the confession. And now there is cost-benefit anaylsis, moral philosophy imitating the accountant and the merchant, and game-theoretic approaches, in which the moral philosopher imitates the military strategist. We need to survey the array of possible styles, and, if we are to imitate, to be aware of why we choose the model we do. Philosophy, these days, seems in its methods not the queen of the sciences, expecting others to listen to her, but the social mime, drawing her procedures as well as her economic support from other sources. Such heteronomy need be no disgrace—by imitating, extending, transferring, and perhaps distorting the methods of other disciplines we may occasionally do something enlightening, useful, entertaining, or even consoling.

The recent struggles in our profession in this country between the self-named pluralists and what they see as an analytic establishment, or ex-establishment, might be seen as involving a clash of models of philosophical procedure. Those who dislike analytical methods are usually rejecting not merely the assimilation of philosophical thinking to mathematical computation, but also the legalist paradigm, the tyranny of argument. (Of course, to replace what Hume disparagingly called "lawyers' wrangling" with political campaigning is dubious advance.) The alternative ways of doing philosophy here and now seem either to be those of the Marxists, modeled on guerrilla warfare, or those of the phenomenologists, modeled on the gentler moves of religious exercises. Few have taken up Wittgenstein's suggestion that a philosophy book could take the form of a series of jokes—and fewer still have brought it off. To get the earthiness Hume recommended, must we choose between being pretend accountants, pretend lawyers, pretend revolutionaries, failed priests, and unsuccessful comics?

Hume had himself to become a real diplomat and a real historian before many found any of his opinions satisfactory to their minds, before he found many auditors for his social philosophy. History and the human sciences could also provide procedures for us to adapt to our purposes, and, for moral philosophy in particular, history seems an indispensable fellow-discipline. Unless we know the fate of communities that tried to implant and live by the moral principles we consider, how can we have any empirically tested opinion about their soundness? The fate of communities that tried living by those principles, their success or failure in passing them on to successive generations, is not decisive, of course, for the validity of those principles for us now, but it does seem relevant data for the moral philosopher. Unless our moral reflections are historically informed, they will be mere speculation.

The difficulty of providing appropriate support for a moral guide is increased if it is a new untried one. To have any confidence that a proposed new guide will work better than the guides it would replace, will conduce more to the human good of those using it and affected by its use, one would need not merely economic and sociological generalizations confirmed by past history, but also something of the novelist's imagination of the detailed human consequences of its use, its full effect on people's lives. Anticipating such real-world consequences of adoption of a moral principle is different from seeing its logical consequences, or its theoretically appropriate application to concrete cases. In real life the attempts to apply an abstract theory or principle lead to results richer and messier than those foreseen from an armchair. The emotional effects of abortion, for example, and the effects on nurses assisting in abortions, go stubbornly beyond what the liberal defender of the right to abortion envisaged as the consequences of his or her principles. The difficulty of learning, transmitting, applying some new proposed moral guide, or reform of an older one, the frequency of misapplications, the hidden psychic costs of living by it, these are all empirical matters of vital importance to the proper evaluation of that guide, but they are matters which, even with the historians' knowledge and the novelists' imagination to assist us, we can still only guess at from our chairs of moral philosophy, in advance of the actual trial of that guide over several generations. To make even educated guesses here we need more studies not only of the effect on children of moral education of various styles and contents (including the effect on how they try to bring up their own children), but of the effect on adolescents and adults of conversion to new principles. The relative incidence, among the followers of different moral guides, and among those who have changed their moral beliefs in various ways, of suicide, alcoholism, avoidance of parenthood, and other forms of the failure of the will to perpetuate one's way of life, would be relevant information for a philosophical examination of such moral guides—more relevant than calculations about what expert, emotionless bargainers would accept in unreal conditions, or what an uninvolved observer would enjoy contemplating from a god's eye view. It is not easy, of course, to find out what role is played by moral beliefs as distinct from bad health or bad economic, political, or personal luck, in driving a person to some form of life rejection, nor indeed should we want to separate too sharply the influence of moral beliefs from economic and political factors. One's moral beliefs may influence one's willingness to put up with economic and political hardship, as well as with bad health and bad luck, but they also affect one's input into the economic and political processes. Relevant to the moral philosopher's examination of a moral code are such questions as "Will the followers of such a code become exploiters and exploited? Will they be led to war more or less often than others? Will they need to restrict one sex to child-rearing roles to ensure the successful transmission of their morality?" Such questions are not easy to get answers to, but without such answers we cannot know what we are endorsing, in endorsing a particular moral guide, nor could we be endorsing it as satisfactory not only to intellect, but to the whole human mind, in all its emotional and historical complexity. To get, or even to try to get, answers to such questions philosophers will have to get their hands a little dirtier, a little more officially familiar not merely with intellectual arguments but with the other forces that drive human life, for better or worse.

The extension of the work of some moral philosophers into consulting and advising in other professions is bound to confront them with some of the real-world complexities a moral guide encounters. This change in the social role of moral philosophy therefore holds out promise as well as problems. The problems arise because of the lack of relevant special expertise with which most of the philosophical consultants enter their new positions. Advisers and consultants are usually those who have some experience-based expertise in the area where the advice is given—we seek legal advice when our problem is with some law-regulated aspect of life; engineering consultants check what other engineers, or builders, are planning to do, and so on. In such cases the one who is consulted is the one with more experience in the problem area. Any expert theoretical or intellectual knowledge the consultant brings will also be experience-tested theory, knowledge refined by practice. Philosophical consultants in the areas of medicine, law, business, are rarely experts in these areas, and any theories they invoke will have been tested merely by argument. Even granted that for some of the moral issues arising within these professions a wider viewpoint is needed than that internal to the profession, why is the viewpoint from a moral theorist's study better for that purpose than that of any morally sensitive intelligent layman? We philosophers, by having given thought, may have help to give, but only if we are willing to investigate (or subcontract the investigation of) the actual results of trying to live by the principles that commended themselves to us in our armchairs and debating halls.

Most of those philosophers with whom I have spoken who are playing these new philosophical roles in other professions seem to be acutely aware of the need to absorb at least some knowledge of the host profession before they can serve it, and seem properly modest about the scope of their contribution and its tenuous connection with any specifically philosophical special knowledge or special skills. (Arthur Caplan tells the story of his contribution to hospital practice—the suggestion that patients' privacy could easily be better respected if a physician on his rounds were willing to wait until a patient had finished using a bedpan before exposing that patient to his own gaze and that of his retinue of attendant underlings. This is a fine contribution, but as Caplan has noted, a Ph.D. in philosophy scarcely seems a necessary condition of making it.)[20] I think that this new class of moral philosophers can be depended upon to carve out some suitable work niches for themselves in their new environments, given time, sensitivity to wrong moves, humility, and inventiveness. From these philosophers, who perforce have more contact with life outside the study and classroom than the rest of us do, we can hope for new suggestions about method, about ways in which we can better ground our moral theories on the facts—the economic, historical, and psychological facts. From them may also come new theories, but I think that the more important benefit to moral philosophy from its current spread into other professions will be new ideas about ways of examining moral theories, systems, opinions, and practices—ways of continuing Humean reflection on the principles by which we proceed.

Such moral philosophy would merge with other disciplines, and with the reflections of common life, and such a merger might help us to escape from that arrogance of solitary intellect which has condemned much moral theory to sustained self-delusions concerning its subject matter, its methods, and its authority.

NOTES

1. R. M. Hare, *Freedom and Reason* (Oxford: Clarendon Press, 1963), p. 97. Hare in more recent writings has moved to the view that the moral theory we get when we analyze this neutral language is one on which all theorizers agree.

2. John Rawls, *A Theory of Justice* (Cambridge, Mass.: Harvard University Press, 1971), p. 50.

3. Alasdair MacIntyre, *After Virtue* (Notre Dame: University of Notre Dame Press, 1981), ch. 6.

4. Ibid. p. 69.

5. Ibid. p. 58.

6. I discuss this further in "Theory and Reflective Practices."

7. David Hume, *Dialogues Concerning Natural Religion,* ed. Nelson Pike (Indianapolis: Bobbs-Merrill, 1970), pt. 8.

8. See my discussion of this move in "Theory and Reflective Practices."

9. Alan Donagan, *The Theory of Morality* (Chicago: University of Chicago Press, 1977), p. 7.

10. Alan Gewirth, *Reason and Morality* (Chicago: University of Chicago Press, 1978).

11. Richard B. Brandt, *A Theory of the Good and the Right* (Oxford: Clarendon Press, 1979).

12. See David Gauthier, *Morals by Agreement* (Oxford: Clarendon Press, 1986).

13. Hegel uses the phrase "Kammerdiener der Moralit" at in *Phänomenologie des Geistes,* ch. 6, p. 468, in the Hoffmeister edition (Hamburg: Felix Meiner Verlag, 1952.

14. See "Civilizing Practices" for more on this.

15. David Hume, *Enquiries,* ed. L. A. Selby-Bigge and P. H. Nidditch (Oxford: Clarendon Press, 1978). Further references to Hume's writings will be to the Selby-Bigge and Nidditch editions of *A Treatise of Human Nature* (T) and *Enquiries* (E).

16. Hume, E. 12.

17. Hume, T. 271.

18. Hume, T. 262.

19. Hume, E. 10.

20. See Arthur L. Caplan "Can Applied Ethics be Effective in Health Care, and Should It Strive to Be?" *Ethics* 93 (1983), 311–12.

Chapter 2

Normative Ethical Theories

CHERYL N. NOBLE

The recent production of major treatises devoted to elaborating normative ethical theories and the eruption of lively debates concerning the merits of opposed normative systems have been greeted with applause. This reaction is an historical about-face, since for forty or fifty years "ethical" treatises had been attacking the pretensions of traditional moral philosophy, calling for its demise or at the least severely limiting its claims. These skeptical attacks had succeeded in seriously undermining the academic status of moral philosophy and consequently moral philosophy was transformed into "metaethics," a highly abstract and technical discipline considered much less necessary to the general education of students than what it replaced and with a diminished role in the curriculum. The recent resurgence of interest in normative ethics has generally been lauded as a sign that philosophy has rededicated itself to its proper and time-honored tasks. There is a widespread feeling that the overblown claims of twentieth century skepticism have been whittled down to innocuous proportions and thus that nothing stands in the way of proceeding to construct ethical theories. The study of normative ethical theory now enjoys such respectability and popularity that it is difficult to raise once more the uncomfortable ideas that the ideal of normative ethical theory is a false one, that vanquishing the spectre of noncognitivism is not sufficient for legitimizing it, and that the popular new justifications for the enterprise fail in mischievous ways.[1]

THE UNITY AND AUTONOMY OF MORALITY AND THE POSSIBILITY OF NORMATIVE ETHICAL THEORIES

Moral philosophers today assume that the possibility of genuine moral knowledge is the same as the possibility of valid normative ethical theories. Thus in the contemporary framework one either accepts the possibility of normative ethical theory or is regarded as holding a skeptical view of moral knowledge. An alternative point of view might escape the horns of this dilemma by regarding the moral realm and moral knowledge as atheoretical, as inappropriately subsumed under the scientific model. This point of view could therefore regard a denial of the possibility of normative ethical theory as not skeptical in that it would have rejected the scientific standard, not as too high, but as inapplicable. It goes without saying that the philosophers who are presently engaging themselves in the formulation and analysis of normative theories regard themselves as having rejected a scientific model for ethics, but in fundamental ways they have not done so.

An unavoidable assumption for the moral theorist is that there is some coherence or unity among all moral standards—unavoidable because as a moral theorist his goal is to reduce the apparently endless diversity of particular moral judgments to some order, absolute or relative. He will attempt to do so by finding the basic or underlying principles which, when combined with a certain spirit of judgment and knowledge of fact, would lead to the acceptance of these particular moral judgments. The theorist may admit that absolute order or unity may not be available in that there may be a plurality of basic principles which have no set order of priority, but even in this case he is searching for whatever degree of order or unity there is, and he tends to believe that a small number of basic principles can be found. To put the point in such a way as to reveal the scientific analogy that guides his search for the fundamental laws, the moral theorist hypothesizes that among various dissimilar moral phenomena such as the rights and duties of friendship, marriage, sexual behavior, work, and the exchange of property there exists some such relation as that between the dissimilar physical phenomena of a lightning storm, the motions of a compass, the appearance of a rainbow, and the formation of an optical image in the range finder of a camera. As Ernest Nagel, whose examples these are, says of them: they all can be accounted for by a "single set of integrally related principles," those of modern electromagnetic theory.[2] A like set of principles is the ideal for moral theory and to the extent that the basic principles cannot be ordered, there is an acknowledgment (as there would be in science) that an ideal has been failed of.

Proving this assumption of the unity of morality false would be an impossible task, but it is less difficult to suggest reasons why this hypothesis underlying the whole enterprise of contemporary normative theory is implausible on the face of it, and not because morality is subjective or emotive or anything of the kind. Rather it is because there are perspectives from which the hypothesized coherence of moral phenomena appears unlikely. Only the habit of rigidly separating thought about morality from historical, sociological, or other empirical and social scientific points of view, in fact, permits the assumption to go unquestioned. Many thinkers, beginning with Hegel, in the nineteenth and early twentieth century rejected this kind of moral theorizing for reasons that grew out of appreciation of the extent to which morality could be understood in the context of cultural, historical, and what would now be called psychoanalytical inquiries. This kind of distrust of moral theory has nothing to do with positivist and related critiques of ethics, i.e., those that underlay English and American skepticism in the twentieth century. Positivism and its near relatives, in fact, have been just as likely to support naive ethical naturalisms as emotivism or other forms of noncognitivism.

This other source of skepticism about traditional moral philosophy hypothesizes that moral standards arise as part of the structures of various cultures, economies, and social forms, and its hypothesis is confirmed by the methods and results of modern history, sociology, and other social scientific inquiry. And if in fact what is good or right within some realm of life is a function of a wide variety of conditioning factors ranging from psychoanalytic to economic ones, then how could it also be possible that, nevertheless, taken as *moral* phenomena, they all stem from a common, relatively unitary source?[3] The point here is not that morality is "merely" disguise for economics or is reducible to psychology or anything of the kind. Rather it is that the moral dimensions of conduct are inseparable from the others and are good or rational only taken as part of the realms of life they are born in. These diverse realms of life are again diverse in historical origin and sociological function and they present imperatives of conduct of their own. It will inevitably be the case that the reasons, historically, why property has come to be respected in certain forms and not others has little to do with the reasons why certain rules of sexual conduct are also regarded as binding (although, of course, there may be fascinating linkages). But a normative ethical theorist must assume that in spite of diverse and unrelated historical origins and social functions—perhaps the one rests almost entirely on economic and the other on psychological factors—these different sets of moral standards, insofar as they are good and valid, are traceable to a more or less simple and unitary logical source. Furthermore, he may find himself willy-nilly committed to the idea that people have all through history accepted the right ideas morally for all the wrong reasons as he tries to reconcile his *theoretical* justifications for the standards history (no doubt wisely) has handed down to him with the actual reasons why certain practices got accepted.

The objective, to repeat, is not that it is impossible for these reasons to believe that all valid moral standards flow logically from a common source. Certainly it is possible in spite of what has been said against the idea. But without some reason, as yet invisible, to think the contrary, it does appear improbable. And one begins to suspect that the hypothesis of the unity of morality has far more to do with the traditions of moral philosophy than any actual study of the relations between moral standards. In the ancient cosmologies and metaphysics of the Greeks and Christians, there were indeed reasons supplied to make the search for the underlying moral principles appear plausible. These reasons, however, have long since ceased to convince and without them, why *suspect* that behind the diversity of moral rights and wrongs which we acknowledge is a common fount of underlying fundamental principles? With the weight of tradition behind him, what the normative theorist has done is to reason from his practical desire for some handle on the realm of moral phenomena to the theoretical claim that *qua* moral phenomena there is some such key or handle to them. This hypothesis is simply more extravagant than its contrary.

It has often been pointed out that were someone actually to produce a normative ethical theory, all doubts such as these would be silenced; the most recent version of this argument will be attended to below. In the meantime, the overwhelming failure of any normative ethical theory to gain anything approaching universal acceptance is not promising. This fact too ought to lead us to take as a more reasonable starting point for moral philosophy the idea that what "makes right acts right" is not a function of their relation to one another or to a common source, basis, or foundation, but is a function of the particular dimension of life and practice they form part of and of the relations between these various parts of life. Moral values and standards, after all, lack a substance of their own. There are no purely moral acts, but only moral and immoral ways of working, buying and selling, engaging in friendships, and so forth. Moral standards always qualify practices, habits, and kinds of conduct which are not at bottom "moral," but political, familial, and the like. The hypothesis that the moral standards which ought to qualify all these practices are an independent function of the requirements of the moral realm is the assumption which, it has been argued, ought no longer be plausible to us. That moral standards exist that govern conduct in all these interdependent realms of life attests not nec-

1

essarily to the existence of an independent moral realm, but to the *moral* point that in all parts of life questions of character and conduct may arise and that the ideal of leading a good life as a whole can develop in consequence. The unity and autonomy of morality, in other words, may be only moral, and not theoretical.[4]

The notion of the unity of morality leads one to think of it as a "realm" superimposed on other realms of life, economic, familial, or political, rather than as the dimension or integral part of them it appears from the points of view of the various social sciences, or for that matter from the point of view of everyday life. But moral philosophy has come to see morality as *governing* political or economic life—which, of course, it does in a manner of speaking in that the moral dimensions of these realms express the forbidden and enjoined manners of behaving in them—rather than seeing them as sets of practices which by their nature will embody certain moral standards. If morality is conceived as a realm apart from but governing these others, it is easy also to think that the same ends or values are being morally met and served in all of them such that, if adultery is wrong, that is true in the long run for the same reasons as not repaying a bank loan or lying about the opposition in an election. Such a view of the nature of morality will inevitably have unfortunate consequences for moral inquiry, since it will unavoidably lead thought away from concrete study of social institutions. And only that kind of study holds out hope of improving our understanding of moral standards, how they in fact operate, originate, and generalize themselves from one part of life to another, and thus how they may be improved, reformed, or better served. The autonomy contemporary moral philosophers have been carving out for their discipline, which has been a way of turning the failure of ethical naturalism to good account, dissolves when morality is considered in its concrete social settings. And thus, also, the recent attempts to develop ethical theories entirely apart from empirical inquiries into the historical and social origins of the ethical ideas that are defended can only fail. These remarks should by no means be read as a defense of naturalism. Learning the historical origins or sociological meaning of the operation of moral standards is not sufficient to tell us whether or not they are good. But, on the other hand, it is impossible to tell whether they are good without knowing these things, for the obvious reason that without knowing them, we do not understand what we are for or against because we lack the kind of self-consciousness that is essential to good judgment.

Intuitionist moral philosophy particularly, but to some degree
the whole tradition of moral philosophy within which contemporaries
locate themselves, has always attempted to theorize about moral
phenomena as they appear to the enculturated moral mind. It has
been entirely indifferent to the goals of social scientific understanding
of the values that inform different cultures and thus to the goal of
historical and social self-consciousness as conditions for intelligent
study of morality. Intuitionism, beginning from the standpoint of the
enculturated mind, studies its intuitions for the "data" of moral
theory, and then attempts to systematize or theorize about those
data, dismissing the idea that the key to the contents of moral
consciousness may lie largely outside it. Contemporary philosophy
has reverted to the idea that the mysteries of morality can be
unraveled in this way, but it has added a new justification for thinking
so. It has borrowed from the philosophy of science a whole set of
categories designed to explain the successful workings of science and
the structure of scientific justifications and tried to show how they
do or can work in the same way for morality. In this way they have
tried to make moral theory into a respectable science among sciences,
but with an independent subject matter.

THE PHILOSOPHY OF SCIENCE AS A MODEL FOR MORAL
PHILOSOPHY

The tendency in thought with which we are concerned is sufficiently widespread to constitute a school which will here be called
"neointuitionism" because of the central role it allots to intuition in
the justification of normative ethical theories.[5] Neointuitionism generally regards it as a foremost goal of moral philosophy to establish
such theories. But since the possibility of giving objective justification
to moral theories is challenged by the dominant skeptical trends of
metaethics of the past decades, neointuitionism has developed several
methodological claims in order to justify circumvention of metaethics.
It has claimed that normative ethics is methodologically prior to or
independent of metaethics. Questions about the possibility of moral
knowledge and the logic of moral justification need not first be settled
(nonskeptically) in order to engage in normative ethical inquiry. It
is entirely possible, neointuitionism suggests, that answers to the
metaethical questions will be forthcoming only if we first develop
general theories of obligation to base them on.

Underlying such methodological claims is an analogy of ethics
with science. In this analogy, moral knowledge is likened implicitly

to scientific or factual knowledge without being assimiliated to it; normative ethical theories are likened to substantive scientific theories; and metaethics is likened to the philosophy of science. Normative ethics is held to be prior to metaethics because it is believed that questions about the nature of moral knowledge, justification, etc., are answerable only by paying close attention to real cases of moral knowledge and thought. Just as philosophers of science can clarify science and evaluate its claims to give us knowledge only by studying the nature and justifications of actual scientific theories as they have developed through history, so metaethicists must study "actual" theories of ethics and perhaps no answers to the thorny questions of justification and meaning can arise except by these means. To require normative ethics to wait for an encouraging nod from metaethics would be rather like waiting for a theory of scientific meaning and justification before attempting to develop theories of gases, genetics, or relativity.

This analogy aims ultimately to rebut moral skepticism, as one might scientific skepticism, by presenting the skeptic with the actual success of a theory—assuming, as may be too generous, that this makes sense as a description of how scientific skepticism might be refuted. Normative ethics, according to the analogy, might define standards of truth for itself and might have internally determined criteria of what is to count as success and failure in its theorizing. If it did, then a theory which was successful by these standards could not be rejected metaethically except by a different, and irrelevant, set of standards. But this scheme for rebutting skepticism requires that moral knowledge be *theoretical*, just as science is, so that all that contemporary philosophy has to say about the structure and justification of theories in general can be applied to normative ethics as well as to any of the sciences. This assumption, which is intimately related to that of the unity of morality, is far from necessary despite its widespread acceptance.

Why believe that a normative ethical theory is the ultimate form and foundation of moral knowledge? A normative ethical theory, as a systematic account of rightness or goodness, is intended to be useful in solving concrete moral and social dilemmas and in resolving moral doubts by prescribing certain conduct, or the establishment of certain institutions, directly or indirectly through the prescription of actions, practices, rules, maxims, or non-basic principles. If underlying principles of right and and wrong could be found, we would be able to claim to know right and wrong. However, even though such theories might enable us to know right and wrong, it does not follow that without them we are ignorant of right and wrong. It follows only given the assumption that moral knowledge is essentially theoretical and that therefore without a moral theory we are as ignorant of right and wrong as we would be of the mechanisms of heredity without genetic theory—an idea which should give us pause. Here, it is possible to play the normative theorist's analogies of science with morality against him.

If normative ethical theories are indeed theories, then like all theories there must be jobs for them to perform, which only they can perform, in the shape of questions they are to answer. If a theory is not necessary for the answering of a question, it will be superfluous and uncompelling, a kind of pseudo-theory. In the case of the phenomena of heredity, for example, we are in a sense driven to accept genetic theory in that it performs a task for us that only it or some similar theory can perform; and if we experienced no mystery or ignorance about the phenomena it proposes to explain, it would then be in a manner of speaking unemployed and therefore uncompelling and superfluous. But as a matter of fact genetic theory does have a job and there are certain questions to which it alone provides the answers. Having these answers is having the theory and lacking them is lacking the theory. Although there may be people who are quite expert at animal breeding who are nonetheless ignorant of genetics, there are limits to their expertise and certain matters of which they must remain ignorant unless they understand the modern science of genetics. But is anything like this ever the case with normative ethical theories? Distressingly enough, the situations are entirely dissimilar.

A rather too flippant critic of normative ethical theories might object to them on the simple grounds that since the job they are supposed to do has always been done without them, they could not possibly be indispensable for doing it. That moral theories are unnecessary for answering moral questions is proved in that moral dilemmas have been getting settled all through history without moral theories. Even those who claim to accept some moral theory do not seem to have different moral opinions from other people; nor do they seem to use a moral theory to resolve moral questions. To such flippancy, of course, there are ready responses. Settling dilemmas and settling them properly or rightly are very different things and it is the latter for which moral theories are indispensable. This claim is taken up more thoroughly below. In the meantime, there is more to this objection than first meets the eye. It is undeniable that any question that a moral theory can answer can be answered without a moral theory, the correctness of the answer aside. More problematically, any answer dictated by a normative ethical theory can be, and in every case I can think of, has been arrived at in some other way, and herein lies the problem. In order for a theory not to be superfluous, we ought to be able to point to some conclusions not reachable except by its means and in the case of normative ethical theories we cannot. If utilitarianism tells us to free our slaves, so do our consciences or our "intuitive" beliefs that all men are created equal. The categorical imperative may tell us to keep our promises, but we knew it all along anyway. We are in general always able to come up with the answer the theory dictates without relying on any theory. And that is as though all the predictions of atomic theory were to be arrived at without relying on the use of atomic theory at all, or as though all the hypotheses which could be formulated and tested on the basis of relativity theory could have been formulated without relativity theory.

This peculiarity of normative ethical theories compared with scientific theories is only one of many, all of which deserve more attention than it is possible to give to them here. Our willingness to make up our minds without moral theories and to be satisfied with atheoretical moral thinking has already been mentioned and will be touched on below. There is the further difficulty of discovering which conclusions any particular theory actually dictates, which the interminable debates about the forms of utilitarianism or whether Kant's Categorical Imperative does or does not commit us to informing the would-be murderer of our friend's whereabouts attest to. There is the still more troublesome fact that without being actually sure what conclusions the theory truly dictates we are nonetheless to decide the truth of the theory in the end by considering what courses of action it enjoins. And worse, one has somehow to know independently of that theory whether those courses of action are the right ones. Finally, and this issue is wholly ignored by moral philosophy, there is a difficulty in understanding what role normative ethical theories are to play in the moral life and how they are to be integrated into our choices of action and conduct. For example, are good people drawn to accept true normative ethical theories while bad people think they are false? How could a bad person see that a true moral theory were in fact true, if he does not believe that he is bad? If the theory conflicts with the considered judgment of a very good man, are we to believe the theory or the man? If the theory conflicts with strong feelings of conscience, is it possible that the theory is nonetheless true? And if the answer to the last question is "yes," as it seems it must be, in what sense do adherents to a moral theory maintain moral autonomy if they must override their sense of moral obligation with their loyalty to a theory? All of these issues arise whether or not one accepts an intuitionist account of the justification of normative ethical theories, but some of them are exacerbated by the neointuitionism favored by many philosophers.

NEOINTUITIONISM AND THE JUSTIFICATION OF NORMATIVE ETHICAL THEORIES

If moral theories are necessary in order to know right and wrong, it was just suggested, there arises some difficulty in explaining how we ever knew what was right and wrong before we had the theory. No one suggests that we did not, oddly enough, since it would be strange to think that we knew everything about heredity and natural selection without genetic theory. On the other hand, if we did know what was wrong and right without the theory, then the question posed earlier of how the theory is of any use arises. Neointuitionism has implicit answers to these questions. It resolves the apparent dilemma by the claim that in developing normative ethical theories, philosophers are laying out what we already know *in a sense*. Moral theories are said to be composed of principles we already operate on, albeit blindly, unclearly, unsystematically, inconsistently, etc. We know right and wrong pre-theoretically, but imperfectly. As we clarify the underlying principles which inform our intuitions, those intuitions themselves become more clear. We clarify theory and particular ideas of right and wrong in relation to one another in a way which this school calls the justification of the theory. Although we normally act on a number of disparate common sense precepts, these can conflict, give ambiguous guidance or fail to give any guidance. Moral philosophy is supposed to find the underlying principles that will systematize these, resolve their apparent contradictions and, where the contradiction is more than apparent, give some basis for a reform of common sense, intuitive morality. In morality, as in science, there is a web of belief in which the justification of any intuition or principle is to be referred to the structure of belief as a whole.

In this theory of justification, intuitions (less straightforward intuitionists will speak of attitudes or prereflective beliefs, but their function is the same) play the role in moral theory that observations do in science. They are to be the subject of theory, what is to be explained, and as well what justifies the theories that are developed. If a theory accounts for all our intuitions in that it prescribes more or less what they would prescribe, then it may safely be extended to cases we either have never encountered, have no intuitions about, or have mixed intuitions about. This is thought to be similar to the way in which a law in science which accounts for all past observations may safely be extended to predict what will happen in future cases. Without denying some real parallels between science and morality, the overall pictures are dissimilar in ways that make the analogy profoundly misleading.

To begin with, calling unreflective moral beliefs "intuitions" grants them an unearned cognitive status. It is a philosophical convention so well established that it is now useless to flout it, but it cannot too often be pointed out that in no way do intuitions or attitudes deserve to be treated as though they could function for morality as observation does for science.[6] Whereas in science, statements of observation are those on which universal agreement is almost certain, in morals there is almost equally certain to be disagreement about what is intuitively right and wrong. While good philosophical explanations of the reliability of observational statements exist, which draw upon our understanding of the nature of language and perception, there is every philosophical reason to *doubt* (given the nature of moral language and the origin of moral belief) the reliability of moral intuitions. It is a well-established fact that our considered moral judgments vary both intra-and interculturally, and vary also according to social class, economic structures, and other factors as well. Since these reasons to be suspicious of moral intuition are so well-known, it is curious that it now comes to be used in such an important way in moral theory.

What has happened is that moral philosophy has tried to rescue intuition from such difficulties with its new understanding of the nature of justification which it has borrowed from the philosophy of science. The juggling between intuition and theory is supposed to result in the sifting out of those intuitions which are truly reliable, which say something basic about our moral sense. The effort is simultaneously to shore up intuitions by means of theories and theories by means of intuition; theory and intuitive data are to succor one another and to have together a strength that neither has separately. But this will not work for the inescapable reason that intuitions are different from observations in the ways already mentioned. Following this method of justification, it is entirely possible that we should weave a tight web of moral belief which, unfortunately, would appear even remotely plausible only to a given class of people in a given historical epoch and culture. This is because, in implicit recognition of the differences between intuitions and observation, moral philosophers do not and can not permit intuitions to serve as the court of appeal that observation is in science, even for a Quinean.

As remarked above, it is often held that if some moral intuitions contradict principles which by and large are satisfactory, those intuitions can be rejected and this idea is troublesome. On what bases can intuitions be rejected? There are several possibilities. An intuition might be rejected on the basis of its weakness, and at times this seems to be the criterion in use. At other times, however, the criterion seems to have nothing to do with its strength or weakness but with how much company it has.[7] In other words, if one has safely covered most of one's intuitions with principles and has just one stubborn one which does not fit, perhaps it may be dropped. At still other times, the criterion seems to depend on how often in life the situation it concerns arises. An intuition which deals with a relatively rare situation or one with heroic dimensions may apparently be dropped sometimes. Perhaps a strong intuition concerning a not uncommon but rather unimportant sort of case could also be dropped—at least, it is not obvious why it should be forbidden, given the permissibility of these other cases. Perhaps, also, various combinations of these factors might also instigate dropping an intuition.

But why rejecting intuitions in any such circumstances should be permitted is hard to understand. This web of belief gains consistency by ignoring the data which make for contradiction. The parallel phenomenon in science could not be tolerated. Although there are special circumstances in which contradictory data in science are ignored and questioned, these are narrowly circumscribed. No observation in science would be rejected *solely* because it was the only kind not to conform to a theory, nor because it concerned exceptional or unimportant circumstances. This is true even though a theory that leaves certain factors unaccounted for or is apparently contradicted by some observations may continue to be accepted failing a more adequate alternative theory. Observations, we are forced to admit, are simply more pushy than intuitions.

Recognition of the lack of compelling power of theories established by this method is evident in that people will not in fact regard a theory as more reliable than a conflicting intuition and will jettison the theory and not the intuition—a perfectly rational attitude considering there is no reason to think the intuitions it accounts for are truer or more important than those it does not. In *any* case in which an intuition disagrees with a theory, therefore, in practice the theory

must and will be questioned. And since it is universally admitted
that this situation will arise with all theories, the theories in the end
turn out to be no contribution to the moral life to speak of. In cases
where the theory concurs with intuitions, one might just as well
trust them. In cases where it does not, one has to find a new theory
anyway. William James, in giving a similar criticism of a "useless"
theory of truth, illustrated his point with a story of an Irishman
being carried to a funeral in a sedan with no floor. He runs along
inside it saying, "Faith, if it weren't for the honor of the thing, I
might just as well walk." Moral theories, likewise, look rather like
ceremonial theories, there for the appearance, but doing not much
else.[8]

Even in the best of all possible worlds, moral theories are said
to offer an advantage over uninstructed intuition only because they
may be extended to cases where we have no intuitions or where
our intuitions are inchoate or weak. The question is, why trust what
such theories would dictate about these cases? Is it because what
they dictate is what we *would* intuitively feel to be right if we
thoroughly understood the complexities of the situation and were
utterly consistent and systematic in our thinking? If that is so, then
one wonders why we simply do not intuit the answer when we
study the case thoroughly and cautiously? What reason is there to
assume our intuitions need aid of this kind? After all, intuitions are
attitudes and finding out what one's attitude should be is, normally,
finding out what one's attitude *is* when one is fully understanding,
consistent, etc. On the other hand, if the theories dictate something
that we would not intuit, given understanding, consistency, and the
rest, we may feel perfectly within our rights to ignore the theory.
In such a case, there would be a clash between the idea of moral
theory and moral autonomy which moral theorists have not recognized.

In the end, the final and all too obvious problem with the
method of justification is that it leads only to self-consistency in
thought and not to objective truth; and it has nothing like a Quinean
notion of observation to save it from the perniciousness of such a
result. In the end this theory leads to a kind of relativism. Thus it
has all of the vices and none of the virtues of classical intuitionism,
which at least gave us a guarantee of truth and objectivity in return
for our swallowing intuition as the inexplicable surd of moral philosophy. These considerations should make us suspicious of the use
of the word 'justification' with regard to the establishing of general
principles on the basis of intuitions and, as well, of the use of the

language and trappings of scientific methods and theories in this connection.

If the doubts raised earlier about the appropriateness of morality as the subject of theorizing of this sort were correct, then we have a new vantage point for understanding the contemporary work in normative ethical theory. The principles these theories lay out as basic may be understood as the selection of particular facets of morality, usually those of present historical importance, which are then said to be the basis for the others. The intuitionist methods begin to appear as vain efforts to achieve a kind of scientific unity where none is possible or desirable. Ironically, although moral philosophy engages in this misleading imitation of science and assumes its trappings, where a genuine and appropriate empiricism is desirable in ethics, it is absent. Rather than basing searches for wise or otherwise valid moral generalizations on serious inquiries into the proper social questions, human nature, or whatever the case may require, moral philosophers consult their intuitions, which is considerably less trouble. There is no attempt to gain awareness of the sources and conditions of our common sense moral judgments. Of course, there may be no escaping reliance upon them, but they can amount to nothing if not informed by such knowledge as historians, sociologists, psychologists and other practitioners of concrete empirical disciplines can provide us with. In place of a difficult methodological empiricism as a corrective to the pseudo-scientific pretensions of contemporary moral philosophy, moral philosophers substitute the idea of being "well-informed." In consequence, philosophers' efforts to tackle problems in normative and applied ethics cannot hope to advance understanding very far. Recent developments in moral philosophy must be viewed as vain attempts to achieve objectivity and reliability in moral belief in that they sacrifice any methods that might actually bring us closer to those goals.

NOTES

1. The criticisms of the idea of normative ethical theory offered here are not intended as criticisms of the idea of normative ethics. Rather, they are aimed at a particular conception of what normative ethics should be.

2. Ernest Nagel, *The Structure of Science* (New York: Harcourt, Brace and World, Inc., 1961), p. 462.

3. The validity or rationality of moral standards is not impugned when it is denied that they are or could be derived from a set of basic moral

principles. In denying the need for normative ethical theories, moreover, one is not denying a need for moral thought, knowledge, inquiry, objectivity, etc., but that these will take a certain form.

4. Surprisingly enough, the view that normative ethical theories are not a proper goal of moral philosophy was not foreign to the thinking of the two foremost British classical intuitionists of the earlier half of the century, H. A. Prichard and Sir David Ross—suprisingly in that the argument here rests in large part on anti-intuitionism. H. A. Prichard, in his famous essay, "Does Moral Philosophy Rest on a Mistake?" (A. I. Melden, ed., *Ethical Theories* [Englewood Cliffs, New Jersey: Prentice-Hall, Inc., 1967], pp. 526–38), gives an argument profoundly different in inspiration from the one here, but which does lead also to the conclusion that the demand for normative ethical theory is misguided. But Prichard thought so because he thought moral theories were always demanded as proofs for what cannot be proved but only "apprehended directly by an act of moral thinking." Sir David Ross argued against the idea that there was something that made right acts right (*The Right and the Good* [London: Oxford University Press, 1930]). Unfortunately as an intuitionist, he believed that right acts were made right only by their intuited rightness. His efforts to disprove one particular kind of normative ethical theory, utilitarianism, at times seems to take the form of what is really an attack on the idea of normative ethical theory *per se.*

5. Although John Rawls can be classified as a neointuitionist, I am not using this term to mean what he does by "intuitionism." By the latter he means any theory that has a plurality of basic principles but provides no priority rule for determining how the basic principles are to be balanced against each other (*A Theory of Justice* [Cambridge: Harvard University Press, 1971], p. 34). Intuition comes into play in the balancing of these principles. However Rawls makes ample use of intuition in other ways that make his theory neointuitionist. See particularly in *A Theory of Justice*, Secs. 4, 7–9, and 87.

Neointuitionism, as described here, is not intended to represent the ideas of any particular philosopher exactly—the resemblance to Rawls's views will be clear—but is intended to be a plausible, broad, and general representation of a view similar to many now in vogue. There are, of course, philosophers who deal with normative ethical theories who are not neointuitionists, but this form of intuitionism is now the dominant theory of justification.

6. Rawls, unlike most philosophers who accept such views, does point out (*A Theory of Justice*, p. 49) that there is no parallel in science to the revising of moral judgments in the light of "regulative principles." "To take an extreme case," he remarks, "if we have an accurate account of the motions of the heavenly bodies that we do not find appealing, we cannot alter these motions to conform to a more attractive theory." Having said so, however,

he does not continue to ask whether this unfortunate dissimilarity has serious consequences for his views on justification, or if not, why not.

7. A "weak" intuition is sometimes treated like an unreliable observation, but this is misleading. A weak intuition always (but, as it were, lackadaisically) intuits one and the same thing. An unreliable observation is one that cannot be readily repeated.

8. All this assumes that principles successfully accounting for all of these intuitions can be formulated. I grant the assumption for the sake of argument, having already given reasons to doubt it. In addition, I do not defend the reliance on intuition to form moral judgments. I only question whether moral theories based on intuition are an improvement over intuition alone.

Chapter 3

The Scientific and the Ethical[1]

BERNARD WILLIAMS

Discussions of objectivity often start from considerations about disagreement. We might ask why this should be so. It makes it seem as though disagreement were surprising, but there is no reason why that should be so (the earliest thinkers in the Western tradition found conflict at least as obvious a feature of the world as concord). The interest in disagreement comes about, rather, because neither agreement nor disagreement is universal. It is not that disagreement needs explanation and agreement does not, but that in different contexts disagreement requires different sorts of explanation, and so does agreement.

The way in which one understands a given kind of disagreement, and explains it, has important practical effects. It can modify one's attitude to others and one's understanding of one's own outlook. In relation to other people, one needs a view of what is to be opposed, rejected, and so forth, and in what spirit; for oneself, disagreement can raise a warning that one may be wrong, and if truth or correctness is what one is after, one may need to reform one's strategies.

Disagreement does not necessarily have to be overcome. It may remain an important and constitutive feature of one's relations to others, and also be seen as something that is merely to be expected in the light of the best explanations that we have of how such disagreement arises. There can be tension involved here, if one at once feels that the disagreement is about very important matters, and that there is a good explanation of why the disagreement is only to be expected. The tension is specially acute when the disagreement is not only important, but expresses itself in judgments that seem to demand assent from others.

Among types of disagreement, and the lessons that can be learned from them, there is a well-known polarity. At one extreme there is the situation of two children wanting one bun, or two heroes wanting one slave girl. The disagreement is practical and it is entirely explicable, and the explanation of it is not going to cast much doubt on the cognitive powers of the people involved. It may be said that this kind of case is so primitively practical that it hardly even introduces any judgment over which there is disagreement. Even at the most primitive level, of course, there is disagreement about *what is to be done*, but this is so near to desire and action that no one is going to think that the disagreement shows any failure of knowledge or understanding on anyone's part. It is simply that two people want incompatible things. But the conflict may well not remain as blank as that, and if the parties want to settle it by ordered speech rather than by violence, they will invoke more substantive judgments, usually of justice, and the children will talk about fairness, or the heroes about precedence.

In their most basic form, at least, these disagreements need not make anyone think that someone has failed to recognize or understand something, or that they cannot speak the language. At the opposite pole of the traditional contrast are disagreements that do make one think that. What these typically are depends on the theory of knowledge favored by the commentator, but they often involve the observation under standard conditions of what J. L. Austin used to call 'middle-sized dry goods'. A feature of these examples that will be important later in the discussion is that the parties are assumed to share the same concepts, and to be trained in the recognition of furniture, pens, pennies or whatever it may be.

Around these paradigms there have been formed various oppositions: between practical and theoretical, or value and fact, or *ought* and *is*. Each of these has been thought to represent a fundamental difference in what disagreement means, and they are often taken to suggest contrasting hopes for resolving it. However, it is a mistake to suppose that these oppositions are different ways of representing just one distinction. Indeed, the two paradigm examples that I have mentioned significantly fail to correspond to the two ends of any one of these contrasts. The quarrel about the allocation of a good is certainly an example of the practical, but until one gets to the stage of taking seriously the claims of justice, it is not yet a disagreement about value. A disagreement in the perception of furniture is without doubt a disagreement about a matter of fact, but is not yet a disagreement about what is most often contrasted with the practical, namely the theoretical. To assemble these kinds of examples into some one contrast requires more work to be done. It has been done, characteristically, by reducing the evaluative to the practical, and extending the factual to the theoretical. Both these maneuvres are of positivist inspiration, and they are both suspect. It is not surprising that some philosophers now doubt whether there is any basic distinction at all that can be constructed to the traditional pattern.

I accept that there is no one distinction that is in question here. I also accept that the more positivistic formulations that have gone into defining each side of such a distinction are misguided. However, I believe that in relation to ethics there is a genuine and profound difference to be found, and also—it is a further point—that the difference is enough to motivate some version of the feeling (itself recurrent, if not exactly traditional) that science has some chance of being more or less what it seems, a systematized theoretical account of how the world really is, while ethical thought has no chance of being everything that it seems. The tradition is right, moreover, not only in thinking that there is such a distinction, but also in thinking that we can come to understand what it is through understanding disagreement. However, it is not a question of how much disagreement there is, nor even of what methods we have to settle disagreement, though that of course provides many relevant considerations. The basic difference lies rather in our reflective understanding of the best hopes that we could coherently entertain for eliminating disagreement in the two areas. It is a matter of what, under the most favourable conditions, would be the best explanation of disagreement being removed: the explanation—as I shall say from now on—of convergence.

The two 'areas,' as I have called them, are the *scientific* and the *ethical*. I hope to explain why one end should be labelled the 'scientific', rather than, say, the 'factual'. It can be explained quite briefly why the other end, the ethical, is not called by any of several other familiar names. It is not called 'the evaluative', because that additionally covers at least the area of aesthetic judgment, and that raises many questions of its own. It is not called 'the normative', which covers only part of the interest of the ethical (roughly, the part concerned with rules), and also naturally extends to such things as the law, which again raise different questions. Last, it is not called 'the practical', because that would displace a large part of the problem. It is not hard to concede that there is a distinction between the practical and (let us say) the non-practical. There is clearly such a thing as practical reasoning or deliberation, and that is not the same as thinking about how things are. It is *obviously* not the same, and that is why positivism thought that it had validated the traditional distinction by reducing the evaluative to the practical. But that reduction is mistaken, and it makes the whole problem look easier than it is.[2]

The basic idea behind the distinction between the scientific and the ethical, expressed in terms of convergence, is very simple. In a scientific inquiry there should ideally be convergence on an answer, where the best explanation of that convergence involves the idea that the answer represents how things are, whereas in the area of the ethical, at least at a high level of generality (the issue of generality is one that we shall come back to), there is no such coherent hope. The distinction does not turn on any difference in whether convergence will actually occur, and it is important that this is not what the argument is about. It might well turn out that there will be convergence in ethical outlook, at least among human beings. The point of the contrast is that even if that happens, it will not be correct to think that it has come about because convergence has been guided by how things actually are, whereas convergence in the sciences might be explained in that way if it does happen. This means, among other things, that we understand differently in the two cases the existence of convergence or, alternatively, its failure to come about.

I shall come back to ways in which we might understand ethical convergence. First, however, we must face certain arguments that suggest there is really nothing at all in the distinction, expressed in these terms. There are two different directions from which that objection can come. In one version, it says that the notion of a convergence that comes about because of how things are is an empty notion. In the other, it says that the notion of such a convergence is not empty, but that it is available as much in ethical cases as in scientific—that is to say, the notion has some content, but it does nothing to help the distinction.

I have already said that the point of the distinction and of its explanation in terms of convergence does not turn on the question whether convergence as a matter of fact occurs. On the scientific side, however, it would be unrealistic to disconnect these ideas totally from the ways in which the history of Western science since the seventeenth century is to be understood. For one thing, any aspiration for the convergence of science that conceded at the same time that it had not occurred up to now might well seem merely Utopian and only fit to obscure the real issues, like the once fashionable hopes for a Galileo of the social sciences. More importantly, the conception of scientific progress in terms of convergence cannot be divorced from the history of Western science because it is the history of Western science that has done most to encourage it.

It is quite hard to deny that history displays a considerable degree of convergence. What has been claimed is that this appearance has no real significance, because it is a cultural artifact, a product of the way in which we choose to narrate the history of science. Richard Rorty has written:[3]

> It is less paradoxical . . . to stick to the classical notion of 'better describing what was already there' for physics. This is not because of deep epistemological or metaphysical considerations, but simply because, when we tell our Whiggish stories about how our ancestors gradually crawled up the mountain on whose (possibly false) summit we stand, we need to keep some things constant throughout the story . . . Physics is the paradigm of 'finding' simply because it is hard (at least in the West) to tell a story of changing universes against the background of an unchanging moral law or poetic canon, but very easy to tell the reverse sort of story.

There are two notable faults in such a description of scientific success and what that success means. One is its attitude to the fact that it is easy to tell one kind of story and hard to tell the other. *Why* is the picture of 'the world already there', helping to control our descriptions of it, so compelling? This seems to require some explanation on Rorty's account, but it does not get one. If the reference to 'the West' implies a cultural or anthropological explanation, it is totally unclear what it would be: totally unclear, indeed, what it could be, if it is not going itself to assume an already existing physical world in which human beings come into existence and develop their cultures, and by which they are affected in various ways.

The point that an assumption of that kind is going to lie behind any explanations of what we do leads directly to the second fault in Rorty's account, that it is self-defeating. If the story he tells were true, then there would be no perspective from which he could express it in this way. If it is overwhelmingly convenient to say science describes what is already there, and if there are no deep metaphysical or epistemological issues here, but only a question of what is convenient (it is 'simply because' of that that we speak as we do), then what everyone should be saying, including Rorty, is that science describes a world that is already there. But Rorty urges us not to say that, and in doing so, and in insisting, as *opposed to that*, on our talking of what it is convenient to say, he is trying to reoccupy the transcendental standpoint outside human speech and activity which is precisely what he wants us to renounce.[4]

A more effective level of objection lies in a negative claim that Rorty and others make, that no convergence of science, past or future, could possibly be explained in any contentful way by reference to the way that the world is, because there is an insoluble difficulty with the notion of 'the world' as determining belief. It comes out as a dilemma. On the one hand, 'the world' may be characterized in terms of our current beliefs about what it contains; it is a world of stars, people, grass, tables and so forth. When 'the world' is taken in this way, we can of course say that our beliefs about the world are affected by the world, in the sense that for instance our beliefs about grass are affected by grass, but there is nothing illuminating or contentful in this—our conception of the world as the object of our beliefs can do no better than repeat the beliefs that we take to represent it. If, on the other hand, we try to form some idea of a world that is prior to any description of it, the world that all systems of belief and representation are trying to represent, then we have a quite empty notion of something completely unspecified and unspecifiable.[5] So either way we fail to have a notion of 'the world' that will do what is required of it.

Each side of this dilemma takes all our representations of the world together, in the one case putting them all in, and in the other leaving them all out. But there is a third and more helpful possibility, that we should form a conception of the world that is 'already there' in terms of some but not all of our representations, our beliefs and theories. In reflecting on the world that is there *anyway*, independent of our experience, we must concentrate not in the first instance on what our beliefs are about, but on how they represent what they are about. We can select among our beliefs and features of our world-picture some which we can reasonably claim to represent the world in a way that is to the maximum degree independent of our perspective and its peculiarities. The resultant picture of things, if we can carry through this task, can be called the 'absolute conception' of the world.[6] In terms of that conception, we may hope to explain the possibility of our attaining that conception itself, and also the possibility of other, more perspectival, representations.

This notion of an absolute conception can serve to *make effective* a distinction between 'the world as it is independently of our experience' and 'the world as it seems to us'. It does that by understanding 'the world as it seems to us' as 'the world as it seems peculiarly to us'; the absolute conception will, correspondingly, be that conception of the world that might be arrived at by any investigators, even if they were very different from us. What counts as a relevant difference from us, and indeed what for various levels of description will count as 'us', will itself be explained on the basis of that conception itself; we shall be able to explain, for instance, why one kind of observer can make observations that another kind cannot make. It is centrally important that these ideas relate to science, not to all kinds of knowledge. We can *know* things, the content of which is perspectival: we can know that grass is green, for instance, though *green*, for certain, and probably *grass*, are concepts that would not be available to every competent observer of the world, and would not figure in the absolute conception. (As we shall see very soon, people can know things even more locally perspectival than that.) The point is not to give an account of knowledge, and the opposition that we are discussing is not to be expressed in terms of knowledge, but of science. The aim is to outline the possibility of a convergence characteristic of science, one that could contentfully be said to be a convergence on how things (anyway) are.

That possibility, as I have explained it, depends heavily on notions of explanation. The substance of the absolute conception (as opposed to those vacuous or vanishing ideas of 'the world' that were offered before) lies in the idea that it could non-vacuously explain how itself, and the various perspectival views of the world, should be possible. It is an important feature of modern science that it contributes to explaining how creatures who have the origins and characteristics that we have can understand a world that has the properties this same science ascribes to the world. The achievements of evolutionary biology and the neurological sciences are substantive in these respects, and the notions of explanation involved are not vacuous. It is true, however, that such explanations cannot themselves operate entirely at the level of the absolute conception, because what they have to explain are psychological and social phenomena, such as beliefs and theories and conceptions of the world, and there may be little reason to suppose that they, in turn, could be adequately characterized in non-perspectival terms. How far this may be so is a central philosophical question. But even if we allow that the explanations of such things must remain to some degree perspectival, this does not mean that we cannot operate the notion of the absolute conception. It will be a conception consisting of non-perspectival materials which will be available to any adequate investigator, of whatever constitution, and it will also help to explain to us, though not necessarily to those alien investigators, such things as our capacity to grasp that conception. Perhaps more than that will turn out to be available, but no more is necessary, in order to give substance to the idea of 'the world' and to defeat the first line of objection to the distinction, in terms of possible convergence, between the scientific and the ethical.

The opposite line of objection urges that the idea of 'converging on how things are' is available, to some adequate degree, in the ethical case as well. The place where this is to be seen is above all with those 'thick' ethical concepts that possess a lot of substantive content. Many exotic examples of these can be drawn from other cultures, but there are enough left in our own: *coward, lie, brutality, gratitude,* and so forth. They are characteristically related to reasons for action. If a concept of this kind applies, this often provides someone with a reason for action, though that reason need not be a decisive one, and may be outweighed by other reasons. Of course, exactly what reason for action is provided, and to whom, depends on the situation, in ways that may well be governed by this and by other ethical concepts, but the general connection with action is clear enough. We may say, summarily, that such concepts are 'action-guiding'.

At the same time, their application is guided by the world. A concept of this sort may be rightly or wrongly applied, and people who have acquired it can agree that it applies or fails to apply to some new situation. In many cases that agreement will be spontaneous, while in other cases there is room for judgment and comparison. Some disagreement at the margin may be irresoluble, but that does not mean the use of the concept is not controlled by the facts or by the users' perception of the world. (As with other concepts that are not totally precise, marginal disagreements can indeed help to show how their use *is* controlled by the facts.) We can say, then, that the application of these concepts is at the same time world-guided and action-guiding. How can it be both of these at once?

Prescriptivism gave a very simple answer to that question. According to prescriptivism, any such concept can be analyzed into a descriptive and a prescriptive element: it is guided round the world by its descriptive content, but has a prescriptive flag attached to it. It is the first feature that allows it to be world-guided, while the second makes it action-guiding. Some of the difficulties with this picture concern the prescriptive element, and how that is supposed to guide action in the relevant sense. (Telling yourself to do something is not an obvious model for recognizing that one has a reason to do it.) But the most significant objection, for this discussion, applies to the other half of the analysis. Prescriptivism claims that what governs the application of the concept to the world is the descriptive element, and that the evaluative interest of the concept plays no part in this. All the input into its use is descriptive, just as all the evaluative aspect is output. It follows that for any concept of this sort, one could produce another which picked out just the same features of the world, but worked simply as a descriptive concept, lacking any prescriptive or evaluative force.

Against this, critics[7] have made the effective point that there is no reason to believe a descriptive equivalent will necessarily be available. How we 'go on' from one application of a concept to another is a function of the kind of interest the concept represents, and one should not assume that one could see how people 'go on' in their use of a concept of this sort, if one did not share the evaluative perspective in which the concept has its point. An insightful observer can indeed come to understand and anticipate the use of the concept without actually sharing the values of the people who use it: that is an important point, and we shall come back to it. But in imaginatively anticipating the use of the concept, he also has to grasp imaginatively its evaluative point. He cannot stand quite outside the evaluative interests of the community he is observing, and pick up the concept simply as a device for dividing up in a rather strange way certain neutral features of the world.

This seems a very plausible account, and certainly a possible one, of what is involved in mastering concepts of this kind and understanding their use. It needs, in fact, to be not much more than possible to play an important part in this argument, by reminding moral philosophy of what the demands made by an adequate philosophy of language or by the philosophy of social explanation may turn out to be. If it is not only possible but plausible, moral philosophy will be well advised to consider what needs to be said if it is true.

The sympathetic observer can follow the practice of the people he is observing; he can report, anticipate, and even take part in discussions of the use that they make of their concept. But, as with some other concepts of theirs, relating to religion, for instance, or to witchcraft, he is not ultimately identified with the use of this concept: it is not really his.[8] This possibility, of the insightful but not totally identified observer, bears on an important question, whether those who use ethical concepts of this kind can have ethical knowledge in virtue of properly applying those concepts. Let us assume, artificially, that we are dealing with a society that is maximally homogeneous and minimally given to general reflection; its members simply, all of them, use certain ethical concepts of this sort. (We may call it the 'hypertraditional' society.) What would be involved in their having ethical knowledge? According to the best available accounts of propositional knowledge,[9] they would have to believe the judgments that they made; those judgments would have to be true; and their judgments would have to satisfy a further condition, which has been extensively discussed in the philosophy of knowledge, but which can be summarized by saying that those first two conditions must be non-accidentally linked: granted the way that the people have gone about their inquiries, it must be no accident that the belief they have acquired is a true one, and if the truth on the subject had been otherwise, they would have acquired a different belief, true in those different circumstances. Thus I may know, by looking at it, that the die has come up 6, and that (roughly[10]) involves the claim that if it had come up 4, I would have come to believe, by looking at it, that it had come up 4 (the alternative situations to be considered have to be restricted to those moderately like the actual one.) Taking a phrase from Robert Nozick, we can say that the third requirement— it involves a good deal more elaboration than I have suggested—is that one's belief should 'track the truth'.

The members of the hypertraditional society apply their 'thick' concepts, and in doing so they make various judgments. If any of those judgments can ever properly be said to be true, then their beliefs, in those respects, can track the truth, since they can withdraw judgments of this sort if the circumstances turn out not to be what was supposed, can make an alternative judgment if it would be more appropriate, and so on. They have, each, mastered these concepts, and they can perceive the personal and social happenings to which the concepts apply. If there is truth here, their beliefs can track it. The question left is whether any of these judgments can be true.

An objection can be made to saying that they are. If they are true, then the observer can correctly say that they are; letting 'F' stand in for one of their concepts, he can say for instance, 'The headman's statement, *That is F*, is true'. But then (the objection goes) he should be able to invoke a very basic principle about truth, the *disquotation principle*,[11] and say, in his own person, *that is F*. But he is not prepared to do that, since F is not one of his concepts.

How strong is this objection? It relies on the following principle: A cannot correctly say that B speaks truly in uttering S unless A could say something tantamount to S himself. (A lot of work has to be done to spell out what counts as something 'tantamount' to S, if this is not going to run into merely technical difficulties, but let us suppose all such problems solved.) Imagine then a certain school slang, which uses special names for various objects, places and institutions in the school. It is a rule that these words are appropriately used only by someone who is a member of the school, and this rule is accepted and understood by a group wider than the members of the school themselves (it would have to be, if it is to be *that* rule at all). People know that if they use these terms in their own person they will be taken for members of the school, or else criticized, and so forth. This provides an exception to the principle, since observers cannot use these terms, but they can correctly say that members of the school, on various occasions, have spoken truly in using them.

In this simple case, it is of course true that the observers have other terms that refer to just the same things as the slang-terms, and that is not so, we are supposing, with the local ethical terms. That makes a difference, since in the school case the observer can clearly factor out what makes a given slang statement true, and what, as contrasted with that, makes it appropriate for a particular person to make it. But we can see the use of the ethical concept as a deeper example of the same thing. In both cases, there is a condition that has to be satisfied if one is to speak in that way, a condition that is satisfied by the local and not by the observer. In both cases, it is a matter of belonging to a certain culture. In the school case it is, so far as the example goes, only a variance of speech, while in the ethical case there is a deeper variance which means the observer has no term that picks out exactly the same things as their term picks out, and is independent of theirs. He has, of course, an expression such as 'what they call "F"' and the fact that he can use that, although it is not independent of their term, is important: his intelligent use of it shows that he can indeed understand their use of their term, although he cannot use it himself.

We can understand in these circumstances why disquotation is not possible, and the fact that it is not gives us no more reason, it seems to me, than it does in the school case to deny that the locals can speak truly in using their own language. However, there is a different, and stronger, objection to saying, in the ethical case, that is what they do. In the school case, the observer did not think the locals' use of their terms implied anything that he actually believed to be false. In other cases, however, an observer may see local statements as false in this way. I am not referring to statements the locals might equally have seen as false, those that are mistaken even in local terms. I mean the case in which the observer sees some whole segment of their discourse as involving a mistake. It is a complex question in social theory, in what cases that might be so.

Social anthropologists have discussed whether ritual and magical conceptions should be seen as mistaken in our terms, or rather as operating at a different level, not commensurable with our scientific ideas. Whatever may be said more generally, it is quite hard to deny that magic, at least, is a causal conception, with implications that overlap with scientific conceptions of causality.[12] To the extent that that is so, magical conceptions can be seen from the outside as false, and then no one will have known to be true any statements claiming magical influence. Those criteria do not reach to do everything that, on this view of the matter, is involved in such claims. In cases of this sort, the problem with conceding truth to the locals' claims is the opposite of the one just discussed. It is not that their notions are different from the observer's, so that he cannot assert what they assert. The problem is that their statements imply notions that are similar enough to some of his, for him to deny what they assert.

One may see the local ethical statements in a way that raises that difficulty. On this reading, the locals' statements imply something that can be put in the observer's terms, and which he rejects: that it is *right*, or *all right*, to do things that he thinks it is not right, or all right, to do. Prescriptivism sees things in this way. The local statements entail, together with their descriptive content, an all-purpose *ought*. We have rejected the descriptive half of that analysis; is there any reason to accept the other half?

Of course, there is a quite minimal sense in which the locals think it 'all right' to act as they do, and they do not merely imply this, but reveal it, in the practice under which they use these concepts and live accordingly. To say that they 'think it all right' merely at this level is not to mention any further and disputable judgment of theirs, but merely to record their practice. Must we agree that there is a judgment, to be expressed by using some universal moral notion, which they accept and the observer may, very well, reject?

I do not think that we have to accept that idea. More precisely, I do not think that we can decide whether to accept it until we have a more general picture of the whole question; this is not an issue that by itself can force more general conclusions on us. The basic question is how we are to understand the relations between practice and reflection. The very general kind of judgment that is in question here—a judgment, that is to say, using a very general concept—is essentially a product of reflection, and it comes into question when someone stands back from the practices of the society and its use of these concepts and asks whether this is the right way to go on, whether these are good ways in which to assess actions, whether the kinds of character that are admired are good kinds of character to admire. Of course, in many traditional societies some degree of reflective questioning and criticism exists, and that itself is an important fact. It is for the sake of the argument, to separate the issues, that I have been using the idea of the hypertraditional society, where there is no reflection.

In relation to that society, the question now is this: does the practice of that society, in particular the judgments that members of the society make, imply answers to reflective questions about that practice, questions they have never raised? Some judgments made by members of a society do have implications at a more general or theoretical level which they have never considered. That may be true of their magical judgments, if those are taken as causal claims, and it is true of their mathematical judgments, and of their judgments about the stars. We may be at some liberty whether to construe what they were saying as expressing mathematical judgments or opinions about the stars, but if we do interpret them as making those judgments and expressing those opinions, they will have those implications. If what a statement expresses is an opinion about the stars, one thing that follows is that it can be contradicted by another opinion about the stars.

There are two different ways in which we can see the activities of the hypertraditional society, which depend on different models of ethical practice. (They are in fact mere sketches or shells, rather than models: they still need their content to be supplied. But they can already have an effect.) One of them can be called an 'objectivist' model. According to this, we shall see the members of the society as trying, in their local and limited way, to find out the truth about values, an activity in which we and other human beings, and perhaps creatures who are not human beings, are all engaged. We shall then see their judgments as having these implications, rather as we see primitive statements about the stars as having implications that can be contradicted by more sophisticated statements about the stars. On the other, contrasted, model we shall see their judgments rather as part of their way of living, a cultural artifact they have come to inhabit (though they have not consciously built it). On this, non-objectivist, model, we shall take a different view of the relations between that practice and critical reflection. We shall not be disposed to see the level of reflection as, implicitly, already there, and we shall not want to say that their judgments have, just as they stand, these implications.

The choice between these two different ways of looking at their activities will determine whether we say the people in the hyper-traditional society have ethical knowledge or not. It is important to be quite clear what ethical knowledge is in question. It is knowledge involved in their making judgments in which they use their 'thick' concepts. We are not considering whether they display knowledge *in using those concepts rather than some others:* that would be an issue at the reflective level. The question 'does that society possess ethical knowledge?' is seriously ambiguous in that way. The collective reference to the society invites one to take the perspective in which their ethical representations are compared with other societies' ethical representations, and that is the reflective level, at which they certainly do not possess knowledge. There is another sense of the question in which it asks whether members of the society could, in exercising their concepts, express knowledge about the world to which they apply them, and the answer to that might be 'yes'.

The interesting result of this discussion is that the answer will be 'yes' if we take the non-objectivist view of their ethical activities: on that view, various members of the society will have knowledge, when they deploy their concepts carefully, use the appropriate criteria, and so on. But on the objectivist view, they do not have knowledge, or at least, it is immensely unlikely that they do, since their judgments have (on that view) extensive implications at the reflective level which they have never considered, and we have every reason to believe that when those implications are considered, the traditional use of ethical concepts will be seriously affected.

The objectivist view, while it denies knowledge to the unreflective society, may seem to promise knowledge at the reflective level. Indeed, it is characteristic of it to expect that it would be at that level that the demands of knowledge would for the first time be properly met. But there is no reason to think that, at least as things are, there is knowledge at the reflective level which is not either common to all ethical systems and has not much content ('one has to have a special reason to kill someone'), or else has simply survived from the unreflective level. The objectivist view sees the practice of the hypertraditional society, and the conclusions that we might reach at the reflective level, equally in terms of beliefs, and its idea is that we shall have a better hold on the truth about the ethical, and will be in a position to replace belief with knowledge, precisely in virtue of the processes of reflection. I see no reason to think that the demands of knowledge at this level, at least as things are, have been met. At the end of this paper I shall suggest that, so far as propositional knowledge of ethical truths is concerned, this is not simply a matter of how things now are. Rather, at a high level of reflective generality there could not be any ethical knowledge of this sort— or, at most, just one piece.

If we accept that there can be knowledge at the hypertraditional or unreflective level; and if we accept the obvious truth that reflection characteristically disturbs, unseats or replaces those traditional concepts; and if we agree that, at least as things are, the reflective level is not in a position to give us knowledge that we did not have before; then we reach the notably unSocratic conclusion that in ethics, *reflection can destroy knowledge.*

Another consequence, if we allow knowledge at the unreflective level, will be that not all propositional knowledge is additive. Not all pieces of knowledge can be combined into a larger body of knowledge. We may well have to accept that conclusion anyway from other contexts that involve perspectival views of the world. A part of the physical world may present itself as one color to one kind of observer, and another to another; to another, it may not exactly be a color that is presented at all. Call those qualities perceived by each kind of observer 'A', 'B', 'C'. Then a skilled observer of one kind can know that the surface is A, of another kind that it is B, and so on, but there is no knowledge that it is A and B and C. This result would disappear if what 'A', 'B', etc., meant were something relational; if, when observers said 'that is A' they meant 'A to observers like us'. It is very doubtful that this is the correct account.[13] If it is not, the coherence of those pieces of knowledge is secured at a different level, when those various perceived qualities are related to the absolute conception. Their relation to that conception is also what makes it clear that the capacities that produce these various pieces of knowledge are all forms of *perception.* Of course, we have good reason to believe this before we possess any such theoretical conception, and certainly before we possess its details, as we still do not. That is because our everyday experience, unsurprisingly, reveals a good deal of what we are and how we are related to the world, and in that way itself leads us toward that theoretical conception.[14]

Some think of the knowledge given by applying ethical concepts as something like perception; but we can now see a vital asymmetry between the case of the ethical concepts, and the perspectival experience of secondary qualities. It lies in the fact that in the case of secondary qualities, what explains also justifies, but in the ethical case, this is not so. The psychological capacities that underlie our perceiving the world in terms of certain secondary qualities have evolved so that the physical world will present itself to us in reliable and useful ways. Coming to know that these qualities constitute our form of perceptual engagement with the world, and how this mode of presentation works, will not unsettle the system.[15] In the ethical case, we have an analogy to the perceptual just to this extent, that there is local convergence under these concepts—the judgments of those who use them are indeed, as I put it before, world-guided. That is certainly enough to refute the simplest oppositions of fact and value. But if this is to mean anything for a wider objectivity, everything depends on what is to be said *next*. With secondary qualities, it is the explanation of the perspectival perceptions that enables us, when we come to reflect on them, to place them in relation to the perceptions of other people and other creatures; and, as we have just noticed, that leaves everything more or less where it was, so far as our perceptual judgments are concerned. The question is whether we can find an ethical analogy to that. Here we have to go outside the local, perspectival judgments, to a reflective or second-order account of them, and there the analogy gives out.

There is, first, a problem of what the second-order account is to be. An *explanation* of those local judgments and of the conceptual differences between societies will presumably have to come from the social sciences: cultural differences are what are in question. Perhaps no existing explanation of such things goes very deep, and we are not too clear how deep an explanation might go. But we do know that it will not look much like explanations of secondary quality perception. The capacities it will invoke will be those involved in finding our way around in a social world, not merely the physical world, and that, crucially, will mean *in some social world or other*, since it is certain both that human beings cannot live without some culture or other, and that there are many different cultures in which they can live, differing in their local perspectival concepts.

In any case, an explanatory theory is not enough to deal with the problems of objectivity raised by the local ethical concepts. In the case of secondary qualities, the explanation also justified, because it could show how the perceptions are related to physical reality, and how they give knowledge of that reality, which is what they purport to do. The question with them is: is this a method of finding one's way around the physical world? The theoretical account explains how it is. In the ethical case, that is not the kind of question raised by reflection. If one asked the question 'Is this a method of finding one's way around the social world?' one would have to be asking whether it was a method of finding one's way around some social world or other, and the answer to that must obviously be 'Yes,' unless the society were extremely disordered, which is not what we were supposing. The question raised is rather 'Is this a good, acceptable, way of living compared with others?' or, to put it another way, 'Is this the best kind of social world?'

When these are seen to be the questions, the reflective account that we require turns out to involve reflective *ethical* considerations. Some believe that these considerations should take the form of an ethical theory. These reflective considerations will have to take up the job of justifying or unjustifying the local concepts once those have come to be questioned. If a wider objectivity were to come from all this, then the reflective ethical considerations would have themselves to be objective. This brings us back to the question that we touched on just now, whether the reflective level might generate its own ethical knowledge. If this is understood as our coming to have propositional knowledge of ethical truths, then we need some account of what 'tracking the truth' will be. The idea that our beliefs can track the truth at this level must at least imply that a range of investigators could rationally, reasonably and unconstrainedly come to converge on a determinate set of ethical conclusions. What are the hopes for such a process? I do not mean of its actually happening, but rather of our forming a coherent picture of how it might happen. If it is construed as convergence on a body of ethical truths which is brought about and explained by the fact that they are truths— that would be the strict analogy to scientific objectivity—then I see no hope for it. In particular, there is no hope of extending to this level the kind of world-guidedness that we have been considering in the case of the 'thick' ethical concepts. Discussions at the reflective level, if they are to have the ambition of considering all ethical experience and arriving at the truth about the ethical, will necessarily use the most general and abstract ethical concepts such as 'right,' and those concepts do not display that world-guidedness (which is why they were selected by prescriptivism in its attempt to find a pure evaluative element from which it could *detach* world-guidedness).

I cannot see any convincing theory of knowledge for the convergence of reflective ethical thought 'on ethical reality' in even distant analogy to the scientific case. Nor is there a convincing analogy with mathematics, a case in which the notion of an independent reality is at least problematical. Every non-contradictory piece of mathematics is part of mathematics, though it may be left aside as too trivial or unilluminating or useless, but not every non-contradictory structure of ethical reflection can be part of one such subject, since they conflict with one another in ways that not only lack the kind of explanation that could form a credible theory of error, but have too many credible explanations of other kinds.

I do not believe, then, that we can understand the reflective level through a model in which we can come to know ethical propositions at that level, while in less reflective states we aim to possess that truth, but can at best arrive at beliefs. We must reject the objectivist view of ethical life as, in that way, a pursuit of ethical truth. But that does not rule out all forms of objectivism. There is a different project, of trying to give an objective grounding or foundation to ethical life, by showing that a certain kind of ethical life was the best for human beings, was most likely to meet their needs. The question asked by this approach is: granted that human beings need, in general, to share a social world, is there anything to be known about their needs and their most basic motivations that will show us what that world should best be?

I cannot argue the question here, but I doubt that there will turn out to be a very satisfying answer to that question. It is probable that any such considerations will radically under-determine the ethical options even in a given social situation (we must remember that what we take the situation to be is itself, in part, a function of what ethical options we can see). They may under-determine it in several different dimensions. Any ethical life is going to contain restraints on such things as killing, injury and lying, but those restraints can take very different forms. Again, with respect to the virtues, which is the most natural and promising field for this kind of inquiry, we only have to compare Aristotle's catalogue of the virtues with any that might be produced now to see how pictures of life that can be recognized as equally appropriate to human beings may differ very much in their spirit and in the actions and institutions they would call for. We also have the idea that there are many and various forms of human excellence that will not all fit together into a one harmonious whole. On that view, any determinate ethical outlook is going to represent some kind of specialization of human possibilities. That idea is deeply entrenched in any naturalistic or, again, historical conception of human nature—that is to say, in any adequate conception of it—and I find it hard to believe that that will be overcome by an objective inquiry or that human beings could turn out to have a much more determinate nature than is suggested by what we already know, one that timelessly demanded a life of a particular kind.

The project of giving to ethical life, in any very determinate form, an objective grounding in considerations about human nature is not, in my view, very likely to succeed. But it is at any rate a comprehensible project, and I believe it represents the only form of ethical objectivity at the reflective level that is intelligible. For that reason, it is worth asking what would be involved in its succeeding. If it succeeded, that would not simply be a matter of agreement on a theory of human nature. The convergence itself would be partly on scientific matters, in a very broad social and psychological sense, but what would matter would be a convergence to which these scientific conclusions would provide only part of the means. Nor, on the other hand, would there be a convergence directly on to ethical truths, as in the other objectivist model. There would be one ethical belief which might perhaps be said to be in its own right an object of knowledge at the reflective level, to the effect that a certain kind of life was best for human beings. But that will not yield other ethical truths directly. The reason for this, to put it summarily, is that the excellence or satisfactoriness of a life does not stand to the beliefs involved in that life as premise to conclusion. Rather, an agent's (excellent or satisfactory) life is characterized by *having* those beliefs, and most of the beliefs will not be about that agent's dispositions or life, or about other people's dispositions, but about the social world. That life will involve, for instance, the agent's using some 'thick' concepts rather than others. Reflection on the excellence of the life does not itself establish the truth of judgments using those concepts, or of the agent's other ethical judgments. It rather shows there is good reason (granted a commitment to an ethical life at all) to live a life that involves those concepts and those beliefs.

The convergence that signaled the success of this project would be a convergence of practical reason, by which people came to lead the best kind of life and to have the desires that belonged to that; convergence in ethical belief would largely be a part and consequence of that process. One very general ethical belief would, indeed, be an object of knowledge at that level. Many particular ethical judgments, involving the favored 'thick' concepts, could be known to be true, but then judgments of that sort (I have argued) can very often be known to be true anyway, even when they occur, as they always have occurred, in a life that is not grounded at the objective level. The objective grounding would not bring it about that judgments using those concepts were true or could be known: that was so already. But it would enable us to recognize that certain of them were the best or most appropriate 'thick' concepts to use. Between the two extremes of the one very general proposition, and the many quite concrete ones, other ethical beliefs would be true only in the oblique sense that they were the beliefs that would help us to find our way around in a social world which—on this optimistic program—would have been shown to be the best social world for human beings.

That would be a structure very different from that of the objectivity of science. There is, then, a radical difference between ethics and science. Even if ethics were objective in the only way in which it could intelligibly be objective, its objectivity would be quite different from that of science. In addition, it is probably not objective in that way. However, that does not mean that there is a clear distinction between (any) fact and (any) value; nor does it mean that there is no ethical knowledge. There is some, and in the less reflective past there has been more.

NOTES

1. The lecture that I gave to the Royal Institute of Philosophy on this subject was subsequently much revised, and has become Chapter 8 ('Knowledge, Science, Convergence') of a book, *Ethics and the Limits of Philosophy*, Fontana Press, London, 1985. It seemed more sensible not to go back to an earlier version of the text, and what appears here (with the agreement of Fontana Books) is a slightly abbreviated version of that chapter.

2. See David Wiggins, 'Truth, Invention and the Meaning of Life', *British Academy Lecture* (1976); and 'Deliberation and Practical Reason,' in *Essays on Aristotle's Ethics*, ed. Amelie Rorty (Berkeley, University of California Press, 1980).

3. *Philosophy and the Mirror of Nature* (Princeton, Princeton University Press, 1980), 344–345. I have discussed Rorty's views in some detail in a review of his *Consequences of Pragmatism*, *New York Review* XXX, No. 7 (28 April 1983).

4. There is a confusion between what might be called empirical and transcendental pragmatism. Some similar problems arise with the later work of Wittgenstein: see 'Wittgenstein and Idealism', in *Understanding Wittgenstein*, Royal Institute of Philosophy Lectures Vol. 7 (London, Macmillan, 1974), and reprinted in *Moral Luck* (Cambridge, Cambridge University Press, 1981); and Jonathan Lear, 'Leaving the World Alone', *Journal of Philosophy* 79 (1982).

5. Rorty, 'The World Well Lost', in *Consequences of Pragmatism*, 14. See also Donald Davidson, 'The Very Idea of a Conceptual Scheme', *Proceedings and Addresses of the American Philosophical Association* 67 (1973/4).

6. Cf. *Descartes: The Project of Pure Enquiry* (Harmondsworth, Penguin Books, 1978). See also N. Jardine, 'The Possibility of Absolutism,' in *Science, Belief, and Behaviour: Essays in Honour of R. B. Braithwaite*, D. H. Mellor (ed.) (Cambridge, Cambridge University Press, 1980); and Colin McGinn, *The Subjective View* (Oxford, Clarendon Press, 1983).

7. Notably John McDowell, 'Are Moral Requirements Hypothetical Imperatives?', *Proceedings of the Aristotelian Society* Supplementary Volume 52 (1978); 'Virtue and Reason', *Monist* 62 (1979). McDowell is above all concerned with the state of mind and motivations of a virtuous person, but I understand his view to have the more general implications discussed in the text. The idea that it might be impossible to pick up an evaluative concept unless one shared its evaluative interest I take to be basically a Wittgensteinian idea. I first heard it expressed by Philippa Foot and Iris Murdoch in a seminar in the 1950s. For the application of ideas from Wittgenstein's later philosophy to ethics, see e.g. Hanna F. Pitkin, *Wittgenstein and Justice* (Berkeley, University of California Press, 1972), and Sabina Lovibond, *Realism and Imagination in Ethics* (Oxford, Blackwell, 1983). McDowell himself draws important consequences in the philosophy of mind, rejecting the 'belief and desire' model of rational action. I do not accept these consequences, but I shall not try to argue the question here. Some considerations later in this paper, about the differences between ethical belief and sense perception, bear closely on it.

8. McDowell ('Virtue and Reason') allows for this possibility, but he draws no consequences from it, and ignores intercultural conflict altogether. He traces scepticism about objectivity in ethics, revealingly, to what he calls a 'philistine scientism', on the one hand, and to a philosopical pathology on the other, of vertigo in the face of unsupported practices. Leaving aside his attitude to the sciences, McDowell seems rather unconcerned even about history, and says nothing about differences in outlook over time. It is significant that in a discussion of the virtues that mostly relates to Aristotle, he takes as an example kindness, which is not an Aristotelian virtue.

9. The most subtle and ingenious discussion of propositional knowledge I know is that of Robert Nozick in Chapter 3 of his *Philosophical Explanations* (Cambridge, Mass., Harvard University Press, 1981). Some central features of Nozick's account, notably its use of subjunctive conditionals, had been anticipated by Fred Dretske, as Nozick acknowledges in his note 53 to that chapter (op. cit. 630), which gives references.

10. How rough? Perhaps he cannot read four dots as 4, though he can read six dots as 6. What if he can only read six dots as 6, and everything else as not 6?

11. A. Tarski, 'The Concept of Truth in Formalized Languages', in *Logic, Semantics, Meta-Mathematics* (Oxford, Oxford University Press, 1956). On the present issue, cf. David Wiggins, 'What Would be a Substantial Theory of Truth?', in *Philosophical Subjects: Essays Presented to P. F. Strawson*, Z. van Straaten (ed.) (Oxford, Blackwell, 1980). Wiggins' discussion raises a further issue, whether the observer could even understand what the sentences mean, unless he could apply a disquotational truth formula to them. (In this he is influenced by Donald Davidson, 'Truth and Meaning', *Synthese* 17 (1967). The fact that there can be a sympathetic but non-identified observer shows that it cannot be impossible to understand something although one is unwilling to assert it oneself.

12. See John Skorupski, *Symbol and Theory* (Cambridge, Cambridge University Press, 1976).

13. Cf. Wiggins, 'Truth, Invention and the Meaning of Life'; Colin McGinn, *The Subjective View* (Oxford, Oxford University Press, 1983), 9–10, 119–120.

14. A formulation of the distinction between primary and secondary qualities is very nearly as old in the Western tradition as the self-conscious use of a principle of sufficient reason.

15. I have taken two sentences here from an article, 'Ethics and the Fabric of the World', to appear in *Morality and Objectivity*, ed., Ted Honderich (London, Routledge and Kegan Paul, 1985). A volume of essays in memory of John Mackie, it discusses Mackie's views on these subjects, and in particular his idea that perceptual and moral experience each involve a comparable error. See also McGinn, op. cit., especially Ch. 7.

Chapter 4

Virtue and Reason

JOHN McDOWELL

1. Presumably the point of, say, inculcating a moral outlook lies in a concern with how people live. It may seem that the very idea of a moral outlook makes room for, and requires, the existence of moral theory, conceived as a discipline which seeks to formulate acceptable principles of conduct. It is then natural to think of ethics as a branch of philosophy related to moral theory, so conceived, rather as the philosophy of science is related to science. On this view, the primary topic of ethics is the concept of right conduct, and the nature and justification of principles of behaviour. If there is a place for an interest in the concept of virtue, it is a secondary place. Virtue is a disposition (perhaps of a specially rational and self-conscious kind) to behave rightly; the nature of virtue is explained, as it were, from the outside in.

My aim is to sketch the outlines of a different view, to be found in the philosophical tradition which flowers in Aristotle's ethics. According to this different view, although the point of engaging in ethical reflection still lies in the interest of the question "How should one live?"[1] that question is necessarily approached *via* the notion of a virtuous person. A conception of right conduct is grasped, as it were, from the inside out.

2. I shall begin with some considerations which make it attractive to say, with Socrates, that virtue is knowledge.

What is it for someone to possess a virtue? "Knowledge" implies that he gets things right; if we are to go any distance toward finding plausibility in the Socratic thesis, it is necessary to start with examples whose status as virtues, and hence as states of character whose possessor arrives at right answers to a certain range of questions about how to behave, is not likely to be queried. I shall use the example of kindness; anyone who disputes its claim to be a virtue should substitute a better example of his own. (The objectivity that "knowledge" implies will recur later.)

A kind person can be relied on to behave kindly when that is what the situation requires. Moreover, his reliably kind behavior is not the outcome of a blind, non-rational habit or instinct, like the courageous behavior—so called only by courtesy—of a lioness defending her cubs.[2] Rather, that the situation requires a certain sort of behavior is (one way of formulating) his reason for behaving in that way, on each of the relevant occasions. So it must be something of which, on each of the relevant occasions, he is aware. A kind person has a reliable sensitivity to a certain sort of requirement that situations impose on behavior. The deliverances of a reliable sensitivity are cases of knowledge; and there are idioms according to which the sensitivity itself can appropriately be described as knowledge; a kind person knows what it is like to be confronted with a requirement of kindness. The sensitivity is, we might say, a sort of perceptual capacity.[3]

(Of course a kind person need not himself classify the behavior he sees to be called for, on one of the relevant occasions, as kind. He need not be articulate enough to possess concepts of the particular virtues; and even if he does, the concepts need not enter his reasons for the actions that manifest those particular virtues. It is enough if he thinks of what he does, when—as we put it—he shows himself to be kind, under some such description as "the thing to do." The description need not differ from that under which he thinks of other actions of his, which we regard as manifesting different virtues; the division into actions that manifest kindness and actions that manifest other virtues can be imposed, not by the agent himself, but by a possibly more articulate, and more theoretically oriented, observer.)

The considerations adduced so far suggest that the knowledge constituted by the reliable sensitivity is a necessary condition for possession of the virtue. But they do not show that the knowledge is, as in the Socratic thesis, to be identified with the virtue. A preliminary case for the identification might go as follows. On each of the relevant occasions, the requirement imposed by the situation, and detected by the agent's sensitivity to such requirements, must exhaust his reason for acting as he does. It would disqualify an action from counting as a manifestation of kindness if its agent needed some extraneous incentive to compliance with the requirement—say, the rewards of a good reputation. So the deliverances of his sensitivity constitute, one by one, complete explanations of the actions that manifest the virtue. Hence, since the sensitivity fully accounts for its deliverances, the sensitivity fully accounts for the actions. But the concept of the virtue is the concept of a state whose possession accounts for the actions that manifest it. Since that explanatory role is filled by the sensitivity, the sensitivity turns out to be what the virtue is.[4]

That is a preliminary case for the identification of particular virtues with, as it were, specialized sensitivities to requirements. *Mutatis mutandis*, a similar argument applies to virtue in general. Indeed, in the context of another Socratic thesis, that of the unity of virtue, virtue in general is what the argument for identification with knowledge really concerns; the specialized sensitivities which are to be equated with particular virtues, according to the argument considered so far, are actually not available one by one for a series of separate identifications.

What makes this plausible is the attractive idea that a virtue issues in nothing but right conduct. Suppose the relevant range of behavior, in the case of kindness, is marked out by the notion of proper attentiveness to others' feelings. Now sometimes acting in such a way as to indulge someone's feelings is not acting rightly: the morally important fact about the situation is not that A will be upset by a projected action (though he will), but, say, that B has a right—a consideration of a sort, sensitivity to which might be thought of as constituting fairness. In such a case, a straightforward propensity to be gentle to others' feelings would not lead to right conduct. If a genuine virtue is to produce nothing but right conduct, a simple propensity to be gentle cannot be identified with the virtue of kindness. Possession of the virtue must involve not only sensitivity to facts about others' feelings as reason for acting in certain ways, but also sensitivity to facts about rights as reasons for acting in certain ways; and when circumstances of both sorts obtain, and a circumstance of the second sort is the one that should be acted on, a possessor of the virtue of kindness must be able to tell that that is so.[5] So we cannot disentangle genuine possession of kindness from the sensitivity that constitutes fairness. And since there are obviously no limits on the possibilities for compresence, in the same situation, of circumstances of the sorts proper sensitivities to which constitute all the virtues, the argument can be generalized: no one virtue can be fully possessed except by a possessor of all of them, that is, a possessor of virtue in general. Thus the particular virtues are not a batch of independent sensitivities. Rather, we use the concepts of the particular virtues to mark similarities and dissimilarities among the manifestations of a single sensitivity which is what virtue, in general, is: an ability to recognize requirements that situations impose on one's behavior. It is a single complex sensitivity of this sort that we are aiming to instill when we aim to inculcate a moral outlook.

3. There is an apparent obstacle to the identification of virtue with knowledge. The argument for the identification requires that the deliverances of the sensitivity—the particular pieces of knowledge with which it equips its possessor—should fully explain the actions that manifest virtue. But it is plausible that appropriate action need not be elicited by a consideration apprehended as a reason—even a conclusive reason—for acting in a certain way. That may seem to open the following possibility: a person's perception of a situation may precisely match what a virtuous person's perception of it would be, although he does not act as the virtuous person would. But if a perception that corresponds to the virtuous person's does not call forth a virtuous action from this non-virtuous person, then the virtuous person's matching perception—the deliverance of his sensitivity—cannot, after all, fully account for the virtuous action that it does elicit from him. Whatever is missing (in the case of the person who does not act virtuously) must be present as an extra component, over and above the deliverance of the sensitivity, in a complete specification of the reason why the virtuous person acts as he does.[6] That destroys the identification of virtue with the sensitivity. According to this line of argument, the sensitivity can be at most an ingredient in a composite state which is what virtue really is.

If we are to retain the identification of virtue with knowledge, then, by contraposition, we are committed to denying that a virtuous person's perception of a situation can be precisely matched in someone who, in that situation, acts otherwise than virtuously. Socrates seems to have supposed that the only way to embrace this commitment is in terms of ignorance, so that, paradoxically, failure to act as a virtuous person would cannot be voluntary, at least under that description. But there is a less extreme possibility, sketched by Aristotle.[7] This is to allow that someone who fails to act virtuously may, in a way, perceive what a virtuous person would, so that his failure to do the right thing is not inadvertent; but to insist that his failure occurs only because his appreciation of what he perceives is clouded, or unfocused, by the impact of a desire to do otherwise. This preserves the identification of virtue with a sensitivity; contrary to the counter-argument, nothing over and above the unclouded deliverances of the sensitivity is needed to explain the actions that manifest virtue. It is not that some extra explanatory factor, over and above the deliverances of the sensitivity, conspires with them to elicit action from the virtuous person, but rather that the other person's failure to act in that way is accounted for by a defectiveness in the approximations to those deliverances that he has.

It would be a mistake to protest that one can fail to act on a reason, and even on a reason judged by oneself to be better than any reason than one has for acting otherwise, without there needing to be any clouding or distortion in one's appreciation of the reason that one flouts.[8] That is true; but to suppose it constitutes an objection to Aristotle is to fail to understand the special nature of the conception of virtue that generates Aristotle's interest in incontinence.

One way to bring out the special nature of the conception is to note that, for Aristotle, continence is distinct from virtue, and just as problematic as incontinence. If someone needs to overcome an inclination to act otherwise, in getting himself to act as, say, temperance or courage demand, then he shows not virtue but (mere) continence. Suppose we take it that a virtuous person's judgment as to what he should do is arrived at by weighing, on the one side, some reason for acting in a way that will in fact manifest, say, courage, and, on the other side, a reason for doing something else (say a risk to life and limb, as a reason for running away), and deciding that on balance the former reason is the better. In that case, the distinction between virtue and continence will seem unintelligible. If the virtuous person allows himself to weigh the present danger, as a reason for running away, why should we not picture the weighing as his allowing himself to feel an inclination to run away, of a strength proportional to the weight that he allows to the reason? So long as he keeps the strength of his inclinations in line with the weight that he assigns to the reasons, his actions will conform to his judgment as to where, on balance, the better reason lies; what more can we require for virtue? (Perhaps that the genuinely courageous person simply does not care about his own survival? But Aristotle is rightly anxious to avert this misconception.[9]) The distinction becomes intelligible if we stop assuming that the virtuous person's judgment is a balancing of reasons for and against. The view of a situation that he arrives at by exercising his sensitivity is one in which some aspect of the situation is seen as constituting a reason for acting in some way; this reason is apprehended, not as outweighing or overriding any reasons for acting in other ways which would otherwise be constituted by other aspects of the situation (the present danger, say), but as silencing them. Here and now the risk to life and limb is not seen as any reason for removing himself. Aristotle's problem about incontinence is not "How can one weigh considerations in favor of actions X and Y, decide that on balance the better reasons are in favor of X, but nevertheless perform Y?" (a question which, no doubt, does not require the idea of clouded judgment for its answer); but rather (a problem equally about continence) "How can one have a view of a situation in which considerations which would otherwise appeal to one's will are silenced, but nevertheless allow those considerations to make themselves heard by one's will?"—a question which clearly is answerable, if at all, only by supposing that the incontinent or continent person does not fully share the virtuous person's perception of the situation.[10]

A more pressing objection is directed against the special conception of virtue: in particular, the use of cognitive notions in characterizing it. According to this objection, it must be a misuse of the notion of perception to suppose that an unclouded perception might suffice, on its own, to constitute a reason for acting in a certain way. An exercise of a genuinely cognitive capacity can yield at most part of a reason for acting; something appetitive is needed as well. To talk of virtue—a propensity to act in certain ways for certain reasons— as consisting in a sensitivity, a perceptual capacity, is to amalgamate the required appetitive component into the putative sensitivity. But all that is achieved thereby is a projection of human purposes into the world. (Here it becomes apparent how the objection touches on the issue of objectivity.) How one's will is disposed is a fact about oneself; whereas a genuinely cognitive faculty discloses to one how the world is independently of oneself, and in particular independently of one's will. Cognition and volition are distinct: the world—the proper sphere of cognitive capacities—is in itself an object of purely theoretical contemplation, capable of moving one to action only in conjunction with an extra factor—a state of will—contributed by oneself. I shall return to this objection.

4. Presented with an identification of virtue with knowledge, it is natural to ask for a formulation of the knowledge which virtue is. We tend to assume that the knowledge must have a statable propositional content (perhaps not capable of immediate expression by the knower). Then the virtuous person's reliably right judgments as to what he should do, occasion by occasion, can be explained in terms of interaction between this universal knowledge and some appropriate piece of particular knowledge about the situation at hand; and the explanation can take the form of a "practical syllogism," with the content of the universal knowledge, or some suitable part of it, as major premiss, the relevant particular knowledge as minor premiss, and the judgment about what is to be done as deductive conclusion.

This picture is congenial to the objection mentioned at the end of §3. According to this picture, the problematic concept of a requirement figures only in the major premiss, and the conclusion, of the syllogism which reconstructs the virtuous person's reason for acting. Knowledge of the major premiss, the objector might say, is none other than the disposition of the will that is required, according to the objection, as a further component in the relevant reasons for acting, and hence as a further component in virtue, over and above any strictly cognitive state. (We call it "knowledge" to endorse it, not to indicate that it is genuinely cognitive.) What a virtuous person really perceives is only what is stated in the minor premiss of the syllogism: that is, a straightforward fact about the situation at hand, which—as the objection requires—would be incapable of eliciting action on its own.

This picture fits only if the virtuous person's views about how, in general, one should behave are susceptible of codification, in principles apt for serving as major premisses in syllogisms of the sort envisaged. But to an unprejudiced eye it should seem quite implausible that any reasonably adult moral outlook admits of any such codification. As Aristotle consistently says, the best generalizations about how one should behave hold only for the most part.[11] If one attempted to reduce one's conception of what virtue requires to a set of rules, then, however subtle and thoughtful one was in drawing up the code, cases would inevitably turn up in which a mechanical application of the rules would strike one as wrong—and not necessarily because one had changed one's mind; rather, one's mind on the matter was not susceptible of capture in any universal formula.[12]

A deep-rooted prejudice about rationality blocks ready acceptance of this. A moral outlook is a specific determination of one's practical rationality: it shapes one's views about what reasons one has for acting. Rationality requires consistency; a specific conception of rationality in a particular area imposes a specific form on the abstract requirement of consistency—a specific view of what counts as going on doing the same thing here. The prejudice is the idea that acting in the light of a specific conception of rationality must be explicable in terms of being guided by a formulable universal principle. This prejudice comes under radical attack in Wittgenstein's discussion, in the *Philosophical Investigations*, of the concept of following a rule.

Consider an exercise of rationality in which there is a formulable rule, of which each successive action can be regarded as an application, appropriate in the circumstances arrived at: say (Wittgenstein's example) the extending of a series of numbers. We tend to picture the understanding of the instruction "Add 2"—command of the rule for extending the series 2,4,6,8, . . .—as a psychological mechanism which, aside from lapses of attention and so forth, churns out the appropriate behavior with the sort of reliability that a physical mechanism, say a piece of clockwork, might have. If someone is extending the series correctly, and one takes his behavior to be compliance with the understood instruction, then, according to this picture, one has postulated such a psychological mechanism, underlying his behavior, by an inference analogous to that whereby one might hypothesize a physical structure underlying the observable motions of some inanimate object. But this picture is profoundly suspect.

What manifests the pictured state of understanding? Suppose the person says, when asked what he is doing, "Look, I'm adding 2 each time." This apparent manifestation of understanding (or any other) will have been accompanied, at any point, by at most a finite fragment of the potentially infinite range of behavior which we want to say the rule dictates. Thus the evidence for the presence of the pictured state is always compatible with the supposition that, on some future occasion for its exercise, the behavior elicited by the occasion will diverge from what we would count as correct. Wittgenstein dramatizes this with the example of the man who continues the series, after 1000, with 1004, 1008, . . .[13] If a possibility of the 1004, 1008, . . . type were to be realized (and we could not bring the person to concede that he had simply made a mistake), that would show that the behavior hitherto was not guided by the psychological conformation that we were picturing as guiding it. The pictured state, then, always transcends the grounds on which it is allegedly postulated.

There may be an inclination to protest: "This is merely inductive skepticism about other minds. After all, one knows in one's own case that one's behavior will not come adrift like that." But this misses the point of the argument.

First, if what it is for one's behavior to come adrift is for it suddenly to seem that everyone else is out of step, then clearly the argument bears on one's own case just as much as on the case of others. (Imagine that the person who goes on with 1004, 1008, . . . had said, in advance, "I know in my own case that my behavior will not come adrift.")

Second, it is a mistake to interpret the argument as making a skeptical point: that one does not know, in the case of another person (or in one's own case either, once we have made the first correction), that the behavior will not come adrift. The argument is not meant to suggest that we should be in a state of constant trepidation lest possibilities of the 1004, 1008, . . . type be realized.[14] We are confident that they will not: the argument aims, not at all to undermine this confidence, but to change our conception of its ground and nature. We tend to picture our transition to this confident expectation, from such grounds as we have, as being mediated by the postulated psychological mechanism. But we can no more find the putatively mediating state manifested in the grounds for our expectation than we can find manifested there the very future occurrences we expect. Postulation of the mediating state is an idle intervening step; it does nothing to underwrite the confidence of the expectation.

(The content of the expectation is not purely behavioral. We might have a good scientific argument, mediated by postulation of a physiological mechanism, for not expecting any particular train of behavior, of the 1004, 1008, . . . type, which we might contemplate. Here postulation of the mediating physiological state would not be an idle intervening step. But the parallel is misleading. We can bring this out by considering a variant of Wittgenstein's example, in which, on reaching 1000, the person goes on as we expect, with 1002, 1004, . . ., but with a sense of dissociation from what he is doing. What he does no longer strikes him as going on in the same way; it feels as if a sheer habit has usurped his reason in controlling his behavior. We confidently expect this sort of thing will not happen; once again, postulation of a psychological mechanism does nothing to underwrite this confidence.)

What *is* the ground and nature of our confidence? About the competent use of words, Stanley Cavell writes:

> We learn and teach words in certain contexts, and then we are expected, and expect others, to be able to project them into further contexts. Nothing insures that this projection will take place (in particular, not the grasping of universals nor the grasping of books of rules), just as nothing insures that we will make, and understand, the same projections. That on the whole we do is a matter of our sharing routes of interest and feeling, modes of response, senses of humour and of significance and of fulfilment, of what is outrageous, of what is similar to what else, what a rebuke, what forgiveness, of when an utterance is an assertion, when an appeal, when an explanation—all the whirl of organism Wittgenstein calls "forms of life." Human speech and activity, sanity and community, rest upon nothing more, but nothing less, than this. It is a vision as simple as it is difficult, and as difficult as it is (and because it is) terrifying.[15]

The terror of which Cavell speaks at the end of this marvelous passage is a sort of vertigo, induced by the thought that there is nothing but shared forms of life to keep us, as it were, on the rails. We are inclined to think that is an insufficient foundation for a conviction that when we, say, extend a number series, we really are, at each stage, doing the same thing as before. In this mood, it seems to us that what Cavell describes cannot be a shared conceptual framework within which something is, given the circumstances, objectively the correct move;[16] it looks, rather, like a congruence of subjectivities, with the congruence not grounded as it would need to be to amount to an objectivity. So we feel we have lost the objectivity of (in our case) mathematics (and similarly in other cases). We recoil from this vertigo into the idea that we are kept on the rails by our grasp of rules. This idea has a pair of twin components: first, the idea (as above) that grasp of the rules is a psychological mechanism which (apart from mechanical failure, which is how we picture mistakes and so forth) guarantees that we stay in the straight and narrow; and, second, the idea that the rails—what we engage our mental wheels with when we come to grasp the rules—are objectively there, in a way which transcends the "mere" sharing of forms of life (hence, for instance, platonism about numbers). This composite idea is not the perception of some truth, but a consoling myth, elicited from us by our inability to endure the vertigo.

Of course, this casts no doubt on the possibility of putting explanations of particular moves, in the extending of a number series, in a syllogistic form: universal knowledge of how to extend the series interacts with particular knowledge of where one is in it, to produce a non-accidentally correct judgment as to what the next number is. In this case we can formulate the explanation so as to confer on the judgment explained the compellingness possessed by the conclusion of a proof. What is wrong is to take that fact to indicate that the explanation lays bare the inexorable workings of a machine: something whose operations, with our understanding of them, would not depend on the deliverances, in particular cases, of (for instance, and centrally) that shared sense of what is similar to what else, which Cavell mentions. The truth is that it is only because of our own involvement in our "whirl of organism" that we can understand the words we produce as conferring that special compellingness on the judgment explained.

Now it is only this misconception of the deductive paradigm that leads us to suppose that the operations of any specific conception of rationality in a particular area—any specific conception of what counts as doing the same thing—must be deductively explicable; that is, that there must be a formulable universal principle suited to serve as major premiss in syllogistic explanations of the sort considered above.

Consider, for instance, a concept whose application gives rise to hard cases, in this sense: there are disagreements that resist resolution by argument, as to whether or not the concept applies. Convinced that one is in the right on a hard case, one will find oneself saying, as one's arguments tail off without securing assent, "You simply aren't seeing it, " or "But don't you see?" In such cases the prejudice takes the form of a dilemma. One horn is that the inconclusiveness of one's arguments stems merely from an inability, in principle remediable, to articulate what one knows. It is possible, in principle, to spell out a universal formula that specifies the conditions under which the concept, in that use of it which one has mastered, is correctly applied. That would elevate one's argument to deductiveness. (If one's opponent refused to accept the deductive argument's major premiss, that would show that he had not mastered the same use of the concept, so that there would be, after all, no substantive disagreement.) If this assimilation to the deductive paradigm is not possible, then—this is the other horn of the dilemma—one's conviction that one is genuinely making a correct application of a concept (genuinely going on in the same way as before) must be an illusion. The case is revealed as one that calls, not for finding (seeing) the right answer to a question about how things are, but (perhaps) for a creative decision as to what to say.[17] Thus, either the case is not really a hard case, since sufficient ingenuity in the construction of arguments will resolve it; or, if its hardness is ineliminable, that shows that the issue cannot, after all, be one about whether an application of a concept is correct.

In a hard case, the issue turns on that appreciation of the particular instance whose absence is deplored, in "You simply aren't seeing it," or which is unsuccessfully appealed to, in "But don't you see?" The dilemma reflects the view that a putative judgment that is grounded in nothing firmer than that cannot really be going on in the same way as before. This is an avoidance of vertigo. The thought is: there is not enough there to constitute the rails on which a genuine series of consistent applications of a concept must run. But in fact it is an illusion to suppose that the first horn of the dilemma yields a way of preserving from risk of vertigo the conviction that we are dealing with genuine concept-application. The illusion is the misconception of the deductive paradigm: the idea that deductive explicability characterizes an exercise of reason in which it is, as it were, automatically compelling, without dependence on our partially shared "whirl of organism." The dilemma registers a refusal to accept that when the dependence that induces vertigo is out in the open, in the appeal to appreciation, we can genuinely be going on in the same way; but the paradigm of a genuine case, that with which the rejected case is unfavorably compared, has the same dependence, only less obviously.[18]

Contemplating the dependence should not induce vertigo at all. We cannot be whole-heartedly engaged in the relevant parts of the "whirl of organism," and at the same time achieve the detachment necessary to query whether our unreflective view of what we are doing is illusory. The cure for the vertigo, then, is to give up the idea that philosophical thought, about the sorts of practice in question, should be undertaken at some external standpoint, outside our immersion in our familiar forms of life.[19] If this cure works where explanations of exercises of rationality conform to the deductive paradigm, it should be no less efficacious where we explicitly appeal to appreciation of the particular instance in inviting acceptance of our judgments. And its efficacy in cases of the second kind is direct. Only the illusion that the deductive cases are immune can make it seem that, in order to effect the cure in cases of the second kind, we must first eliminate explicit dependence on appreciation, by assimilating them, as the prejudice requires, to the deductive paradigm.

If we make the assimilation, we adopt a position in which it is especially clear that our picture of a psychological mechanism, underlying a series of exercises of rationality, is a picture of something that transcends the grounds on which it is ascribed to anyone. In the cases in question, no one can express the envisaged universal formula. This transcendence poses difficulties about the acquisition of the pictured state. We are inclined to be impressed by the sparseness of the teaching that leaves someone capable of autonomously going on in the same way. All that happens is that the pupil is told, or shown, what to do in a few instances, with some surrounding talk about why that is the thing to do; the surrounding talk, *ex hypothesi* given that we are dealing with a case of the second kind, falls short of including actual enunciation of a universal principle, mechanical application of which would constitute correct behavior in the practice in question. Yet pupils do acquire a capacity to go on, without further advice, to novel instances. Impressed by the sparseness of the teaching, we find this remarkable. But assimilation to the deductive paradigm leaves it no less remarkable. The assimilation replaces the question "How is it that the pupil, given that sparse instruction, goes on to new instances in the right way?" with the question "How is it that the pupil, given that sparse instruction, divines from it a universal formula with the right deductive powers?" The second question is, if anything, less tractable. Addressing the first, we can say: it is a fact (no doubt a remarkable fact) that, against a background of common human nature and shared forms of life, one's sensitivities to kinds of similarities between situations can be altered and enriched by just this sort of instruction. This attributes no guess-work to the learner; whereas no amount of appealing to common human nature and shared forms of life will free the second question from its presupposition—inevitably imported by assimilation to the deductive—that the learner is required to make a leap of divination.[20]

It is not to be supposed that the appreciation of the particular instance, explicitly appealed to in the second kind of case, is a straightforward or easy attainment on the part of those who have it; that either, on casual contemplation of an instance, one sees it in the right light, or else one does not, and is then unreachable by argument. First, "Don't you see?" can often be supplemented with words aimed at persuasion. A skillfully presented characterization of an instance will sometimes bring someone to see it as one wants; or one can adduce general considerations, for instance about the point of the concept a particular application of which is in dispute. Given that the case is one of the second kind, any such arguments will fall short of rationally necessitating acceptance of their conclusion in the way a proof does.[21] But it is only the prejudice I am attacking that makes this seem to cast doubt on their status as arguments: that is, appeals to reason. Second, if effort can induce the needed appreciation in someone else, it can also take effort to acquire it oneself. Admitting the dependence on appreciation does not imply that, if someone has the sort of specific determination of rationality we are considering, the right way to handle a given situation will always be clear to him on unreflective inspection of it.

5. If we resist the prejudice, and respect Aristotle's belief that a view of how one should live is not codifiable, what happens to our explanations of a virtuous person's reliably right judgments as to what he should do on particular occasions? Aristotle's notion of the practical syllogism is obviously meant to apply here; we need to consider how.

The explanations, so far treated as explanations of judgments about what to do, are equally explanations of actions. The point of analogy that motivates the quasi-logical label "practical syllogism" is this. If something might serve as an argument for a theoretical conclusion, then it can equally figure in an account of someone's reasons for believing that conclusion, with the premisses of the argument giving the content of the psychological states—beliefs, in the theoretical case—which we cite in the reason-giving explanation. Now actions too are explained by reasons; that is, by citing psychological states in the light of which we can see how acting in the way explained would have struck the agent as in some way rational. The idea of a practical syllogism is the idea of an argument-like schema for explanations of actions, with the "premisses," as in the theoretical case, giving the content of the psychological states cited in the explanation.[22]

David Wiggins has given this account of the general shape of a practical syllogism:

> The first or major premiss mentions something of which there could be a desire, *orexis*, transmissible to some practical conclusion (i.e., a desire convertible *via* some available minor premiss into an action). The second premiss pertains to the feasibility in the particular situation to which the syllogism is applied of what must be done if the claim of the major premiss is to be heeded.[23]

The schema fits most straightforwardly when reasons are (in a broad sense) technical: the major premiss specifies a determinate goal, and the minor premiss marks out some action as a means to it.[24]

The role played by the major premiss, in these straightforward applications of the schema, is to give the content of an orectic psychological state: something we might conceive as providing the motivating energy for the actions explained. Aristotle's idea seems to be that what fills an analogous role in the explanation of virtuous actions is the virtuous person's conception of the sort of life a human being should lead.[25] If that conception were codifiable in universal principles, the explanations would take the deductive shape insisted on by the prejudice discussed in §4. But the thesis of uncodifiability means that the envisaged major premiss, in a virtue syllogism, cannot be definitively written down.[26] Any attempt to capture it in words will recapitulate the character of the teaching whereby it might be instilled: generalizations will be approximate at best, and examples will need to be taken with the sort of "and so on" that appeals to the cooperation of a hearer who has cottoned on.[27]

If someone guides his life by a certain conception of how to live, then he acts, on particular occasions, so as to fulfill suitable concerns.[28] A concern can mesh with a noticed fact about a situation, so as to account for an action: as, for instance, a concern for the welfare of one's friends, together with awareness that a friend is in trouble and open to being comforted, can explain missing a pleasant party in order to talk to the friend. On a suitable occasion, that pair of psychological states might constitute the core of a satisfying explanation of an action which is, in fact, virtuous. Nothing more need be mentioned for the action to have been given a completely intelligible motivation. In Aristotle's view, the orectic state cited in an explanation of a virtuous action is the agent's entire conception of how to live, rather than just whatever concern it happened to be; and this may now seem mysterious. But the core explanation, as so far envisaged, lacks any indication that the action explained conformed to the agent's conception of how to live. The core explanation would apply equally to a case of helping one's friend because one thought it was, in the circumstances, the thing to do, and to a case of helping one's friend in spite of thinking it was not, in the circumstances, the thing to do.

A conception of how one should live is not simply an unorganized collection of propensities to act, on this or that occasion, in pursuit of this or that concern. Sometimes there are several concerns, fulfillment of any one of which might, on a suitable occasion, constitute acting as a certain conception of how to live would dictate, and each of which, on the occasion at hand, is capable of engaging with a known fact about the situation and issuing in action. Acting in the light of a conception of how to live requires selecting and acting on the right concern. (Compare the end of §1, on the unity of virtue.) So if an action whose motivation is spelled out in our core explanation is a manifestation of virtue, more must be true of its agent than just that on this occasion he acted with that motivation. The core explanation must at least be seen against the background of the agent's conception of how to live; and if the situation is one of those on which any of several concerns might impinge, the conception of how to live must be capable of actually entering our understanding of the action, explaining why it was this concern rather than any other that was drawn into operation.

How does it enter? If the conception of how to live involved a ranking of concerns, or perhaps a set of rankings each relativized to some type of situation, the explanation of why one concern was operative rather than another would be straightforward. But uncodifiability rules out laying down such general rankings in advance of all the predicaments with which life may confront one.

What I have described as selecting the right concern might equally be described in terms of the minor premiss of the core explanation. If there is more than one concern that might impinge on the situation, there is more than one fact about the situation that the agent might, say, dwell on, in such a way as to summon an appropriate concern into operation. It is by virtue of his seeing this particular fact rather than that one as the salient fact about the situation that he is moved to act by this concern rather than that one.[29] This perception of saliences is the shape taken here by the appreciation of particular cases that I discussed in §4: something to which the uncodifiability of an exercise of rationality sometimes compels explicit appeal when we aim to represent actions as instances of it. A conception of how to live shows itself, when more than one concern might issue in action, in one's seeing, or being able to be brought to see, one fact rather than another as salient. And our understanding of such a conception enters into our understanding of actions—the supplementation that the core explanation needs—by enabling us to share, or at least comprehend, the agent's perception of saliences.[30]

It is not wrong to think of the virtuous person's judgments about what to do, or his actions, as explicable by interaction between knowledge of how to live and particular knowledge about the situation at hand. (Compare the beginning of §4.) But the thought needs a more subtle construal than the deductive paradigm allows. With the core explanations and their supplementations, I have in effect been treating the complete explanations as coming in two stages. It is at the first stage—hitherto the supplementation—that knowledge of how to live interacts with particular knowledge: knowledge, namely, of all the particular facts capable of engaging with concerns whose fulfillment would, on occasion, be virtuous. This interaction yields, in a way essentially dependent on appreciation of the particular case, a view of the situation with one such fact, as it were, in the foreground. Seen as salient, that fact serves, at the second stage, as minor premiss in a core explanation.[31]

6. We can go back now to the non-cognitivist objection outlined at the end of §3. Awareness that one's friend is in trouble and open to being comforted—the psychological state whose content is the minor premiss of our core explanation—can perhaps, for the sake of argument, be conceded to be the sort of thing that the objection insists cognitive states must be: something capable of eliciting action only in conjunction with a non-cognitive state, namely, in our ex-

ample, a concern for one's friends.³² But if someone takes that fact to be the salient fact about the situation, he is in a psychological state that is essentially practical. The relevant notion of salience cannot be understood except in terms of seeing something as a reason for acting which silences all others (compare §3). So classifying that state as a cognitive state is just the sort of thing the objection attacks.

The most natural way to press the objection is to insist on purifying the content of what is genuinely known down to something that is, in itself, motivationally inert (namely, given the concession above, that one's friend is in trouble and open to being comforted); and then to represent the "perception" of a salience as an amalgam of the purified awareness with an additional appetitive state. But what appetitive state? Concern for one's friends yields only the core explanation, not the explanation in which the "perception" of salience was to figure. Perhaps the conception of how to live? That is certainly an orectic state. But, given the thesis of uncodifiability, it is not intelligible independently of just such appreciation of particular situations as is involved in the present "perception" of a salience; so it is not suitable to serve as an element into which, together with some genuine awareness, the "perception" could be regarded as analyzable. (This non-cognitivist strategy is reflected in assimilation to the deductive paradigm: that the assimilation is congenial to the non-cognitivist objection was noted early in §4. The failure of the strategy is reflected in the failure of the assimilation, given the thesis of uncodifiability.)

If we feel the vertigo discussed in §4, it is out of distaste for the idea that a manifestation of reason might be recognizable as such only from within the practice whose status is in question. We are inclined to think there ought to be a neutral external standpoint from which the rationality of any genuine exercise of reason could be demonstrated. Now we might understand the objection to be demanding a non-cognitive extra which would be analogous to hunger: an appetitive state whose possession by anyone is intelligible in its own right, not itself open to assessment as rational or irrational, but conferring an obvious rationality, recognizable from outside, on behavior engaged in with a view to its gratification. In that case it is clear how the objection is an expression of the craving for a kind of rationality independently demonstrable as such. However, it is highly implausible that all the concerns that motivate virtuous actions are intelligible, one by one, independently of appreciating a virtuous person's distinctive way of seeing situations. And even if they were, the various particular concerns figure only in the core explanations.

We do not fully understand a virtuous person's actions—we do not see the consistency in them—unless we can supplement the core explanations with a grasp of his conception of how to live. And though this is to credit him with an orectic state, it is not to credit him with an externally intelligible over-arching desire; for we cannot understand the content of the orectic state from the envisaged external standpoint. It is, rather, to comprehend, essentially from within, the virtuous person's distinctive way of viewing particular situations.[33]

The rationality of virtue, then, is not demonstrable from an external standpoint. But to suppose that it ought to be is only a version of the prejudice discussed in §4. It is only an illusion that our paradigm of reason, deductive argument, has its rationality discernible from a standpoint not necessarily located within the practice itself.

7. Although perceptions of saliences resist decomposition into "pure" awareness together with appetitive states, there is an inclination to insist, nevertheless, that they cannot be genuinely cognitive states. We can be got into a cast of mind in which—as it seems to us—we have these problematic perceptions, only because we can be brought to care about certain things; hence, ultimately, only because of certain antecedent facts about our emotional and appetitive make-up. This can seem to justify a more subtle non-cognitivism: one which abandons the claim that the problematic perceptions can be analyzed into cognitive and appetitive components, but insists that, because of the anthropocentricity of the conceptual apparatus involved, they are not judgments, true or false, as to how things are in an independent reality; and that is what cognitive states are.[34]

I cannot tackle this subtle non-cognitivism properly now. I suspect that its origin is a philistine scientism, probably based on the misleading idea that the right of scientific method to rational acceptance is discernible from a more objective standpoint than that from which we seem to perceive the saliences. A scientistic conception of reality is eminently open to dispute. When we ask the metaphysical question whether reality is what science can find out about, we cannot, without begging the question, restrict the materials for an answer to those that science can countenance. Let the question be an empirical question, by all means; but the empirical data that would be collected by a careful and sensitive moral phenomenology—no doubt not a scientific enterprise—are handled quite unsatisfyingly by non-congnitivism.[35]

It would be a mistake to object that stress on appreciation of the particular, and the absence of a decision procedure, encourages everyone to pontificate about particular cases. In fact resistance to non-cognitivism, about the perception of saliences, recommends humility. If we resist noncognitivism, we can equate the conceptual equipment which forms the framework of anything recognizable as a moral outlook with a capacity to be impressed by certain aspects of reality. But ethical reality is immensely difficult to see clearly. (Compare the end of §4.) If we are aware of how, for instance, selfish fantasy distorts our vision, we shall not be inclined to be confident that we have got things right.[36]

It seems plausible that Plato's ethical Forms are, in part at least, a response to uncodifiability: if one cannot formulate what someone has come to know when he cottons on to a practice, say one of concept-application, it is natural to say that he has seen something. Now in the passage quoted in §4, Cavell mentions two ways of avoiding vertigo: "the grasping of universals" as well as what we have been concerned with so far, "the grasping of books of rules." But though Plato's Forms are a myth, they are not a consolation, a mere avoidance of vertigo; vision of them is portrayed as too difficult an attainment for that to be so. The remoteness of the Form of the Good is a metaphorical version of the thesis that value is not in the world, utterly distinct from the dreary literal version which has obsessed recent moral philosophy. The point of the metaphor is the colossal difficulty of attaining a capacity to cope clear-sightedly with the ethical reality which *is* part of our world. Unlike other philosophical responses to uncodifiability, this one may actually work toward moral improvement; negatively, by inducing humility, and positively, by an inspiring effect akin to that of a religious conversion.[37]

8. If the question "How should one live?" could be given a direct answer in universal terms, the concept of virtue would have only a secondary place in moral philosophy. But the thesis of uncodifiability excludes a head-on approach to the question whose urgency gives ethics its interest. Occasion by occasion, one knows what to do (if one does) not by applying universal principles but by being a certain kind of person: one who sees situations in a certain distinctive way. And there is no dislodging, from the central position they occupy in the ethical reflection of Plato and Aristotle, questions about the nature and (hardly discussed in this paper) the acquisition of virtue.

It is sometimes complained that Aristotle does not attempt to outline a decision procedure for questions about how to behave. But we have good reason to be suspicious of the assumption that there must be something to be found along the route he does not follow.[38] And there is plenty for us to do in the area of philosophy of mind where his different approach locates ethics.

NOTES

1. Aristotle, *Nicomachean Ethics* (henceforth cited as *NE*), e.g., 1103b 26–31; cf. Plato, *Republic* 352d 5–6.

2. Cf. *NE* VI. 13 on the distinction between "natural virtue" and "virtue strictly so called."

3. Non-cognitivist objections to this sort of talk will be considered later.

4. There is a gap here. Even if it is conceded that the virtuous person has no further *reason* for what he does than the deliverance of his sensitivity, still, it may be said, two people can have the same reason for acting in a certain way, but only one of them act in that way. There must then be some further *explanation* of this difference between them: if not that the one who acts has a further reason, then perhaps that the one who does not is in some state, standing or temporary, which undermines the efficacy of reasons, or perhaps of reasons of the particular kind in question, in producing action. This suggests that if we are to think of virtue as guaranteeing action, virtue must consist not in the sensitivity alone but in the sensitivity together with freedom from such obstructive states. These issues recur in §3.

5. I do not mean to suggest that there is always a way of acting satisfactorily (as opposed to making the best of a bad job); nor that there is always one right answer to the question what one should do. But when there is a right answer, a virtuous person should be able to tell what it is.

6. If we distinguish the reason why he acts from his reason for acting, this is the objection of n4 above.

7. *NE* VII. 3.

8. Cf. Donald Davidson, "How is Weakness of Will Possible?," in Joel Feinberg, ed., *Moral Concepts* (Oxford: Oxford University Press, 1969), 93–133, at 99–100.

9. *NE* III. 9.

10. On this view, genuine deliverances of the sensitivity involved in virtue would necessitate action. It is not that action requires not only a deliverance of the sensitivity but also, say, freedom from possibly obstructive factors, for instance distracting desires. An obstructive factor would not interfere with the efficacy of a deliverance of the sensitivity, but rather preclude genuine achievement of that view of the situation. This fills the gap mentioned in n4 above. (My discussion of incontinence here is meant

to do no more than suggest that the identification of virtue with knowledge should not be dismissed out of hand, on the ground that it poses a problem about incontinence. I have said a little more in §§9, 10 of my "Are Moral Requirements Hypothetical Imperatives?," *Proceedings of the Aristotelian Society Supplementary Volume 52* (1978), 13–29; but a great deal more would be needed in a full treatment.)

11. See, e.g., *NE* I. 3.

12. See *NE* V. 10, especially 113b 19–24.

13. *Philosophical Investigations* (Oxford: Basil Blackwell, 1953), §185.

14. Nor even that we really *understand* the supposition that such a thing might happen. See Barry Stroud, "Wittgenstein and Logical Necessity," *Philosophical Review* 74 (1965), 504–518.

15. *Must We Mean What We Say?* (New York: Charles Scribner's Sons, 1969), 52.

16. Locating the desired objectivity *within* the conceptual framework is intended to leave open, here, the possibility of querying whether the conceptual framework itself is objectively the right one. If someone wants to reject the question whether this rather than that moral outlook is objectively correct, he will still want it to be an objective matter whether one has, say, succeeded in inculcating a particular moral outlook in someone else; so he will still be susceptible to the vertigo I am describing.

17. Why not abandon the whole practice as fraudulent? In some cases something may need to be said: for instance by a judge, in a lawsuit. Against the view that in legal hard cases judges are free to *make* the law, see Ronald Dworkin, "Hard Cases," in *Taking Rights Seriously* (London: Duckworth, 1977), 81–130.

18. In the rejected case, the dependence is out in the open in an especially perturbing form, in that the occasional failure of the appeal to appreciation brings out how the "whirl of organism" is only partly shared; whereas there are no hard cases in mathematics. This is indeed a significant fact about mathematics. But its significance is not that mathematics is immune from the dependence.

19. I am not suggesting that effecting this cure is a simple matter.

20. See Wittgenstein, *Philosophical Investigations*, e.g., §210.

21. If general considerations recommend a universal formula, it will employ terms that themselves give rise to hard cases.

22. I distinguish practical reason from practical reasoning. From *NE* 1105a 28–33, with 1111a 15–16, it might seem that virtuous action, in Aristotle's view, must be the outcome of reasoning. But this doctrine is both

incredible in itself and inconsistent with 1117a 17–22. So I construe Aristotle's discussion of deliberation as aimed at the reconstruction of reasons for action not necessarily thought out in advance; where they were not thought out in advance, the concept of deliberation applies in an "as if" style. See John M. Cooper, *Reason and Human Good in Aristotle* (Cambridge, Mass., and London: Harvard University Press, 1975), pp. 5–10. (It will be apparent that what I say about Aristotle's views on practical reason runs counter to Cooper's interpretation at many points. I am less concerned here with what Aristotle actually thought than with certain philosophical issues; so I have not encumbered this paper with scholarly controversy.)

23. David Wiggins, "Deliberation and Practical Reason," *Proceedings of the Aristotelian Society* 76 (1975–76); 29–51, at 40. The quoted passage is an explanation of Aristotle, *De Motu Animalium* 701a 9ff. My debt to Wiggins's paper will be apparent.

24. There is an inclination to insist on the only, or best, means. But this is the outcome of a suspect desire to have instances of the schema which *prove* that the action explained is the thing to do.

25. *NE* 1144a 31–33.

26. This is distinct from the claim that a person may at any stage be prone to change his mind (cf. §3 above). Wiggins (cited in n23 above) appears at some points to run the two claims together, no doubt because he is concerned with practical reason generally, and not, as I am, with the expression in action of a specific conception of how to live. The line between realizing that one's antecedent conception of how to live requires something that one had not previously seen it to require, on the one hand, and modifying one's conception of how to live, on the other, is not a sharp one. But I do not want to exploit cases most happily described in the second way.

27. Cf. Wittgenstein, *Philosophical Investigations* §208.

28. I borrow this excellent term from Wiggins (cited in n23 above), 43ff.

29. This use of "salient" follows Wiggins, 45.

30. On the importance of the appreciation of the particular case, see *NE* 1142a 23–30, 1142a 25–b5; discussed by Wiggins, cited in n23, 46–49. (For the point of "or at least comprehend," see n33 below.)

31. That the interaction, at the first stage, is with *all* the potentially reason-yielding facts about the situation allows us to register that, in the case of, say, courage, the gravity of the risk, in comparison to the importance of the end to be achieved by facing it, makes a difference to whether virtue really does require facing the risk; even though at the second stage, if the risk is not seen as salient, it is seen as no reason at all for running away. I am indebted here to a version of Wiggin's (f) (cited in n23 above, p. 45),

importantly modified for a revised excerpt from his paper in Joseph Raz, ed., *Practical Reasoning* (Oxford: Oxford Univ. Press, 1978).

32. Actually this is open to question, because of special properties of the concept of a friend.

33. The qualification "essentially" is to allow for the possibility of appreciating what it is like to be inside a way of thinking without actually being inside it, on the basis of a sufficient affinity between it and a way of thinking of one's own. These considerations about externally intelligible desires bear on Philippa Foot's thesis, in "Morality as a System of Hypothetical Imperatives," *Philosophical Review* 81 (1972), pp. 305–16, that morality should be construed, or recast, in terms of hypothetical imperatives, on pain of being fraudulent. Her negative arguments seem to me to be analogous to an expose of the emptiness of platonism, as affording a foundation for mathematical practice external to the practice itself. In the mathematical case it is not a correct response to look for another external guarantee of the rationality of the practice, but that seems to me just what Mrs Foot's positive suggestion amounts to in the moral case. (If the desires are not externally intelligible the label "hypothetical imperative" loses its point.) See, furher, my "Are Moral Requirements Hypothetical Imperatives?" cited in n10 above.

34. On anthropocentricity, see David Wiggins, "Truth, Invention, and the Meaning of Life," *Proceedings of the British Academy* 62 (1976), 331–78, at 348–49, 360–63.

35. See Wiggins, cited in n34, above; and Iris Murdoch, *The Sovereignty of Good* (London: Routledge and Kegan Paul, 1970).

36. Cf. Iris Murdoch, cited n35, above. I am indebted here to Mark Platts.

37. This view of Plato is beautifully elaborated by Iris Murdoch.

38. The idea, for instance, that something like utilitarianism *must* be right looks like a double avoidance of vertigo: first, in the thought that there must be a decision procedure; and second, in the reduction of practical rationality to the pursuit of neutrally intelligible desires.

Chapter 5

"Finely Aware and Richly Responsible": Literature and the Moral Imagination

MARTHA CRAVEN NUSSBAUM

"The effort really to see and really to represent is no idle business in face of the constant force that makes for muddlement."[1] So Henry James on the task of the moral imagination. We live amid bewildering complexities. Obtuseness and refusal of vision are our besetting vices. Responsible lucidity can be wrested from that darkness only by painful, vigilant effort, the intense scrutiny of particulars. Our highest and hardest task is to make ourselves people "on whom nothing is lost."[2]

This is a claim about our ethical task, as people who are trying to live well. In its context it is at the same time a claim about the task of the literary artist. James often stresses this analogy: the work of the moral imagination is in some manner like the work of the creative imagination, especially that of the novelist. I want to study this analogy and to see how it is more than analogy: why this conception of moral attention and moral vision finds in novels its most appropriate articulation. More: why, according to this conception, the novel is itself a moral achievement, and the well-lived life is a work of literary art.

Although the moral conception according to which James's novels have this value will be elicited here from James's work, my aim is to commend it as of more than parochial interest—as, in fact, the best account I know of these matters. But if I succeed only in establishing the weaker claim that it is a major candidate for truth, deserving of our most serious scrutiny when we do moral philosophy, this will be reason enough to include inside moral philosophy those texts in which it receives its most appropriate presentation. I shall argue that James's novels are such texts. So I shall provide further support for my contention that certain novels are, irreplaceably, works of moral philosophy. But I shall go further. I shall try to articulate and define the claim that the novel can be a paradigm of moral activity. I confine myself to *The Golden Bowl*,[3] so as to build on my previous interpretation.[4]

I begin by examining the nature of moral attention and insight in one episode, in which two people perform acts of altruism without reliance upon rules of duty, improvising what is required. This leads to some reflection about the interaction of rules and perceptions in moral judging and learning: about the value of "plainness," about the "mystic lake" of perceptual bewilderment, about "getting the tip" and finding a "basis." Finally I probe James's analogy (and more) between moral attention and our attention to works of art, between moral achievement and the creation of a work of art. In short: I begin assessing the moral contribution of texts that narrate the experiences of beings committed to value, using that "immense array of terms, perceptional and expressional, that. . . in sentence, passage and page, simply looked over the heads of the standing terms—or perhaps rather, like alert winged creatures, perched on those diminished summits and aspired to a clearer air" (GB, pref., 17–18).

I

How can we hope to confront these characters and their predicament, if not in these words and sentences, whose very ellipses and circumnavigations rightly convey the lucidity of their bewilderment, the precision of their indefiniteness? Any pretense that we could paraphrase this scene without losing its moral quality would belie the argument that I am about to make. I presuppose, then, the quotation of chapter 37 of *The Golden Bowl*. Indeed, honoring its "chains of relation and responsibility," I presuppose the quotation of the entire novel. What follows is a commentary.

This daughter and this father must give one another up. Before this "they had, after all, whatever happened, always and ever each other . . . to do exactly what they would with: a provision full of possibilities" (GB, 471). But not all possibilities are, in fact, compatible with this provision. He must let her go, loving her, so that she can live with her husband as a real wife; loving him, she must discover a way to let him go as a "great and high" man and not a failure, his dignity intact. In the "golden air" of these "massed Kentish woods" (472) they "beat against the wind" and "cross the bar" (478): they reach, through a mutual and sustained moral effort, a resolution and an end. It is, moreover (in this Tennysonian image), their confrontation with death: her acceptance of the death of her own childhood and an all-enveloping love (her movement out of Eden into the place of birth and death); his acceptance of a life that will be from now on, without her, a place of death. She, bearing the guilt that her birth as a woman has killed him; he, "offering himself, pressing himself upon her as a sacrifice—he had read his way so into her best possibility" (481). It is a reasonable place for us to begin our investigation; for the acts to be recorded can be said to be paradigmatic of the moral: his sacrifice, her preservation of his dignity, his recognition of her separate and autonomous life.

The scene begins with evasion, a flight from dilemma into the lost innocence of childhood. For "it was wonderfully like their having got together into some boat and paddled off from the shore where husbands and wives, luxuriant complications, made the air more tropical" (471). They "slope" off together as "of old" (470); they rest "on their old bench," far from the "strain long felt but never named" (471), the conflicts imposed by other relations. They might have been again the only man and woman in the garden. They immerse themselves in "the inward felicity of their being once more, perhaps, only for half an hour, simply daughter and father." Their task will be to depart from this felicity without altogether defiling its beauty.

The difficulty is real enough. Could it be anything but a matter of the most serious pain and guilt for her to give up, even for a man whom she loves passionately, this father who has raised her, protected her, loved her, enveloped her, who really does love only her and who depends on her for help of future happiness? In these circumstances she cannot love her husband except by banishing her father. But if she banishes her father he will live unhappy and die alone. (And won't she, as well, have to see him as a failure, his life as debased, as well as empty?) It is no wonder, then, that Maggie finds herself wishing "to keep him with her for remounting the stream of time and dipping again, for the softness of the water, into the contracted basin of the past" (473–74). To dare to be and do what she passionately desires appears, and is, too monstrous, a cruel refusal of loyalty. And what has her whole world been built on, if not on loyalty and the keen image of his greatness? It is no wonder that the feeling of desire for her husband is, in this crisis, felt as a numbing chill, and she accuses it: "I'm at this very moment. . . frozen still with selfishness" (478).

This is moral anguish, not simply girlish fear. Keeping down her old childish sense of his omnipotence exacerbates and does not remove her problem: for seeing him as limited and merely human (as Adam, not the creator) she sees, too, all the things he cannot have without her. And in her anguish she has serious thought of regression and return: "Why . . . couldn't they always live, so far as they lived together, in a boat?" (471) In pursuit of that idea she calls upon her ability to speak in universal terms, about what "one must always do." The narrator says of this "sententious[ness]" that it "was doubtless too often even now her danger" (473)—linking the propensity for abstractness and the use of "standing terms" with her past and present refusals to confront the unique and conflict-engendering nature of her own particular context.

I say this to show the moral difficulty of what is going on here, the remarkable moral achievement, therefore, in his act of sacrifice which resolves it. The general sacrificial idea—that he will go off to America with Charlotte—is in itself no solution. For it to become a solution it has to be offered in the right way at the right time in the right tone, in such a way that she can take it; offered without pressing any of the hidden springs of guilt and loyalty in her that he knows so clearly how to press; offered so that he gives her up with greatness, with beauty, in a way that she can love and find wonderful. To give her up he must, then, really give her up; he must wholeheartedly *wish* to give her up, so that she sees that he *has* "so read himself into her best possibility."

Maggie has spoken of her passion for Amerigo, saying that when you love in the deepest way you are beyond jealousy—"You're beyond everything, and nothing can pull you down" (476). What happens next is that her father perceives her in a certain way:

> The mere fine pulse of passion in it, the suggestion as of a creature consciously floating and shining in a warm summer sea, some element of dazzling sapphire and silver, a creature cradled upon depths, buoyant among dangers, in which fear or folly, or sinking otherwise than in play, was impossible—something of all this might have been making once more present to him, with his discreet, his half shy assent to it, her probable enjoyment of a rapture that he, in his day, had presumably convinced no great number of persons either of his giving or of his receiving. He sat awhile as if he knew himself hushed, almost admonished, and not for the first time; yet it was an effect that might have brought before him rather what she had gained than what he had missed . . . It could pass, further, for knowing—for knowing that without him nothing might have been; which would have been missing least of all. "I guess I've never been jealous," he finally remarked.

And she takes it:

> "Oh it's you, father, who are what I call beyond everything. Nothing can pull you down."(477)

This passage records a moral achievement of deep significance. Adam acknowledges, in an image of delicate beauty and lyricism, his daughter's sexuality and free maturity. More: he wishes that she be free, that the suggestion of passion in her voice be translated into, fulfilled in a life of sparkling playfulness. He assents to her pleasure and wishes to be its approving spectator, not its impediment. He renounces, at the same time, his own personal gain—renounces even the putting of the question as to what he might or might not gain. (For even the presence of a jealous or anxious question would produce a sinking otherwise than in play.) The significance of his image resonates the more for us if we recall that he used to see Maggie (and wish her to be) "like some slight, slim draped 'antique' of Vatican or Capitoline hills, late and refined, rare as a note and immortal as a link, . . . keeping still the quality, the perfect felicity of the statue" (153–54). That image denied (with her evident collusion) her active womanliness; it also denied her status as a separate, autonomous center of choice. It expressed the wish to collect and keep her always, keep her far from the dangers so often expressed, in the thought of these characters, by the imagery of water and its motion. Now he wishes her moving and alive, swimming freely in the sea—not even confined to his boat, or to the past's "contracted basin." Not "frozen stiff" with guilt, either.

We can say several things about the moral significance of this picture. First, that, as a picture, it is significant—not only in its casual relation to his subsequent speeches and acts, but as a moral achievement in its own right. It is, of course, of enormous causal significance; his speeches and acts, here and later, flow forth from it and take from it the rightness of their tone. But suppose that we rewrote the scene to give him the same speeches and acts (even, *per impossibile*, their exact tonal rightness), with a different image—perhaps one expressing conflict, or a wish to swim alongside her, or even a wish for her drowning—in any of these cases, our assessment of him would be altered.[5] Furthermore, the picture has a pivotal role in his moral activity here that would not be captured by regarding it as a mere precondition for action. We want to say, *here* is where his sacrifice, his essential moral choice, takes place. Here, in his ability to picture her as a sea creature, is the act of renunciation that moves us to pain and admiration. "He had read his way so into her best possibility"—here James tells us that sacrifice is an act of imaginative interpretation; it is a perception of her situation as that of a free woman who is not bound by his wish. As such it is of a piece with the character of his overt speech, which succeeds as it does because of his rare power to take the sense and nuance of her speeches and "read himself into" them in the highest way.

The image is, then, morally salient. I need to say more about what is salient in it. What strikes us about it first is its sheer gleaming beauty. Adam sees his daughter's sexuality in a way that can be captured linguistically only in language of lyrical splendor. This tells us a great deal about the quality of his moral imagination—that it is subtle and high rather than simple and coarse; precise rather than gross; richly colored rather than monochromatic; exuberant rather than reluctant; generous rather than stingy; suffused with loving emotion rather than mired in depression. To this moral assessment the full specificity of the image is relevant. If we had read, "He thought of her as an autonomous being," or "He acknowledged his daughter's mature sexuality," or even "He thought of his daughter as a sea creature dipping in the sea," we would miss the sense of lucidity, expressive feeling, and generous lyricism that so move us here. It is relevant that his image was not a flat thing but a fine work of art; that it had all the detail, tone, and color that James captures in these words. It could not be captured in any paraphrase that was not itself a work of art.

The passage suggests something further. "It could pass, further, for knowing—for knowing that without him nothing might have been." To perceive her as a sea creature, in just this way, is precisely, to know her, to know their situation, not to miss anything in it— to be, in short, "a person on whom nothing is lost." Moral knowledge, James suggests, is not simply intellectual grasp of propositions; it is not even simply intellectual grasp of particular facts; it is perception.[6] It is seeing a complex, concrete reality in a highly lucid and richly responsive way; it is taking in what is there, with imagination and feeling. To know Maggie is to see and feel her separateness, her felicity; to recognize all this is to miss least of all. If he had grasped the same general facts without these responses and these images, in all their specificity, he would not really have known her.

Her moral achievement, later, is parallel to his. She holds herself in a terrible tension, close to the complexities of his need, anxiously protecting the "thin wall" (480) of silence that stands between them both and the words of explicit disclosure that would have destroyed his dignity and blocked their "best possibility." Her vigilance, her silent attention, the intensity of her regard, are put before us as moral acts: "She might have been for the time, in all her conscious person, the very form of the equilibrium they were, in their different ways, equally trying to save." (480) She measures her moral adequacy by the fullness and richness of her imaginings: "So much was crowded into so short a space that she knew already she was keeping her head." (480) And her imagination, like his, achieves its moral goal in the finding of the right way of seeing. Like an artist whose labor produces, at last, a wonderful achieved form, she finds, "as the result, for the present occasion, of an admirable traceable effort" (484), a thought of her father "that placed him in her eyes as no precious work of art probably had ever been placed in his own." (484) To see Adam as a being more precious than his precious works of art becomes, for her, after a moment, to see him as "a great and deep and high little man" (484)—as great *in*, not in spite of, his difficulty and his limitation and his effort, great because he is Adam, a little man, and not the omnipotent father. In short, it is to see that "loving him with tenderness was not to be distinguished, one whit, from loving him with pride." (484) Pride in, belief in the dignity of, another human being is not opposed to tenderness toward human limits. By finding a way to perceive him, to imagine him not as father and law and world but as a finite human being whose dignity is in and not opposed to his finitude, Maggie achieves an adult love for him and a basis of equality. "His strength was her strength, her pride was his, and they were decent and competent together." (485) Her perceptions are necessary to her effort to give him up and to preserve his dignity. They are also moral achievements in their own right: expressions of love, protections of the loved, creations of a new and richer bond between them.

Moral communication, too, both here and later in the scene, is not simply a matter of the uttering and receiving of general propositional judgments. Nor is it any sort of purely intellectual activity. It partakes both of the specificity and of the emotional and imaginative richness of their individual moral effort. We see them drawing close in understanding by seeing where they come to share the same pictures. When we hear of "the act of their crossing the bar" and their "having had to beat against the wind" (478), we discover all at once that we cannot say whose image for their situation this is. We can only say that it belongs to both of them: each inhabits, from his or her own point of view, the world of the same picture. "It was as if she had gotten over first and were pausing for her consort to follow." The paragraph melds their two consciousnesses and two viewpoints—not by confounding their separateness, for they see each other, within the picture, as distinct individuals, but by showing the extent to which fine attention to another can make two separate people inhabit the same created world—until, at the end, they even share descriptive language: "At the end of another minute, he found their word." And: "she helped him out with it." Together they give birth, in love and pain, to a lucid description of the moral reality before them. Father and mother both, he carries and nurtures it; she assists in the delivery. The true judgment is the child of their responsive interaction. In the chapter's final moments we hear talk of "their transmitted union" (485)—as if to say that moral like-mindedness is neither, on the one hand, merely a shared relation to something external (a rule, a proposition), nor, on the other, some-thing internal in such a way that awareness is fused and separateness lost. It is the delicate communication of alert beings who always stand separated as by "an exquisite tissue" (480), through which they alertly hear each other breathing.

The final moment of the scene describes the act that is the fruit of this communicating. I have said that these picturings, describings, feelings, and communications—actions in their own right—have a moral value that is not reducible to that of the overt acts they engender.[7] I have begun, on this basis, to build a case for saying that the morally valuable aspects of this exchange could not be captured in a summary or paraphrase. Now I shall begin to close the gap between action and description from the other side, showing that a responsible action, as James conceives it, is a highly context-specific and nuanced and responsive thing whose rightness could not be captured in a description that fell short of the artistic. Again, I quote the passage:

> "I believe in you more than anyone."
> "Than anyone at all?"
> She hesitated, for all it might mean; but there was—oh a thousand times—no doubt of it. "Than anyone at all." She kept nothing of it back now, met his eyes over it, let him have the whole of it; after which she went on: "And that's the way, I think, you believe in me."
> He looked at her a minute longer, but his tone at last was right. "About the way—yes."
> "Well then—?" She spoke as for the end and for other matters—for anything, everything else there might be. They would never return to it.

"Well then—!" His hands came out, and while her own took
them he drew her to his breast and held her. He held her hard
and kept her long, and she let herself go; but it was an embrace
that august and almost stern, produced, for its intimacy, no revulsion
and broke into no inconsequence of tears. (485)

We know, again, that the overt items, the speeches and the
embrace, are not the only morally relevant exchange. There are, we
are told, thoughts and responses behind her "Well then"—thoughts
of ending, feelings of immeasurable love, without which the brief
utterance would be empty of moral meaning. But we can now also
see that even where the overt items are concerned, nuance and fine
detail of tone are everything. "His tone at last was right": that is,
if he had said the same words in a different tone of voice, less
controlled, more stricken, less accepting, the whole rightness of the
act, of his entire pattern of action here, would have been undone.
He would not have loved her as well had he not spoken so well,
with these words at this time and in this tone of voice. (His very
tentativeness and his silences are a part of his achievement.) Again,
what makes their embrace a wonderful achievement of love and
mutual altruism is not the bare fact that it is an embrace; it is the
precise tonality and quality of that embrace: that it is hard and long,
expressive of deep passion on his side, yielding acceptance of that
love on hers; yet dignified and austere, refusing the easy yielding
to tears that might have cheapened it.
    We can say, first, that no description less specific than this could
convey the rightness of this action; second, that any change in the
description, even at the same level of specificity, seems to risk
producing a different act—or at least requires us to question the
sameness of the act. (For example, my substitution of "austere" for
"august" arguably changes things for the worse, suggesting inhibition
of deep feeling rather than fullness of dignity.) Furthermore, a paraphrase such as the one I have produced, even when reasonably
accurate, does not ever succeed in displacing the original prose; for
it is, not being a high work of literary art, devoid of a richness of
feeling and a rightness of tone and rhythm that characterize the
original, whose cadences stamp themselves inexorably on the heart.
A good action is not flat and toneless and lifeless like my paraphrase—
whose use of the "standing terms" of moral discourse, words like
"mutual sacrifice," makes it too blunt for the highest value. It is an
"alert winged creature," soaring above these terms in flexibility and

lucidity of vision. The only way to paraphrase this passage without loss of value would be to write another work of art.

II

In all their fine-tuned perceiving, these two are responsible to standing obligations, some particular and some general. Perceptions "perch on the heads of" the standing terms: they do not displace them. This needs to be emphasized, since it can easily be thought that the morality of these hypersensitive beings is an artwork embroidered for its own intrinsic aesthetic character, without regard to principle and commitment.[8] James, indeed, sees this as its besetting danger; in the characters of Bob and Fanny Assingham, he shows us how perception without responsibility is dangerously free-floating, even as duty without perception is blunt and blind. The right "basis" for action is found in the loving dialogue of the two. Here, Maggie's standing obligations to Adam (and also those of a daughter in general to fathers in general) pull her (in thought and feeling both) toward the right perception, helping to articulate the scene, constraining the responses she can make. Her sense of a profound obligation to respect his dignity is crucial in causing her to reject other possible images and to search until she finds the image of the work of art with which she ends (484). Adam's image of the sea creature, too, satisfies, is right, in part because it fulfills his sense of what a father owes an adult daughter.

So, if we think of the perception as a created work of art, we must at the same time remember that artists, as James sees it, are not free simply to create anything they like. Their obligation is to render reality, precisely and faithfully; in this task they are very much assisted by general principles and by the habits and attachments that are their internalization. (In this sense the image of a perception as a child is better, showing that you can have the right sort of creativity only within the constraints of natural reality.) If their sense of the occasion is, as often in James, one of improvisation, if Maggie sees herself as an actress improvising her role, we must remember, too, that the actress who improvises well is *not* free to do anything at all. She must at every moment—far more than one who goes by an external script—be responsively alive and committed to the other actors, to the evolving narrative, to the laws and constraints of the genre and its history. Consider the analogous contrast between the symphony player and the jazz musician. For the former, all commitments and continuities are external; they come from the score and from the conductor. The player reads them off like anyone else. The jazz player, actively forging continuity, must choose in full awareness of and responsibility to the historical traditions of the form, and must actively honor at every moment his commitments to his fellow musicians, whom he had better know as well as possible as unique individuals. He will be more responsible than the score reader, and not less, to the unfolding continuities and structures of the work. These two cases indicate to us that a perceiver who improvises is doubly responsible: responsible to the history of commitment and to the ongoing structures that go to constitute her context; and especially responsible to these, in that her commitments are internalized, assimilated, perceived, rather than read off from an external script or score.

Furthermore, the case of moral improvisation shows an even deeper role for obligation and rule than do these artistic cases. For a jazz musician, to depart from tradition in a sudden and radical way can be disconcerting, sometimes self-indulgent or irresponsible; but it can equally well be a creative breakthrough before which the sense of obligation to the past simply vanishes. In Jamesian morality this is not, I think, the case. There will be times when a confrontation with a new situation may lead the perceiver to revise her standing conception of value, deciding that certain prima facie obligations are not really binding here. But this never takes the form of leaping above or simply sailing around the standing commitments. And if the perceiver, examining these commitments, decides that they do in fact bind her, then no free departures will be permitted, and the effort of perception will be an effort of fidelity to all elements of the situation, a tense and labored effort not to let anyone down. It is not open to Maggie, as perceiver, to turn her back upon her father, not open to him to depart from her. The task of "the whole process of their mutual vigilance" (480) is to know "that their thin wall might be pierced by the lightest wrong touch" (480); good improvisation preserves, and does not rend, that "exquisite tissue."

How, then, are concrete perceptions prior? (In what sense are the descriptions of the novelist higher, more alert, than the standing terms?) We can see, first, that without the ability to respond to and resourcefully interpret the concrete particulars of their context, Maggie and Adam could not begin to figure out which rules and standing commitments are operative here. Situations are all highly concrete, and they do not present themselves with duty labels on them. Without the abilities of perception, duty is blind and therefore powerless. (Bob Assingham has no connection with the moral realities about him until he seeks the help of his wife's too fanciful but indispensable eyes.)

Second, a person armed only with the standing terms—armed only with general principles and rules—would, even if she managed to apply them to the concrete case, be insufficiently equipped by them to act rightly in it. It is not just that the standing terms need to be rendered more precise in their application to a concrete context. It is that, all by themselves, they might get it all wrong; they do not suffice to make the difference between right and wrong. Here, to sacrifice in the wrong words with the wrong tone of voice at the wrong time would be worse, perhaps, than not sacrificing at all. And I do not mean wrong as judged by some fortuitous and unforeseeable consequences for which we could not hold Adam responsible. I mean wrong in itself, wrong of him. He is responsible here for getting the detail of his context for the context it is, for making sure that nothing is lost on him, for feeling fully, for getting the tone right. Obtuseness is a moral failing; its opposite can be cultivated. By themselves, trusted for and in themselves, the standing terms are a recipe for obtuseness. To respond "at the right times, with reference to the right objects, toward the right people, with the right aim, and in the right way, is what is appropriate and best, and this is characteristic of excellence" (Aristotle *NE*, 1106b21–23).

Finally, there are elements in their good action that cannot even in principle be captured in antecedent "standing" formulations, however right and precise—either because they are surprising and new, or because they are irreducibly particular. The fine Jamesian perceiver employs general terms and conceptions in an open-ended, evolving way, prepared to see and respond to any new feature that the scene brings forward. Maggie sees the way Adam is transforming their relationship and responds to it as the heroic piece of moral creation it is—like an improvising actress taking what the other actor gives and going with it. All this she could not have done had she viewed the new situation simply as the scene for the application of antecedent rules. Nor can we omit the fact that the particularity of this pair and their history enter into their thought as of the highest moral relevance. We could not rewrite the scene, omitting the particularity of Maggie and Adam, without finding ourselves (appropriately) at sea as to who should do what. Again, to confine ourselves to the universal is a recipe for obtuseness. (Even the good use of rules themselves cannot be seen in isolation from their relation to perceptions.)

If this view of morality is taken seriously and if we wish to have texts that represent it at its best (in order to anticipate or supplement experience or to assess this norm against others), it seems difficult not to conclude that we will need to turn to texts no less elaborate, no less linguistically fine-tuned, concrete, and intensely focused, no less metaphorically resourceful, than this novel.[9]

III

The dialogue between perception and rule is evidently a subject to which James devoted much thought in designing *The Golden Bowl*. For he places between us and "the deeply involved and immersed and more or less bleeding participants" (*GB*, pref., 8) two characters who perform the function, more or less, of a Greek tragic chorus. "Participants by fond attention" just as we are (Fanny alone of all the characters is referred to as "our friend"), they perform, together, an activity of attending and judging and interpreting that is parallel to ours, if even more deeply immersed and implicated. James has selected for his "chorus" neither a large group nor a solitary consciousness but a married couple, profoundly different in their approaches to ethical problems but joined by affection into a common effort of vision. In his depiction of their effort to see truly, he allows us to see more deeply into the relationship between the fine-tuned perception of particulars and a rule-governed concern for general obligations: how each, taken by itself, is insufficient for moral accuracy; how (and why) the particular, if insufficient, is nonetheless prior; and how a dialogue between the two, prepared by love, can find a common "basis" for moral judgment.

Bob Assingham is a man devoted to rules and to general conceptions. He permits himself neither surprise nor bewilderment—in large part because he does not permit himself to see particularity:

> His wife accused him of a want, alike, of a moral and intellectual reaction, or rather indeed of a complete incapacity for either . . . The infirmities, the predicaments of men neither surprised nor shocked him, and indeed—which was perhaps his only real loss in a thrifty career—scarce even amused; he took them for granted without horror, classifying them after their kind and calculating results and chances.(72)

Because he allows himself to see only what can be classified beforehand under a universal, he cannot have any moral responses—

including amusement—that require recognition of nuance and idio-
syncrasy. (By presenting him for *our* amusement, as a character
idiosyncratic and unique, James reminds us of the difference between
the novelist's sense of life and his.)

Fanny, on the other hand, takes fine-tuned perception to a
dangerously rootless extreme. She refuses to such an extent the
guidance of general rules that she is able to regard the complicated
people and predicaments of her world with an aestheticizing love,
as "her finest flower-beds"—across which he is, to her displeasure,
always taking "short cuts." (274) She delights in the complexity of
these particulars for its own sake, without sufficiently feeling the
pull of a moral obligation to any. And because she denies herself
the general classifications that are the whole of his vision, she lacks
his straight guidance from the past. Her imagination too freely strays,
embroiders, embellishes. By showing us these two characters and
the different inadequacies of their attempts to see and judge what
stands before them, James asks hard questions about his own idea
of fine awareness. He shows how, pressed in the wrong way, it can
lead to self-indulgent fantasy; he acknowledges, in Bob, "the truth
of his plain vision, the very plainness of which was its value." (217)
So he suggests to us (what we also see in his protagonists, though
less distinctly) that perception is not a self-sufficient form of practical
reasoning, set above others by its style alone. Its moral value is not
independent of its content, which should accurately connect itself
with the moral traditions of the community. This content is frequently
well preserved, at least in general outline, in the plain man's attachment to common sense moral values, which will often thus give
reasonable guidance as to where we might start looking for the right
particular choice.

And in a scene of confrontation between Bob and Fanny, James
shows us how a shared moral "basis," a responsible vision, can be
constructed through the dialogue of perception and rule. Fanny has
been led to the edge of the realization that she has been willfully
blind to the real relationship between Charlotte and the Prince. In
this chapter (23) she and her husband will acknowledge together
what has happened and accept responsibility for nourishing the
intrigue by their blindness. Their preparation for real dialogue is
announced by the contiguity of the metaphors in which they represent
themselves to themselves. She, brooding, becomes a "speechless
Sphinx"; he is "some old pilgrim of the desert camping at the foot
of that monument." (273) As he stands waiting before her, we begin
to sense "a suspension of their old custom of divergent discussion,

that intercourse by misunderstanding which had grown so clumsy now." (273) She begins to perceive in him a "finer sense" of her moral pain (273); and this very sense of her trouble is, on his side, fostered by his old characteristic sense of his duty. He imagines her as dangerously voyaging in a fragile boat; and he responds to this picture, true to his plain, blunt sense of an old soldier's requirement, with the thought that he must then wait for her "on the shore of the mystic lake; he had . . . stationed himself where she could signal to him at need." (274)

As the scene progresses, this very sense of duty brings him to a gradual acknowledgment of her risk and her trouble—and these elements of his old moral view combine with anxious love of her to keep him on the scene of her moral effort, working at a richer and more concrete attention. His sternness, on the other hand, prevents her from finding an evasive or self-deceptive reading of the situation, an easy exit; his questions keep her perceptions honest. Bob, while becoming more "finely aware," never ceases to be himself. Still the duty-bound plain man, but loving his wife concretely and therefore perceiving one particular troubled spot in the moral landscape, he begins to attend more lucidly to all of it; for only in this way (only by being willing to see the surprising and the new) can he love and help her: "He had spoken before in the light of a plain man's vision, but he must be something more than plain man now" (280). Something *more*, and not something *other*: for it is also true that he can help her in *her* effort to perceive well only by remaining true to the plainness of his vision. Because he sees himself as on the shore to help her, she cannot evade her presentiment of moral danger. He keeps her before the general issues, and thus before her own responsibility.

As they move thus toward each other, they begin to share each other's sentences, to fill, by an effort of imagination, each other's gaps. (275) And they move from contiguity in images to the inhabiting of a shared picture that expresses a mutual involvement in moral confrontation and improvisation: they are now "worldly adventurers, driven for relief, under sudden stress, to some grim midnight reckoning in an odd corner." (277) A short time later she presents him with a picture and he "enters into" it. (279) At the climactic moment, Fanny feels (as the result of *his* effort) a sharp pain of realized guilt; and Bob, responding with tenderness to her pain, opens himself fully to her moral adventure, to the concrete perception of their shared situation. She cries, and he embraces her, all with a patience that presently stilled her. Yet the effect of this small crisis, oddly enough, was not to close their colloquy, with the natural result of sending them to bed: what was between them had opened out further, had somehow through the sharp show of her felling, taken a positive stride, had entered, as it were, without more words, the region of the understood, shutting the door after it and bringing them so still more nearly face to face. They remained for some minutes looking at it through the dim window which opened upon the world of human trouble in general and which let the vague light play here and there upon gilt and crystal and colour, the florid features, looming dimly, of Fanny's drawing-room. And the beauty of what thus passed between them, passed with her cry of pain, with her burst of tears, with his wonderment and his kindness and his comfort, with the moments of their silence, above all, which might have represented their sinking together, hand in hand, for a time, into the mystic lake where he had begun, as we have hinted, by seeing her paddle alone—the beauty of it was that they now could really talk better than before, because the basis had at last, once for all, defined itself . . . He conveyed to her now, at all events, by refusing her no gentleness, that he had sufficiently got the tip, and that the tip was all he had wanted.(282)

Both plainness and perception, both sternness and bewilderment, contribute to the found "basis." Perception is still, however, prior. They are, at the end, in the "mystic lake" together, not upon the dry shore. To bring himself to her he has had to immerse himself, to feel the mystery of the particular, leaving off his antecedent "classifying" and "editing." The "basis" itself is not a rule but a concrete way of seeing a concrete case. He could see nothing in this case until he learned her abilities; and he was able to learn them only because there was already something in him that went beyond the universal, namely, a loving, and therefore particular, vision of her. The dialogue between his rules and her perceptions is motivated and sustained by a love that is itself in the sphere of perception, that antecedes any moral agreement. James suggests that if, as members of moral communities, we are to achieve shared perceptions of the actual, we had better love one another first, in all our disagreements and our qualitative differences. Like Aristotle, he seems to say that civic love comes before, and nourishes, civic justice. And he reminds us, too, of Aristotle's idea that a child who is going to develop into a person capable of perception must begin life with a loving perception of its individual parents, and by receiving their highly individualized love. Perception seems to be prior even in time; it motivates and sustains the whole enterprise of living by a shared general picture.

Finally, James's talk (or Bob's talk) of "getting the tip" shows us what moral exchange and moral learning can be, inside a morality based on perception. Progress comes not from the teaching of an abstract law but by leading the friend, or child, or loved one—by a word, by a story, by an image—to see some new aspect of the concrete case at hand, to see it as this or that. Giving a "tip" is to give a gentle hint about how one might see. The "tip," here, is given not in words at all but in a sudden show of feeling. It is concrete, and it prompts the recognition of the concrete.[10]

I have already argued that Jamesian perceiving and correct acting require James's artful prose for their expression. Now I can go further, claiming that the moral role of rules themselves, in this conception, can only be shown inside a story that situates rules in their appropriate place vis-á-vis perceptions. If we are to assess the claim that correct judgment is the outcome of a dialogue between antecedent principle and new vision, we need to see the view embodied in prose that does not take away the very complexity and indeterminacy of choice that gives substance to the view. The moral work involved in giving and getting "the tip" could hardly be shown us in a work of formal decision theory; it could not be shown in any abstract philosophical prose, since it is so much a matter of learning the right sort of vision of the concrete. It could not be shown well even in a philosopher's example, inasmuch as an example would lack the full specificity, and also the indeterminacy, of the literary case, its rich metaphors and pictures, its ways of telling us how characters come to see one another as this or that and come to attend to new aspects of their situation. In the preface to this novel, James speaks of the "duty" of "responsible prose" to be, "while placed before us, good enough, interesting enough and, if the question be of picture, pictorial enough, above all *in itself*." (*GB*, pref., 11) The prose of *The Golden Bowl* fulfills this duty.

I say that this prose itself displays a view of moral attention. It is natural, then, to inquire about the status of my commentary, which supplements the text and claims to say why the text is philosophically important. Could I, in fact, have stopped with the quotation of these chapters, or the whole novel, dropping my commentary on it? Or: is there any room left here for a philosophical criticism of literature?

The text itself displays, and is, a high kind of moral activity. But, I think, it does not itself, self-sufficiently, set itself beside other conceptions of moral attention and explain its differences from them, explaining, for example, why a course in "moral reasoning" that relied only on abstract or technical materials, omitting texts like this one, would be missing a great part of our moral adventure. The philosophical explanation acts, here, as the ally of the literary text, sketching out its relation to other texts, exposing the deficiencies of other forms of moral writing. I find that the critical and distinction-making skills usually associated (not inaccurately) with philosophy do have a substantial role to play here—if they are willing to assume a posture of sufficient humility. As Aristotle tells us, a philosophical account that gives such importance to concrete particulars must be humble about itself, claiming only to offer an "outline" or a "sketch" that directs us to salient features of our moral life. The real content of that life is not found in that outline, except insofar as it quotes from or attentively reconstructs the literary text. And even to be the ally of literature—not to negate the very view of the moral life for which it is arguing—the philosopher's prose may have to diverge from some traditional philosophical styles, toward greater sugges-tiveness. And yet, so long as the temptation to avoid the insights of *The Golden Bowl* is with us—and it will, no doubt, be with us so long as we long for an end to surprise and bewilderment, for a life that is safer and simpler than life is—we will, I think, need to have such "outlines," which, by their greater explicitness, return us to our wonder before the complexities of the novel, and before our own active sense of life.[11]

IV

We must now investigate more closely James's analogy between morality and art and its further implications for the moral status of this text. I speak first of the relationship between moral attention and attention to a work of art; then of the relationship between artistic creation and moral achievement.

Maggie begins, as I argued elsewhere, by viewing people as fine art objects in a way that distances her conveniently from their human and frequently conflicting demands. As she matures, however, she makes a more mature use of analogy; she does not drop it.[12] At the novel's end, her ability to view the other people as composing a kind of living, breathing painting, her attention to them as a response to this work (cf. 459), expresses her commitment to several features of James's moral ideal which are by now familiar to us: a respect for the irreducibly particular character of a concrete moral context and the agents who are its components; a determination to scrutinize all aspects of this particular with intensely focused perception; a determination to care for it as a whole. We see, too, her determination to be guided by the tender and gentle emotions, rather than the blinding, blunt, and coarse—by impartial love for them all not to be "the vulgar heat of her wrong." (459)

But this conception of moral attention implies that the moral/aesthetic analogy is also more than analogy. For (as James frequently reminds us by his use of the author/reader "we") our own attention to his characters will itself, if we read well, be a high case of moral attention. "Participants by a fond attention" (*AN*, 62) in the lives and dilemmas of his participants, we engage with them in a loving scrutiny of appearances. We actively care for their particularity, and we strain to be people on whom none of their subtleties are lost, in intellect and feeling. So if James is right about what moral attention is, then he can fairly claim that a novel such as this one not only shows it better than an abstract treatise, it also elicits it. It calls forth our "active sense of life," which is our moral faculty. The characters' "emotions, their stirred intelligence, their moral consciousness, become thus, by sufficiently charmed perusal, our own very adventure" (*AN*, 70). By identifying with them and allowing ourselves to be surprised (an attitude of mind that storytelling fosters and develops), we become more responsive to our own life's adventure, more willing to see and to be touched by life.

But surely, we object, a person who is obtuse in life will also be an obtuse reader of James's text. How can literature show us or train us in anything, when, as we have said, the very moral abilities that make for good reading are the ones that are allegedly in need of development? James's artistic analogy has already, I think, shown us an answer to this question. When we examine our own lives, we have so many obstacles to correct vision, so many motives to blindness and stupidity. The "vulgar heat" of jealousy and personal interest comes between us and the loving perception of each particular. A novel, just because it is not our life, places us in a moral position that is favorable for perception and it shows us what it would be like to take up that position in life. We find here love without possessiveness, attention without bias, involvement without panic. Our moral abilities must be developed to a certain degree, certainly, before we can approach this novel at all and see anything in it. But it does not seem farfetched to claim that most of us can read James better than we can read ourselves.

The creation side of the analogy is succinctly expressed in James's claim that "to 'put' things is very exactly and responsibly and interminably to do them." (*GB*, pref., 25) The claim has, in turn, two aspects. First, it is a claim about the moral responsibility of the novelist, who is bound, drawing on his sense of life, to render the world of value with lucidity, alert and winged. To "put" things is to do an assessible action. The author's conduct is *like* moral conduct at its best, as we have begun to see. But it is more than like it. The artist's task is a moral task. By so much as the world is rendered well by some such artist, by so much do we "get the best there is of it, and by so much as it falls within the scope of a denser and duller, a more vulgar and more shallow capacity, do we get a picture dim and meagre." (*AN*, 67)[13] The whole moral content of the work expresses the artist's sense of life; and for the excellence of this the novelist is, in James's view, rightly held (morally) accountable:

> The question comes back thus, obviously, to the kind and the degree of the artist's prime sensibility, which is the soil out of which his subject springs. The quality and capacity of that soil, its ability to "grow" with due freshness and straightness any vision of life, represents, strongly or weakly, the projected morality. (*AN*, 45)

On the other side, the most exact and responsible way of doing is, in fact, a "putting": an achievement of the precisely right description, the correct nuance of tone. Moral experience is an interpretation of the seen, "our apprehension and our measure of what happens to us as social creatures." (*AN*, 64–65) Good moral experience is a lucid apprehension. Like the imaginings and doings of Maggie and Adam, it has precision rather than flatness, sharpness rather than vagueness. It is "the union of whatever fulness with whatever clearness." (*AN*, 240) Not that indeterminacy and mystery are not also there, when the context presents them, as so often in human life it does. But then the thing is to respond to that with the right "*quality* of bewilderment" (*AN*, 66), intense and striving.

Again we can see that there is more than analogy here. Our whole moral task, whether it issues in the words of *The Golden Bowl* or in Maisie's less verbally articulated but no less responsive and intense imaginings, is to make a fine artistic creation. James does not give linguistic representation pride of place: he insists that there is something fine that Maisie's imagination creatively does, which is rightly rendered in his words, even though Maisie herself could not have found those words. Perceptions need not be verbal. (*AN*, 145) But he does insist that our whole conduct is *some* form of artistic "putting" and that its assessible virtues are also those for which we look to the novelist.

Two clarifications are in order. First, this is not an aestheticization of the moral; for the creative artist's task is, for James, above all moral,"the expression, the literal squeezing out of value." (*AN*, 312) Second, to call conduct a creation in no way points toward a rootless relativism. For James's idea of creation (like Aristotle's idea of improvisation) is that it is thoroughly committed to the real. "Art deals with what we see . . . it plucks its material in the garden of life." (*AN*, 312) The Jamesian artist does not feel free to create just anything at all: he imagines himself as straining to get it right, not to miss anything, to be keen rather than obtuse. He approaches the material of life armed with the moral and expressive skills that will allow him to "squeeze out" the value that is there.

This ideal makes room, then, for a norm or norms of rightness and for a substantial account of ethical objectivity. The objectivity in question is "internal" and human. It does not even attempt to approach the world as it might be in itself, uninterpreted, unhumanized. Its raw material is the history of human social experience, which is already an interpretation and a measure. But it is objectivity all the same. And this is what makes the person who does the artist's task well so important for others. In the war against moral obtuseness, the artist is our fellow fighter, frequently our guide. We can develop, here, the analogy with our sensory powers that the term *perception* already suggests. In seeing and hearing we are, I believe, seeing not the world as it is in itself, apart from human beings and human conceptual schemes, but a world already interpreted and humanized by our faculties and our concepts. And yet, who could deny that there are some among us whose visual or auditory acuity is greater than that of others; some who have developed their faculties more finely, who can make discriminations of color and shape (of pitch and timbre) that are unavailable to the rest of us? Who miss less, therefore, of what is to be heard or seen in a landscape, a symphony, a painting? Jamesian moral perception is, I think, like this: a fine development of our human capabilities to see and feel and judge; an ability to miss less, to be responsible to more.[14]

V

Is this norm practical? Is there any sense to claiming that the consciousness of a Maggie Verver or a Strether can be paradigmatic of our own responsible conduct? In short (James reports a critic's question), "Where on earth, where roundabout us at this hour," has he found such "supersubtle fry?" (*AN*, 221) And if they are not found, but "squeezed out" from coarser matter by the pressure of the artist's hand, how can they be exemplary for us? James's answer is complex. He grants, first, that he cannot easily cite such examples from daily life. (*AN*, 222) He insists, on the other hand, that these characters do not go so far beyond actual life that their lucidity makes them "spoiled for us," "knowing too much and feeling too much . . . for their remaining 'natural' and typical, for their having the needful communities with our own precious liability to fall into traps and be bewildered" (*AN*, 63). Like Aristotle's tragic heroes,[15] they are high but possible and available, so much so that they can be said to be "in essence an observed reality." (*AN*, 223) And: if the life around us today does not show us an abundance of such examples, "then so much the worse for that life." (222)

Here the opponent responds that it surely seems odd and oddly arrogant to suggest that the entire nation is dense and dull and that only Henry James and his characters are finely sensible enough to show us the way. Surely patterns for public life must be nearer to home, straightforwardly descriptive of something that is readily found. James has moved too far away; his sense of life has lost its connection with real life. James's answer is that there is no better way to show one's commitment to the fine possibilities of the actual than (in protest "against the rule of the cheap and easy") to create, in imagination, their actualization:

> to *create* the record, in default of any other enjoyment of it: to imagine, in a word, the honourable, the producible case. What better example than this of the high and the helpful public and, as it were, civic use of the imagination? . . . Where is the work of the intelligent painter of life if not precisely in some such aid given to true meanings to be born? He must bear up as he can if it be in consequence laid to him that the flat grows salient and the tangled clear, the common—worst of all!—even amusingly rare, by passing through his hands. (*AN*, 223–24)

If he has done this—and I think he has—then these alert winged books are not just irreplaceably fine representations of moral achievement, they are moral achievements on behalf of our community. Like Adam Verver's sacrifice: altruism in the right way at the right time in the right images and the right tone, with the right precision of bewilderment.[16]

NOTES

1. Henry James, *The Art of the Novel* (New York: Scribner, 1934), 149. For reasons of space, individual preface titles will not be given. The title quotation is from *AN*, 62.

2. Henry James, *The Princess Casamassima* (New York: Penguin Books, 1977), 133.

3. All page references to *The Golden Bowl (GB)* are to the Penguin Modern Classics edition (New York, 1966).

4. "Flawed Crystals: James's *The Golden Bowl* and Literature as Moral Philosophy," *New Literary History* 15, no. 4 (1983): 25–50. The issue also contains replies to this paper by Richard Wollheim, Patrick Gardiner, and Hilary Putnam, and my reply to them.

5. See Iris Murdoch, *The Sovereignty of Good* (Boston: Routledge & Kegan Paul, 1970).

6. On Aristotle's similar view, see Nussbaum, *The Fragility of Goodness: Luck and Ethics in Greek Tragedy and Philosophy* (Cambridge: Cambridge University Press, 1986), chap. 10; and also Nussbaum, "The Discernment of Perception: An Aristotelian Model for Private and Public Morality," in *Proceedings of the Boston Area Colloquium in Ancient Philosophy*, 1 (1985): 151–200.

7. See also *AN*, 65, where James attacks "the unreality of sharp distinction . . . between doing and feeling . . . I then see their 'doing' . . . as, immensely, their feeling, their feeling as their doing."

8. For the objection, see Putnam's reply in *New Literary History*. For my reply, see also "The Discernment," where I develop the point about improvisation, with reference to Aristotle.

9. For related arguments, see "Flawed Crystals"; *Fragility*, chaps. 1, 2, 6, 10; and "The Discernment."

10. Compare Ludwig Wittgenstein, *Philosophical Investigations*, trans. G. E. M. Anscombe (New York: Macmillan, 1968) pt. 2, sec. II, 227e:

> Correcter prognoses will generally issue from the judgments of those with better knowledge of mankind.
> Can one learn from this knowledge? Yes; some can. Not, however, by taking a course in it, but through *"experience."*—Can someone else be a man's teacher in this? Certainly. From time to time he gives him the right tip.—This is what "learning" and "teaching" are like here.—What one acquires here is not a technique; one learns correct judgments. There are also rules, but they do not

form a system, and only experienced people can apply them right. Unlike calculating-rules.

What is most difficult here is to put this indefiniteness, correctly and unfalsified, into words.

11. I develop this point further in "Love's Knowledge," *Self-Deception,* ed. Amelie O. Rorty and Brian McLaughlin (Berkeley and Los Angeles: University of California Press, 1987).

12. For development of this point, see Gardiner's reply to "Flawed Crystals," and mine to him.

13. This claim, in context, is actually about the novel's hero or heroine, but it is applied elsewhere to the author: see "Flawed Crystals."

14. This view has strong similarities with the view developed in Nelson Goodman's *Ways of Worldmaking* (Indianapolis: Hackett, 1978). I am grateful to Goodman for helpful comments on an earlier version.

15. On the Aristotelian hero, see *Fragility,* Interlude 2.

16. A shorter version of this article was published under the title "Finely Aware and Richly Responsible: Moral Attention and the Moral Task of Literature," in *Journal of Philosophy* 82 (1985): 516–29, and presented in an American Philosophical Association Symposium on Morality in Literature, 29 December 1985. On that occasion my commentator was Cora Diamond, whose excellent paper (entitled "Missing the Adventure") has contributed in several ways to the development of my views in this present version.

Chapter 6

Morality and Conflict

STUART HAMPSHIRE

I

There is a disturbing phrase in Aristotle's definition of the human good, which (I quote) "turns out to be activity of soul in accordance with virtue, and if there is more than one virtue, in accordance with the best and most complete." But we must add to this "in a complete life. For one swallow does not make a summer." It is not difficult to understand what Aristotle is saying: the deployment of human excellence, and the most complete excellence, will only amount to happiness or well-being (εὐδαιμονία) if the subject's life is not amputated and if he attains the normal life-span. For happiness, in the required sense of that word, nothing must be left out and incomplete in an individual's life, neither his virtue nor his life-span. Why? Because as moral philosophers we must be looking for the perfect specimen of humanity, without defect, lacking nothing that contributes to the ideal whole person and the ideal whole life.

The idea of the human good, presented in this framework, implies that any falling away, any comparative failure in total achievement, will be a defect and a vice, a form of incompleteness: an absence of the complete human being completely active in a complete life. This is how Aristotle did in fact argue in his detailed survey of the virtues, and of virtue as a whole. A person may be deficient as a thinker, or as a practical person, as a citizen, as a politician, as a friend, all these being spheres of activity that are essential to human virtue as a whole and that are constitutive parts of it, and not merely peripheral. Aristotle does not need to deny that there are difficult questions of priority, including the famous conflict between the claims of pure thought and the claims of practical wisdom and of public life, a conflict that had been of such concern to the Platonists. The morally instructed, or wise, person strikes the right balance between conflicting interests and moral requirements at the moment of decision. With good judgment, taste and discretion, the resolution of conflicts can be found by a right ordering of the contrary tendencies in human nature. By deft calculation and educated prudence, a harmonious and complete life can be achieved, with full deployment of all the essential energies that to normal persons will most make life seem worth living. The presupposition of an attainable harmony of moral requirements is buttressed by the analogy between ethics and medicine, between the health of the soul and the health of the body. The health of the body depends upon a balance, particularly a balance in diet; similarly the health of the soul depends upon a balance. Like the life cycle that characterizes a species of plant or an animal species, a human being has a characteristic and typical range of activities to be fitted in at the appropriate times in his life.

This analogy suggests a dubious presupposition behind the Aristotelian argument. The cycle of appropriate activities within an individual's life is being presented as a feature of the species to be properly studied by a biologist; but surely it is also a feature of particular populations whose differences are studied by historians and anthropologists? The expected stages of a complete life, from childhood through adolescence and the middle years to old age, are notoriously marked by moral requirements which are characteristic of some particular way of life, one among the many known to historians and to anthropologists. It is evident that the common sexual and reproductive needs of the species impose constraints upon the variations that are likely to be found in contrasting cultures. But history and anthropology together show that the natural constraints still leave a wide area for diversity: diversity in sexual customs, in family and kinship structures, in admired virtues appropriate to different ages and to the two sexes, in relations between social classes, also in the relation between the sexes, and in attitudes to youth and to old age. Even the notion of completeness is not free from the contamination of moral diversity; varying attitudes to old age, and to death, must modify the prevailing attitude to the completeness of a life, and to the evaluation of longevity.

The diversity in ideas of the standard complete life and of the standard pattern of admired activities is not a merely negative phenomenon, nor is it an accidental one. The diversity is itself a primary, perhaps the primary, feature of human nature, species-wide, and it is a feature that explains many other distinguishing characteristics of the species. An analogy: it is an intrinsic feature of natural languages that they all serve to distinguish a particular group of persons within the species, and that they help to maintain the identity, and the sense of identity, of the particular group. They unite men and women, in part because they also divide them. It is part of the function of a natural language, and of the social customs and moral norms that together constitute a distinct way of life, to mark off a group of men and women, uniting the group and dividing humanity. More generally, the distinct ways of life investigated by historians and anthropologists serve to embellish and to disguise the raw and basic necessities which are common to the whole species; they are clothing for the naked creature, who unclothed can cultivate the abstract virtues that men recognize they need in virtue of their common humanity. Men and women, adopting or conforming to a distinct way of life, realize they have moved away from their natural condition from childhood onwards, as they become morally self-conscious within a particular style of family life and in a particular form of dependence. Not only the Garden of Eden, but many other myths, represent the transition, and represent also the common awareness of it. We therefore usually attach to the phrase 'a complete life' a content that is relative to an envisaged or actual way of life: an order of priority among different required activities and virtues, and a sequence of stages and of approved moral development.

If there is this recognized diversity in ideals of completeness, the presupposition that there is a natural and normal harmony between conflicting moral requirements becomes questionable. How could there be a guaranteed harmony among competing moral requirements and interests, a harmony founded on common human nature, if this common human nature is always overlaid by some specific moral requirements, which are not founded on a universal human nature, the naked man, and which are known to be diverse? At this point the analogy between the diversity of natural languages with their different grammars and the diversity of moral requirements for a complete life can again be invoked. It is a plausible, though still unconfirmed, hypothesis that there is a deep structure of universal grammar, determined in its turn by the needs of learning to hear, to understand, and to speak, and that this natural and universal syntax limits the diversity of historical languages. So also in the morality that governs sexuality, marriage and family relationships, it is difficult to overlook the existence of two layers of moral requirement and moral prohibition, the natural and the conventional. The dependence of very young children on adult nurture, the onset of sexual maturity, the instinctual desires associated with motherhood, the comparative helplessness of the old, are all biological features of a standard outline of human life, which may be appealed to as imposing some limits on moral requirements at all times and in all places. The precise limits may not be very definite and they may admit immense variations within the limits. But there is an argument from the natural dependence of young children to the requirement that they should be nurtured in some kind of family; or, to take account of Plato, if not in a family, that at least they should be nurtured, even if only by the state. That parents and children, or surrogate parents, have obligations and duties toward each other, requirements of reciprocal support, is also a very general moral requirement, which under challenge would probably be traced back to a natural dependence, common to the species as a whole, as well as to the distinguishing necessities of a particular way of life. What particular structure the family has, and the specific forms that the dependence and the duties of support may actually take, do vary widely with different ways of life. This two-layer account of moral requirements and their justification implies that the universal, species-wide requirements, derived from basic human necessities, are very unspecific; they are very general restraints that are compatible with many different conceptions of the good life for men.

Some moral injunctions and prohibitions are explained and justified, when challenged, by reference to the unvarying dispositions and needs of normal human beings, living anywhere in any normal society: for example, the requirement not to cause suffering when this can be avoided. On the other hand, some injunctions and prohibitions, as in duties arising from kinship, duties of politeness, of many kinds of loyalty, are in fact traced back, when challenged, to a particular way of life in which these duties are essential elements. They are essential to the way of life in the sense that they are part of an interconnected set of duties and obligations which, taken together, represent a particular and distinct moral ideal to be expressed in a distinct way of life. Men and women ordinarily know that their own way of life is one of many that have existed and that might exist. When they enter into arguments about moral issues, they often do in fact implicitly distinguish between those duties they think they cannot neglect simply as human beings, and those duties they think arise from a valued way of life that might, however regrettably, change radically and that might not continue forever.

II

The following moral philosophers compete with Aristotle in suggesting theoretical reconstructions of moral arguments: Hume, Kant, the utilitarians (particularly J. S. Mill and G. E. Moore), the deontologists (such as W. D. Ross and H. A. Prichard) and ideal social contract theorists (such as J. B. Rawls). This is a moderately comprehensive list of opposing moral theories, yet they are united and in agreement in one respect: their theories of moral judgment agree with Aristotle, first, in stating or implying that moral judgments are ultimately to be justified by reference to some feature of human beings common throughout the species; secondly, they agree with Aristotle in stating or implying that a morally competent and clear-headed person has, in principle, the means to resolve all moral problems as they present themselves, and that he need not encounter irresoluble problems: the doctrine of moral harmony. Admittedly Ross and Prichard did acknowledge that there occur conflicts of duties which are difficult to resolve by rational method. But their theories of moral judgment do not imply that it is unavoidable that many moral problems should be irresoluble by any constant method.

To deny the possibility of a species-wide human norm, which presents an ideal of the complete life with all the main moral requirements fulfilled, an apparently small modification of Aristotle's account of the distinguishing peculiarity of human beings is needed: he gives reason, theoretical and practical, as the peculiarity of human beings, with practical reason taking the form of deliberation both about ends and about means to ends. The other animals do not deliberate and they do not choose, at least in the special reflective way that human beings deliberate, representing to themselves, and on occasion to others, the alternatives open to them. So far Aristotle goes, but I think not far enough in distinguishing the human animal. The animals of any one species, and particularly the higher animals, often have marked characters as individuals and are often idiosyncratic in their behavior. These differences can be accentuated by skilled breeding and by skilled training. But it remains true that it is only by inheritance, and by environmental influences, which include training, that their salient differences can be maintained and increased. They cannot be maintained by the creatures' own pleased recognition of their differences. They do not possess the power to name, and to record for themselves, the points of difference in their behavior, and therefore they lack the power to think of these differences with pleasure or with displeasure, with pride or with shame. There is therefore a degree and a kind of expected uniformity in the behavior over a lifetime of sub-human creatures who have similar genetic endowments and who have been subject to similar environmental influences. There will be notable individual differences. But the scope for a variety of behavior is not indefinitely wide, and the variety is particularly limited in sexual behavior and in family organization.

The self-conscious and willed reinforcement of differences in behavior and in interests between groups of human beings is the effect of a shared habit of thinking of these differences historically and under descriptions that identify the differences. This source of continual reinforcement of differences is, as far as we know, unique in human beings. It is a cumulative process of differentiation between groups of human beings, who identify themselves as distinct groups by their shared and distinct natural languages and by their distinct ways of life, which are to some extent reflected in the moral vocabulary of their languages. There are many thousands of languages in the different regions of the world, and they are used to preserve the distinct history and habits of a particular population; and this remembered history will in turn reinforce the consciousness of difference.

As soon as it is recognized within moral theory that human beings reflect on their own distinguishing desires and interests, and on their own actions, in their own distinct languages, a duality opens up, which, once opened, cannot be closed; it must infect the whole of moral theory: the Greek duality between nature and convention. The distinguishing capacity for thought, which for Aristotle opened the way to a rational choice between kinds of life and kinds of human excellence, at the same time complicates and multiplies choice, and, more important, puts a limit on its rationality. As a direct consequence of the capacity to recognize and to name differences, a whole range of different complete lives is represented as normal for human beings; and the capacity to conceive these multiple alternatives is recognized as a natural power common to the whole species, alongside the power to calculate and to argue logically. Therefore the capacity to envisage conflicts between norms for a complete life, conflicts of ends and values, is natural in human beings.

Aristotle could reply that men and women are able, as thinkers, to recognize that there are many diets characteristic of different cultures; but this recognition still leaves open the question of which of these diets is best adapted to the independently determined and constant needs of human nature. As there is an ideally healthy diet for men and women of normal physique in a normal climate, should there not be a normal moral regimen correspondingly? The answer is that the power of thought makes our natural dispositions, and the natural targets of our desires, indefinitely variable in accordance with variable conceptions of these dispositions. At least this is true of those desires that are not elementary somatic impulses. The dispositions of the soul are in part constituted by reflexive thought about its dispositions, and are not exclusively to be perceived from some independent standpoint. As soon as the power of reflection develops, our so-called natural dispositions are modified by our beliefs about them, both about what they ought to be, and about their naturalness; and these beliefs are modified by the norms and ideals associated with a particular way of life, the one to which we are committed. Secondly, the ideal of health in the body is underpinned by some independent experimental knowledge of the chemical and other universal mechanisms at work in causing pain and death. We do not have, and do not expect to have, any comparable experimental knowledge of causal mechanisms in the soul; our ideals of happiness and virtue have no such underpinning.

The reinforcement of peculiarities of disposition and character, in pursuit of a distinguishing moral ideal, always entails a sacrifice of some dispositions which are greatly admired elsewhere within other ways of life. Every virtue in any particular way of life entails a specialization of powers and dispositions realized at some cost in the exclusion of other possible virtues that might be enjoyed, except they are part of another way of life, and they cannot be grafted onto the original one. This is an ethical equivalent of the old logical principle: *omnis determinato est negatio*. As children we inherit, and may disown, a particular way of life, and a particular set of prescriptions, which specify, more or less vaguely, the expected virtues and achievements of this particular complete life. To take the Aristotelian examples: some determinate kind of justice or fairness is expected from us, as a disposition that will last a lifetime: some determinate patterns and forms of friendship and of love are expected, as a disposition, or set of dispositions, that persist through a whole life. The conflict comes from the diversification and the specialization in the forms of love and friendship taken as normal in different ways of life. I use the word 'specialization' in the sense that is sometimes given to it in popular expositions of the theory of evolution. A species of animal develops some characteristic sensory mechanism, or some characteristic type of movement, the better to escape predators, or to find food, or to select a mate in a given environment. The new power, which solves a specific problem, often entails a recognizable cost for the organism as a whole within its probable environment. A disposition to a particular form of friendship, or of love, will be at the expense of other possibilities, and will be recognized to be so. For example, the ideal of friendship between young males in some ancient Greek cities is thought to have entailed a cost in the ideal of romantic love between men and women, and perhaps also in ideals of married love, ideals that have prevailed in other places and at other times. Individuals inevitably become conscious of the cost exacted by their own way of life and of the other possibilities of achievement and enjoyment discarded. They feel the cost in internal conflict also. Every established way of life has its cost in repression.

I am not arguing for any type of ethical relativism, or that moralities cannot be compared and criticized. It is a fact that a traveler, or an anthropologist, can come to understand, and can enter into and adopt, an ideal of friendship which is expressed in observances and in patterns of behavior previously unknown to him. He would recognize that he had new friends, though friends of a different type, because of a close similarity in manifest sentiments of reliance and affection. He had come to understand, and to adopt, a part of an alien way of life; history shows that this quite often happens. My point is that in entering into the new norm of friendship or love he will be discarding some part of friendship or love to which he had previously subscribed; he cannot enjoy both specific forms of the virtue together.

For the other sovereign virtue, justice, the argument has to be slightly different. Justice is an abstract virtue, in the sense that a person must perceive certain definite formal relations before he knows that he has a case of justice or injustice before him. The child who exclaims "That's not fair" has an argument of a recurrent form ready in support of his claim. For example, he will ask for an equal distribution of good things, or he will insist on some relevant difference between recipients that justifies an inequality. In spite of this abstract and formal identity, ideals of justice obviously differ greatly in different places and at different times in their specific content, that is, in what actions they specifically prescribe. Aristotle's ideal of justice is not difficult to understand, and his defense of it is intelligible as part of the whole way of life he is advocating, and also as a defense specifically of justice. This way of life, and this moral ideal, have as their center the development of superior character and superior intelligence, and a superior political organization, as the supreme priorities. Other virtues must be sacrificed to these ends, and a particular ideal of justice is required if these ends are to be obtained: unequal advantages to persons of unequal quality. In the modern liberal philosopher, J. B. Rawls, the same formal notion of justice, with its constant relation to equality, is employed to a contrary end: to prescribe that discrimination in access to primary goods should be reduced to a minimum rather than maintained, and this reduction is to be prescribed in the name of justice. The choice and pursuit of either one of these two conceptions of justice entails a cost in the loss of the values realized by the choice of the other.

It may be objected that contemporary liberal thinkers would not admit that any substantial human good is lost when the Aristotelian conception of a just society is abandoned. They may claim one conception is right and the other wrong. On this second-order question Aristotle would be in agreement: not an irresoluble conflict, but a rationally justified choice between that which is finally shown to be the correct conception and the incorrect one. A similar claim may be made for the different forms of friendship and love, though with less immediate plausibility: that one of these forms of friendship is the best or correct form, and the many others known to us are all deviations from the norm. In his two books on friendship Aristotle does argue in this way, unconvincingly, because his specific norm of friendship, in so far as Aristotle describes it, is so evidently part of one particular way of life, which is not ours, and which is not generalizable across other ways of life with their supporting virtues. Similarly the modern liberals' conception of justice in society is not generalizable as a virtue that could be embedded in other admired ways of life without conflict with their other sustaining virtues and ideals.

III

Ways of life are sharply coherent and have their own unity in the trained dispositions that support them, and in the manners and observances and prescriptions which as children we are taught to see as normal. We learn to recognize normal conduct in the same way that we learn our native language; and not principally in the way that we learn mathematics and the law, that is, by methodical instruction, but rather by imitation. At some stage we may be introduced to a museum of normalcies which have accumulated in history. But still we cannot pick and choose bits of one picture to put besides bits of another; the coherence of the pictures comes from their distinct histories: this may be called the no-shopping principle.

There exists a multiplicity of coherent ways of life, held together by conventions and imitated habits, for much the same reasons that there is a multiplicity of natural languages, held together by conventions and imitated habits of speech. As thinking creatures we have to give meaning to our actions as satisfying certain descriptions, and there cannot be meaning without conventions, and any convention is one of an open set of possible conventions. Therefore the formation of dispositions and character, as described by Aristotle, as also the first education in Plato's *Republic*, are inadequate accounts of what actually happens in the formation of character, and inadequate accounts of what could possibly happen. It is as if they had represented the learning of a natural language as learning the language of Adam, that is, the language all men would speak if they had not been divided at the Tower of Babel. There is no Adamic language, and there is no set of natural dispositions which is by itself sufficient to form a normal and natural character, and to which children could be introduced. They have to learn our ways, or to learn someone's foreign or archaic ways, our forms of decent and normal living, our forms of justice and courage and friendship, or someone's alien forms. In acquiring the habits and observances, and the methods of evaluation of dispositions and character which are our methods, children are already becoming specialized as one human type among indefinitely many others. Some potentialities of their nature will never be developed, and they will usually know that; and, perhaps more important, they will feel the repression. No moralist will be able to match the physician's claim to legislate for humanity, showing a picture with the words: "Here is the perfect moral specimen, the complete human being."

The coherence of a way of life, and also the compatibility of the virtues cultivated within it, are clearly matters of degree. A modern, liberal, highly literate, cosmopolitan society is loosely coherent, and a secluded, pre-industrial, sub-literate community is tightly coherent, and there are many intermediate cases. Conflicts that are not easily resolved naturally occur at points of contact between two coherent sets of acknowledged virtues; again there must be uncertainty, and a sense of incompleteness and one-sidedness, which is a recognition of cost. This may typically happen when a person, or a group of persons, change their social role and are moving from one way of life to another. More radical still is the conflict that arises within an individual because his habituation within his own moral tradition has not sealed him off from alternative views of his own dispositions, as he reflects and compares. This subversive reflection may even constitute an essential part of his moral tradition, as constituting a central virtue within it: as part of a liberal tradition, already present in Pericles' speech in Thucydides. The no-shopping principle in its application is, once again, a matter of degree. The virtue of magnificence (μεγαλοπρέπεια) as specified by Aristotle, is not one that I can reasonably want to cultivate, or even can imagine cultivating, in a modern democratic society. It is a virtue that fits naturally into a coherent set of dispositions, which together constitute the moral norm for a number of aristocratic societies known in history. The 'fit' and the 'coherence' in this context are intended to stand for psychological relations, historically illustrated.

IV

We are presented in the *Nicomachean Ethics* with two disjointed accounts, which inevitably we are unable to stitch together into a single account of the one harmonious natural life, as Aristotle intended. First, there are the essential virtues, taken as a mere list—justice, courage, temperance, practical good sense, friendship, theoretical understanding—and with a little imagination we can give them an application in our own setting, in the twentieth-century nation-state, with modern science and industry. The habits and customs that realize these dispositions are now largely different in specific detail; but we can still count the very different patterns of behavior as expressions of the same dispositions, mapping our way of life on to Aristotle's ideal, and observing, for instance, that we still admire and praise genuine knowledge as Aristotle praised contemplation (θεωρία). The second, and disjointed, aspect of the Nicomachean Ethics is the very specific Greek ideal of the free citizen, the man of leisure, prepared to participate in the government of his city, cultivating his intelligence, a leader in his society, rightly deferred to by the lower orders, by slaves and by non-citizens, manly and consciously superior to women, who are dependent on men, respecting always differences of quality among persons and respecting the status that properly attaches to these differences. This disjointedness between the two aspects of the Nicomachean Ethics, the abstract and the specific, is not to be remedied, because to name the virtues is not to describe specific patterns of behavior nor to describe the specific thoughts and feelings that support the behavior; the character of a person, or even of a type of person, is not sufficiently represented by such abstract terms, and the value and nobility, or the mere decency, of his way of living is not to be recognizably reproduced at this level of abstraction. In so far as Aristotle does describe specifically the morally ideal person and the morally normal life, there emerges a person and a way of life very far from the ordinary moral opinions (τἀενδοξα) that now prevail in the industrial West and support a largely different way of life. Aristotle inserts an

ideal, a balance in virtue between, for example, practical and theoretical activities, and which was demanded by the nature of the
mind and of its faculties, as a balance in diet is demanded by our
bodies. But happiness and fulfillment are not analogous to health,
as this ideal of balance requires. If Wittgenstein was, on reflection,
happy that he had devoted his life to philosophy at the expense of
other possibilities, as it is recorded that he was, it cannot be true
that he ought for his own good to have aimed at complete virtue,
in the Aristotelian sense of a balance of virtues, including the practical
and political virtues.

My argument repeatedly returns to this starting point: that the
capacity to think scatters a range of differences and conflicts before
us: different languages, different ways of life, different specializations
of aim within a way of life, different conventions and styles also
within a shared way of life, different prohibitions. A balanced life
is a particular moral ideal to which there reasonably can be, and
have been, alternatives acceptable to thoughtful men at different
times and places: not only to Gauguin and Flaubert, the usual
examples, but to men and women following specialized ways of life
at different places and times: following ideals of courage and en-
durance, ideals of altruism and social service, ideals of detachment
and contemplation, an ideal of maintaining a family tradition, ideals
of science and learning—all of these abstractly named ideals have
been embodied as elements in admired ways of life, and there are
certainly many others. Those who have been governed by one of
these ideals, or by two or more of them in a lifetime, have experienced
conflict in themselves and have seen moral conflict all around them.
They always knew that there were alternatives, and that they have
adopted, or they had been born into and had not rejected, a way
of life which excluded other virtues no less well-known to thoughtful
men and women. They knew that there had been, and would be,
many other admirable ways of living even if they also thought, as
they often did, that their arrangement of priorities was the best.

Our everyday and raw experience is of a conflict between contrary
moral requirements at every stage of almost anyone's life: why then
should moral theorists—Kantians, utilitarians, deontologists, contrac-
tarians—look for an underlying harmony and unity behind the facts
of moral experience? Why should there be a residuary Platonism
here, even today, when Platonism has lost its hold in the theory of
knowledge? The *Nicomachean Ethics* suggest one answer at one level,
the rational level, for the persistence of a partial Platonism, even
among those who, like Aristotle, think they have escaped from Plato.

The phrase 'the things that admit of being otherwise' (ταευδεχομενα αλλωζεχειν) are still not for Aristotle proper objects of the purest and most elevated and most honorable kind of thought, which is concerned with things that must be as they are, and that clearly could not be otherwise. This evaluative proposition about thought and knowledge is the fundamental tenet of Platonism; there is a deep structure of knowable necessity behind contingent appearances. Throughout the *Nicomachean Ethics* Aristotle is trying to show that practical reason is respectably systematic and methodical, and truly deserves its name of reason, within the limits set by the irreducible particularity and contingency of actual situations. There is a similar desire to exhibit a rational structure behind the superficial contingency of moral requirements in Kant, in the utilitarians and in ideal contract theory. If a practice, or an institution, an obligation or a duty or a right, is said to exist by convention, it is implied that things could have been otherwise. Anything that is a matter of convention and admits of alternatives will have an historical explanation. It cannot be part of the necessary structure of reality, to which reason in its most elevated employment can penetrate. Aristotle's ambition in the *Nicomachean Ethics* is to show the deep structure, the foundation in nature, the 'why' of our ordinary moral beliefs. Many different sets of clothes conventionally covering the same body, the natural object beneath, will all reveal something of the structure of the body. We can therefore neglect the superficial diversity of actual moral beliefs and practices, attributing this diversity to the contingency of changing social conditions producing diverse social customs. Beneath the social customs there is a solid structure of moral necessity, and the moral necessities are of overriding importance, while the social customs are comparatively trivial in the demands they make on us.

If this picture is correct, the conflicts we actually experience in plumping for one way of life with its customs are either signs of muddled thinking or they are superficial conflicts, clashes between different cultures and customs only, and not deep ultimate moral conflicts, to be taken with all the seriousness implied by the word 'moral' in contrast with the words 'custom' and 'convention'. Within the single, fully admirable way of life there will be difficult decisions, conflicts between values all of which ought to be included in the complete life, and hence there will be trade-offs. But these admissions fall far short of my claim that there must always be moral conflicts which cannot, given the nature of morality, be resolved by any constant and generally acknowledged method of reasoning. My claim is that morality has its sources in conflict, in the divided soul and between contrary claims, and there is no rational path that leads from these conflicts to harmony and to an assured solution, and to the normal and natural conclusion.

There are the famous sentences and phrases in the *Nicomachean Ethics* where Aristotle seems about to turn away from Plato's ghost. They are the sentences about perception (ἐντῃαἰσθήσει ἡκρισις) and about the observation of the particular circumstances of the particular case being all-important. But the whole framework of the Ethics, in Books I, VI and X, holds Aristotle fast, and he does not escape from the old gradings of thought and of knowledge, as in the divided line of the Republic. There is a snobbery of abstract thought at the expense of perception of the contingent, of the concrete, of the particular, of the historical accident, of the objects of the presumed lower reaches of the mind. It is as if the theory of aristocracy, and of necessary social gradation, had been transferred to the theory of knowledge.

Learning a language, and speaking and understanding and writing a language, are typical thoughtful activities, and typical exercises of intelligence. The kinds of precision and the kinds of clarity required are different from those required in mathematics, and each of these exercises of intelligence presents its own kind of difficulty. There is also the difference that the structures of mathematics to be learnt and their uses to be elaborated are everywhere the same, not confined to particular places and time. There is a history of their discovery, but they do not otherwise have a history, unlike the structures of languages, which all have a history and are best explained and understood through their history. This is not the place to assess the worth and dignity of the study of history and of languages as yielding forms of knowledge; but it is certain that the conventions of behavior and sentiment that enter into our moralities have to be understood by reference to their history, as also do the specific divergences between different ways of life. Against Plato, Oscar Wilde can be quoted: "It is only shallow people who do not judge by appearances," and he meant by "appearances" surfaces, the direct objects of perception, including styles of expression.

That the conventions governing sexual customs and family relationships, and the forms of personal respect and good manners, may greatly vary is no reason for concluding that the morality of sexuality and family is superficial in a person's life, at least if superficial entails unimportant, or even that manners and styles of expression are unimportant. We know that in the average life nothing is more important in moral consciousness than family and sexual relations, and than love and friendship, and their accepted manners of expression also. That which is very variable in human relations, determined by transient habits and social forms and easily susceptible of being otherwise, may have profound moral importance, alongside universal principles of justice and utility. Not only that, but a perception of the variability and of the contingency, even of the merely accidental nature, of a moral prohibition often, in fact, contributes to our sense of its importance. When Flaubert and Proust paid most careful attention to the uses of the past imperfect tense in French, they knew they were concerned with a surface feature of one language and of one literature. But Proust's observations on the uses of the past tense in Flaubert made a point that was also important for literature and language in general, and he knew that it was. Similarly, paying attention to a mode of address, a sexual prohibition, a family ritual, a style of communication between employee and employer, a custom among friends, may be a case of paying attention to an institution that is characteristic of a particular way of life at a particular time, or of the moral character of a particular person who has adopted or inherited a particular way of life. The understanding of these institutions as parts of a way of life is one route to the understanding of morality in general. Certain minutiae of behavior, as they strike a stranger, may be emblematic and have the right or wrong emotional significance for those who understand the behavior, understand in the sense that one understands an idiom in a spoken language.

When the ancient picture is challenged along these lines, the metaphor of superficial and variable contrasted with deep and constant loses its application to morality. Each way of life shows in its regulations a characteristic design and direction. We expect there to be a recognizable vision of humanity and of its particular possibilities, a vision that animates the particular system of moral rules, however transient the vision, now preserved only in a surviving literature or painting. The same rule of politeness which in one way of life may be a triviality of social custom, of no moral significance, may have a significant place in another way of life, marking mutual respect between persons, which is a general moral necessity, differently reflected in wholly different conduct.

V

I am not arguing for moral relativism, taken as the thesis that ways of life, with their priorities among virtues and their dependent moral rules, are not subjects for moral judgment, because there is no independent ground from which they can be evaluated. On the contrary, there are several ways in which they can be judged and ought to be judged. Not only may a way of life fail actually to satisfy the purposes, and to permit the virtues it purports to satisfy and permit, and be internally incoherent, but it may also lead to the destruction of life and to greater misery and degradation and to gross injustice, as Nazism did. These are always and everywhere considerations that count for evil in striking the balance between good and evil. There are obvious limits set by common human needs to the conditions under which human beings flourish and human societies flourish. History records many ways of life that have crossed these limits. Rather I have argued that human nature, conceived in terms of common human needs and capacities, always underdetermines a way of life, and underdetermines an order of priority among virtues, and therefore underdetermines the moral prohibitions and injunctions that support a way of life. I am making three points against the classical moralists: (a) that there cannot be such a thing as the complete human good; nor (b) can there be a harmony among all the essential virtues in a complete life; nor (c) can we infer what is universally the best way of life from propositions about human nature. Human nature includes the capacity to reflect on, and compare, aims and ideals, and to reflect on this reflection, which in turn demands the capacity to evolve conventions of behavior alongside linguistic conventions, and thereby to create a moral order within the natural order. Whether it is Aristotelian, Kantian, Humean, or utilitarian, moral philosophy can do harm when it implies that there ought to be, and that there can be, fundamental agreement on, or even a convergence in, moral ideals—the harm is that the reality of conflict, both within individuals and within societies, is disguised by the myth of humanity as a consistent moral unit across time and space. There is a false blandness in the myth, an aversion from reality. We know that we in fact have essential divisions within us as persons and that we experience moral conflicts arising from them. A person hesitates between two contrasting ways of life, and sets of virtues, and he has to make a very definite, and even final, determination between them. This determination is a negation, and normally the agent will feel that the choice has killed, or repressed, some part of him.

Similarly in the public domain: for example, we know that accelerating natural science and technology often produce effects that are morally ambiguous and uncertain and that they import drastic changes into cherished and admired ways of life. An appeal to the alleged constancies of human nature, to the fixed array of natural powers and to universal virtues, will not represent our natural way of thinking about such problems. The effects of new science and of new technology on ideals of work, on family relations, on local loyalties, and on norms of intelligence and on education, cannot be thought about effectively at a level highly abstracted from historical realities. We have both to perceive and to imagine the effects developing within one, or more, actual ways of life which we understand, and confront the concrete decisions that force a determination between them.

Not all moral determinations are matters of balance; there is also unmixed evil. The Nazis tried to establish a way of life that entirely discarded justice and gentleness, among many other generally recognized virtues, and they deliberately made the claim "anything goes" under these headings. The claim "anything goes" is a sign of evil, because it calls for the destruction of the human world of customary moral claims precariously established within the setting of natural human interests. An uncritical Machiavellianism, or an uncritical consequentialism such as Lenin's, or that of subsequent communist and Fascist leaders, may extend the claim "anything goes" across several of the virtues, draining past ways of life of their value, without a compensating vision of new virtues in a new way of life. The Nazis repudiated justice, and they dismissed considerations of utility and benevolence; they also undermined most of the moral conventions of their society. There is a kind of moral dizziness that goes with such destruction of conventional restraints and of normal decencies in social relations. Because we do not altogether understand why the restraints have developed in precisely the way they have, we respond with moral anxiety and shock to the cry, "anything goes." The normal decencies of behavior evidently might have been different from what they are, if the relevant history had been different. The contingency of the rules does not detract from their stringency: on the contrary, a consciousness of the contingency, a belief that the rules could have been different, with the constancies of human nature remaining the same, tends to reinforce the shared sense that the rule must not be broken, except for an overriding consideration; to break it is to undermine morality more generally. The analogy between linguistic rules and moral rules helps to explain this stringency. The more idiomatic a usage is, whether of grammar or of vocabulary, the more disturbing or absurd is the impression made by a failure to follow the usage. One shows oneself to be a foreigner and a stranger with particular vividness if one's pronunciation of a word is in accordance with consistency and logic, but is at variance with the correct pronunciation, which is usually determined by historical accident as much as by consistency. Every natural language flaunts its idioms and inconsistencies, because they lend the language, spoken and written, its distinctive flavor and spirit. In some important areas of morality, which are the least regulated by rational calculation, the rules that support the distinctive features of a particular way of life, and its determinate conception of the human good, will be particularly stringent rules.

Stringency, necessity: these are the notions that we associate with moral injunctions and prohibitions. Most duties and obligations present themselves as conflicts. Sometimes an individual can present, in a rational reconstruction, the argument that made one final conclusion necessary. This is the Aristotelian picture of practical reason, and it fits many occasions of private life in which utilities are to be calculated, and in which justice as fairness is at stake. This Aristotelian picture even more evidently fits many occasions in public life. Typical difficulties in politics arise when considerations of justice and utility come into conflict. Those who are responsible in politics generally have to be in a position to give a persuasive justificatory account of their decisions to those who are affected by them. Aristotle expressly modeled his account of rational choice on public political debate. But there are many occasions in normal life, particularly in personal relations, when a course of action presents itself as morally necessary, and any alternative as morally impossible, and yet nothing like a clear account could be given of the factors that make the action necessary. If the agent reflects, he will say, "The necessity is not principally a matter of reason, in the sense of calculation; it is more a matter of reflective feeling and of perception, and of a feeling and a perception I am prepared to stand by and to endorse."

The standard objection to accepting the appeal to feeling and to perception is that it is a dangerous form of irrationalism, opening the way to prejudice and bigotry. But it is not irrational not to rely on explicit reasoning and calculation in spheres in which the empirical premises required for the reasoning are known to be, or are likely to be, extremely unclear and indefinite, or difficult to analyze. An action or a policy may be felt to be, or perceived to be, squalid, or mean, or disloyal, or dishonorable, even though the agent can give no very precise and explicit account of why on this particular occasion he perceives the situation in this light. He may be sure that the action or policy has to be rejected as unworthy and repugnant, reasonably trusting his reflective feelings about it, which may have arisen because he has noticed features of the situation that he does not know he has noticed and that he cannot spell out and analyze. Secondly, the contrast between reason and emotion, derived from the old faculty psychology, is not a clear contrast. There are considered and thoughtful mental attitudes, accompanied by strong feeling, which typically come into conflict with each other in difficult moral situations. We have no exact science that can be applied to the study of human feeling, and of admiration and respect and remorse and sense of loss. The usual models of practical reasoning are often too definite to be applicable: the fitting of a particular instance under a general principle, as in law, or the fitting of means to ends, as in engineering. We need not in moral matters aspire always to reason in a scientific style, when the issue is not one of probable consequences, or of articulated law and justice. In some matters of serious moral concern, we ought not to pretend to reason like engineers and technicians and lawyers, or even like doctors, who sometimes have a tested body of knowledge to deploy in their practical syllogisms.

VI

A stable feature of human nature, over and above a normal physical constitution, is the need to possess a distinct history, which is one's own and not that of all mankind, and also to cultivate that which is particular and that is believed to be the best of this time and of that place, alongside and within the universal moral claims that are common to all people as such. In difficult decisions involving conflicts, people are being required to determine what their overriding moral commitments are, and what their priorities are among the activities and achievements they value in their lives. They are always throwing away something they value, or at least they thought they valued. If they are average morally sensitive persons, they know that they have failed to respond to moral claims they had always believed were binding; but they could not have anticipated the contingencies of their experience, in which they found they could not combine loyalty to all the interests, and all the values, which they had believed make life worth living. As they grow older, they will normally perceive that they are going lop-sided to the grave.

This point about moral conflict can be made by contrasting moral requirements with ordinary, morally neutral ambitions and desires. There is no incoherence in the idea that a person might in a lifetime realize every morally insignificant ambition and strong desire he has

154 / Stuart Hampshire

had. The supposition is unlikely often to be true, but it cannot be ruled out *a priori* as incoherent. In retrospect, one comments on one's good luck; circumstances had never imposed the choice between two strong desires and tastes. Why then should a man or woman not be rightly described as having led a morally blameless life, in the sense that they had never rejected a serious moral claim made upon them, having been fortunate in not encountering the worst kind of moral conflict? Clearly these words could be used and they would be understood, and they might even convey a truth, rightly interpreted. But to have a fortunately blameless life, in this negative sense, is not the same as having the best possible life, in a moral sense. The blameless subject would not say of himself that he *happened* only to admire, and to intend to cultivate, only those virtues which in his conduct he had shown himself to possess; and he happened also to be uninterested in all other ways of life, with their supporting virtues, except his own. A person's morality cannot be a matter of what he happens to admire, or believe in, as a matter of psychological fact; but he can, if he chooses, accept his desires and tastes, in so far as he regards them as morally insignificant, as just matter of fact. If a person has lived a blameless life "according to his lights," as the saying goes, the question always arises—"Were his lights good enough, or could they have been better?"; and this question arises for him as agent, as he knows, no less than for unkind observers. For this reason the phrase "a blameless life" is very far from being enthusiastic praise of a person. It suggests confined purposes and an absence of enterprise and absence of large views. Even persons exclusively committed to one clearly delineated way of life, which they are sure is the only right one, ought to admit if they reflect, that the virtues that they cultivate, and the moral claims they act on, both entail a cost; even though they are sure the cost ought to be paid. If they think, like Aristotle, that effective action in public affairs is part of the best way of life, then they will admit that total candor is excluded for them. The Chancellor of the Exchequer is not required to respond honestly to questions about a future devaluation of the currency.

I am not merely arguing the case for the plurality of values, and the impossibility of realizing all positive values in a single life, a case that has been persuasively argued by Isaiah Berlin, among others. My thesis entails the plurality, but it is a stronger thesis and differently grounded. Belief in the plurality of values is compatible with the belief that the different and incompatible values are all eternally grounded in the nature of things, and, more specifically, in human nature. Then Aristotle was in error in supposing ultimate conflicts to be in principle, and with luck, avoidable. But still a definite list of essential virtues, deducible from human nature alone, could be drawn up, even if there will always be conflicts between them; and I deny that such a list is possible. My claim rests on the indispensable and related notions of convention and ways of life, and on the analogy between moralities and natural languages in respect of their plurality; and this analogy, I am claiming, is more than superficial. Just as we know that each of the many natural languages evolves, and that linguistic conventions of grammar and idiom change with changing circumstances, so also the moral conventions that support a particular way of life change.

The attainment of complete virtue, and of the human good deducible from human nature, have been postponed in the theories of philosophers of history in the last century, particularly by Marx and Comte. Historical development, rationally managed, will lead upwards and on to a final perfection. The partial moralities and partial satisfactions of the past should be redeemed in a final stage, in which the potentialities of humanity are realized in full in a final social adjustment. Many reasons have been given in the last few decades for rejecting this linear and teleological view of historical development as ungrounded and not credible. If my thesis about morality is correct, a teleological theory of human development in any form entails an impossibility, the impossibility of human perfection and of the full realization of all human potentialities. We may compare and reasonably praise or condemn past and present established ways of life by reference to their consequences for human welfare, and by standards of justice and fairness we can defend by argument, even if there are no rigorous proofs in this kind of argument. We can make similar, though less fundamental, comparisons between languages in respect of their clarity in communication and of their potentialities in literature, or between legal systems by reference to general standards of equity and clarity. Just as there is no reason to regard all, or any, natural language as an approximation to, or a partial realization of, the ultimate, perfect language, so there is every reason not to think of past and present ways of life, with their supporting and dominant virtues, as phases in the development toward the one perfect way of life.

There is an implication for political thought: we ought not to plan for a final reconciliation of conflicting moralities in a perfect social order; we ought not even to expect that conflicts between moralities, which prescribe different priorities, will gradually disappear, as rational methods in the sciences and in law are diffused. We know virtually nothing about the factors determining the ebb and flow of moral beliefs, conventions and commitments; and we know very little about the conditions under which an intense and exclusive attachment to a particular way of life develops, as opposed to a more selective and critical attitude to the moral conventions that prevail in the environment. We are still in the dark about the dominant phenomenon in contemporary politics: nationalism.

We ordinarily recognize that many moral claims that we accept are to be explained by the history of a particular person or population, and they provoke the question, "Why is this prescription a binding one, given that evidently this moral claim is not to be accepted as valid for all mankind?" There is often no fully rational answer either of Durkheimian form, pointing to the bad consequences of disregarding established conventions, except when they are harmful; or, alternatively, of the functional kind, which might show that the specific practices enjoined contribute to an independently approved goal. Within a particular convention of behavior that prevails in a particular population, a set of actions and reactions which, within conventions prevailing elsewhere, might be repugnant, might here be natural and acceptable. The social context, formed by interlocking conventions, generally makes all the difference to the perception and assessment of types of conduct, which perhaps could be described from a neutral standpoint as identical. There is the analogous fact that there are acceptable and admirable ways of applying paint to canvas within the conventions of abstract expressionism which would be unacceptable within the conventions of Renaissance painting.

I must repeat, to avoid misunderstanding, that strict reasoning, both computational and quasi-legal, certainly has an immense part in moral thought, particularly in public affairs and, more specifically still, in problems of peace and war. Very often, though not universally and necessarily, rational considerations of human welfare and of justice override, and ought to override, all more intuitive perceptions of the value of particular relationships and practices and sentiments. But when we do discard conventions of behavior, or even whole ways of life, on moral grounds that are fully explicit and rational, we shall unavoidably find ourselves entering into other conventions and into another way of life. We shall not find ourselves, as the Enlightenment philosophers hoped, citizens of the world, unclothed in the sole light of reason, computing what is best for mankind as a whole, or computing abstract justice, and guided by no considerations of another less rational kind. If persons do pursue an ideal of pure rationality, such as the one recommended by the utilitarians, they will find that they are disguising from themselves the moral considerations that explain much of their own conduct; these considerations can be classified as moral, because they engage reflective feelings of respect and admiration, or remorse and repugnance. A rational moralist will retort that, as things are, he will be struggling against his upbringing and against ordinary social influences in following his rational morality. And it is this struggle between reason and sentiment that is the essence of morality, he will claim; and the advocacy of a rational morality, whether by a utilitarian or by a Kantian, is a statement of what ought to be, and not a description of the actual state of our unreformed moralities, which are tainted by social custom and by inherited dispositions. I am arguing against such a rational moralist that reason both is, and ought to be, not the slave of the passions in practical matters, but the equal partner of the passions, when these are circumscribed as the reflective passions.

Hume's enlightened theory of moral reasoning can be criticized at two points: first, he accepts a simple and sharp dichotomy between reason, which is calculative reason, and passion and desire, which move to action; and this leaves no clear place for the wide range of reflective thought and judgment which does not consist of explicit calculation and argument. Secondly, Hume argues that nature has so designed us that we tend toward agreement and harmony in moral questions, if we have normal sentiments and sympathies. I have been arguing that nature has so designed us that, taking humanity as a whole and the evidences of history, we tend to have conflicting and divergent moralities imbedded in divergent ways of life, each the product of specific historical memories and local conditions. If a person disclaimed any commitment to any set of conventions, he would lack the normal means of conveying his feelings, and of responding to the feelings of others through shared discriminations and evaluations. Mathematics and the natural sciences do cross frontiers and unite humanity. But we also need to enter into, and to share, the conventions of significant behavior and of speech and of expression that hold a community together as a community, in part thereby creating the frontier that is crossed by mathematics and the natural sciences.

There is a further ground for not rejecting, in the name of reason, moral divergence and moral conflict over and above the values of diversity and individuality, and also the value of community. It is a consideration that is not easily made clear. We stand to the natural order, within which we know ourselves to be a subordinate part, as scientific observers of nature and as manipulators of it in the service of our own interest. There is nothing to prevent our studying ourselves, and studying human beings generally, as natural objects that function in accordance with regularities and laws we find to be universal, or at least general, in nature. We can apply this natural knowledge to change our own physical and mental states and our dispositions in desired and approved directions. We are also apt to adopt toward the natural order, including human nature, an altogether different stance. We decorate it, play variations upon it for our pleasure, disguise it and cover it, enhance it, and leave a personal or communal mark upon it. We enclose, and set boundaries, to parts of the natural environment, not only for use, but for pleasure. As the clearest, concrete example of this attitude to nature, Kant cited gardens, and, more particularly, the English landscape garden of the eighteenth century.

The symbolism of gardens in literature is extensive and old, and I shall not pursue it here. It is at least clear that a garden is a celebration of nature by means of embellishing it and of constraining it for the sake of pleasure. A garden is intended to be a fusion of naturalness and of artificiality, created for the sake of the pleasure and reassurance this fusion brings. Secondly, the shapes and forms of any satisfactory garden show the conventions of the particular type to which the garden belongs, and each type has a history and a sentimental significance. We constrain a tract of nature, unclothed, to take on forms that have a known history and show human invention. We humanize a landscape and an environment in this way and, having lent it a visible history, we are able to feel at home in it. Another relevant example of the embellishment and enhancing of nature in accordance with variable conventions, which have a history, has already been mentioned: the adornment of the body with clothes. Clothes, whether sophisticated or primitive, play variations upon the human body and its shape. They convey both sexual and social ideas, and are linked in several ways to sexuality, as sexuality is conventionally developed and restrained in a particular population. Much clothing is not directly functional, but rather is designed to be pleasing, and usually also to suggest a social role. Approved clothing can be at once capricious and conventional. One would be amazed if one found a people who had no conventions governing the covering or the decoration of their bodies.

Just as there is no ideally rational arrangement of a garden, and no ideally rational clothing, so there is no ideally rational way of ordering sexuality and there is no ideally rational way of ordering family and kinship relationships. The ordering is subject to rational control, specifically in respect of the comparative fairness or unfairness of the arrangements and their tendency under particular conditions to promote happiness or harm. These are the arguable matters, and the arguments can cross frontiers when comparisons between different whole ways of life are made. Within the limits of our biological nature, and restrained by rational calculation of consequences and of fairness within a group or population, we invent our sexual second nature, usually as customs of a particular community; and the customs that constitute a type of family, and a kinship structure, are a second nature also, an embellishment of the naked, biological man, carrier of genes. As raw food has to be cooked and changed in accordance with learnt custom, natural sexuality also has to be trimmed and directed in accordance with some customs or other. When ideally natural arrangements are sought in, for example, clothing or in sexual practices, the result is one more fashion, later seen as characteristic of a particular period and of a particular place.

Christian marriage is one institution among others, entailing a large number of moral claims for those who accept the institution, or accept some variant of it, as part of their way of life. Christian marriage itself has a long history of changing moral claims and virtues—for example, the claims of romantic love, of fidelity, of chastity, of responsible paternity and maternity, of the sharing of property. Whatever choices a man or woman may make among all the variants under these headings, they will be entering into an interconnected set of duties and obligations, many of which are not to be explained and justified by utilitarian calculations; nor as deducible from Kantian imperatives binding on all rational persons; nor adequately justified as instances of justice and fairness. It remains true that we balance, and must always balance, the calculable requirements of justice and utility against the uncalculated requirements of reflective moral sentiment; and neither side, the universal or the customary, can be known *a priori* to be always and in all circumstances overriding.

VII

The word 'institution' must finally come into the discussion because all men and women belong to, or are imbedded in, some institutions, which impose moral claims on them. It is not enough to follow the current habit among moral philosophers who write about 'practices' as distinct from individual actions. An institution is a more formally established, and a more definitely identifiable, entity than a practice; it is generally governed by its own observances and rituals. The moral claims of pure practical reason, calculating consequences, often come into conflict with the duties and obligations that arise from participation in an institution, and there sometimes is no third, independent source of moral arbitration.

The old question arises once again: would it not be better, as a policy for an enlightened and reformed way of life, to subject every institution around us, and every loyalty thereby engendered, to constant rational scrutiny and criticism? If the institution serves a useful purpose from the standpoint of human happiness, or from the standpoint of a just order of things, then its moral claims can be endorsed; if not, not. Marriage as an institution, with its present obligations and rituals, can be evaluated from this double standpoint of utility and justice, and the validity of a range of moral claims would be thereby rationally tested. Has it not already been admitted that we must always evaluate moral claims, and even a whole way of life, by reference to human welfare and to justice as fairness? It is easy to think of institutions loyally preserved, and of whole ways of life long sustained, which have been cruel and oppressive and grossly unjust in their effects, and which ought for these reasons to have been destroyed, and their moral claims repudiated. They were prolonged by lack of rational criticism, by respect for tradition and for the past, and by an inert moral conservatism.

A distinction needs to be made to meet this objection: there is a large difference, and a logical independence, between two moral philosophies, often confused. First, there is a moral philosophy that prescribes rational evaluation of moral claims and institutions and that in normal circumstances prescribes the rejection of moral claims and institutions that damage human welfare or are unjust in their operation; but there sometimes are overriding considerations when the damage caused is not too great and the injustice too extreme and when the opposing values are far from trivial. This moral philosophy, defended here, asserts that there always will be, and that there always ought to be, conflicts between moral requirements arising from universal requirements of utility and justice, and moral requirements that are based on specific loyalties and on conventions and customs of love and friendship and family loyalty, historically explicable conventions. The second moral philosophy asserts that any moral claim is finally valid if and only if it either contributes to human welfare or promotes justice; there is a double criterion that should solve conflicts by entirely rational argument, except when justice and utility conflict. For the second philosophy the only finally acceptable conflict is between utility and justice, the two universal requirements that all reasonable persons must acknowledge. The first moral theory asserts that moral conflicts are of their nature ineliminable and that there is no morally acceptable and overriding criterion, simple or double, to be appealed to, and no constant method of resolving conflicts. Moral considerations are an open set, new ones arise, and old ones disappear, in the natural course of history. The worth and value of a person's life and character, and also of a social structure, are always underdetermined by purely rational considerations.

Many of the moral claims that persons recognize are changed or modified as time passes; but their dispositions and moral beliefs ought to be reasonably consistent over time; and they would be ashamed if there were too many abrupt moral conversions, with their own past repudiated. They recognize moral claims that arise from the requirement that their lives, or some considerable part of their lives, should exhibit some consistency of aim and some coherent character. An explanation of the moral claims would have to be, partly at least, historical, referring to their past and their consciousness of the past. As for persons, so for institutions; they also need some continuity, if their individuality as distinct entities is to be preserved; their history ideally has to make sense as the story of something that had a well-defined character, while it existed, a character of its own. Loyalty is only one of the virtues that derives its necessity from the necessity of continuity, and of continuity through change. A person's family, father and more, origins, and ancestors, in so far as a person knows who they were, contribute to the picture that the person forms of his own nature and place in the world. This place in the world defines some of the obligations and duties. He will probably have reasons for trying to change his nature and place in the world; but the emotional involvement, through conscious and unconscious memories, to some degree ties him or her to the past, and particularly to family relationships, as he sees them. Therefore any person, man and woman alike, will be interested both in explaining and in justifying their present conduct by referring to their personal history. Historical explanation, as a mode of understanding, comes naturally to everyone, because all normal men and women are interested in their own origins and their own history and the history of their family. They are not able to think of themselves, as utilitarians and Kantians demand, as unclothed citizens of the universe, merely rational and sentient beings, deposited in no particular place at no particular time.

Conventions; moral perceptions and feelings; institutions and loyalties; tradition; historical explanations—these are related features, and ineliminable features, of normal thought about the conduct of life and about the character and value of persons. In theoretical reasoning there are two elements analogous to the universal considerations and the conventional considerations in practical reason. These are the methodology of the natural sciences, based on experiment and on quantitative methods, and directed toward the discovery of universal laws, and the methodology of the humanities, specifically history and the study of languages and literatures, based on informed critical judgment of the evidence and on the interpretation of texts. Trying to undermine Descartes' theory of knowledge, with its paradigms of knowledge in mathematics and physics, Vico claimed in *La Scienza Nuova* that there exists also a human world created by men in the course of their development toward full humanity. This is the world of natural languages and of their grammars, of law and legal institutions, of art and poetry and fiction, of social structures, such as republics and monarchy, slavery and aristocracy. The discipline that is the study of this man-made world he called philology. We must use the methods that we use in interpreting languages also in interpreting the laws and legal institutions, the customs, the social structures, and also the poetry and fiction, of the past. According to Vico, because every person has developed in thought and feeling from childhood into full adult rationality, he can, through memory, imaginatively enter into the ages of poetry, with their accompanying social structures, when history, or the history of a particular people, records the childhood of humanity. As microcosms within the macrocosm of history, we can recall the transition from the imaginative, inventive, emotionally unrestrained thoughts and feelings of childhood to the controlled rationality of adults, who are guided principally by concepts and calculations and are not guided, like children, principally by images and fantasies. History is not simply inferior as knowledge to science; it has its own kind of assurance, because we can in fact imaginatively recapture the meaning and spirit of institutions and of languages and literatures which are long past and foreign to us. We can understand them as human inventions, because we have all engaged in similar inventions in our own time. Men and women are influenced by the historical notion of legitimacy. They consequently look for the foundation of their present conduct in the conventions and institutions within which their family and their forebears lived. Social institutions and moral conventions, like the conventions of literature and art, and the conventions of speech, need all to be understood and evaluated as phases of human development. Vico insists that that which is of great value in one phase of thought cannot be successfully reproduced and imitated in a different phase of thought, and cannot be just transplanted from one way of life to another, as the results of natural science can be: the no-shopping principle again.

A rational explanation, answering a "why?" question, is always a case of exhibiting a multiplicity of particular cases as falling under a comparatively simple principle or rule: the simpler, the better the explanation. There is a very substantial part of morality, and of moral concern, that requires the recognition of complexity and not the reduction of complexity to simplicity. Consider a typical intersection of the two kinds of moral thinking: a person may ask, "Is not this sexual and family custom unjust, and therefore to be condemned?" Argument might show that the custom does offend against some entirely general principles of fairness and justice, and this is a very strong ground for condemning it. But the custom might be one of a network of interconnected customary family relationships that could not be radically disturbed without undermining a whole valued way of life. In a particular case, involving individuals and their particular circumstances, the general considerations about justice might reasonably be thought less weighty and action-inducing than complex features of the situation that could not easily and naturally be expressed in general terms, even less reduced to general principles. At any time, and particularly, but not solely, in private life, the practical need is often for sensitive observation of the easily missed features of the situation, not clear application of principles. There is no overriding reason why we should look for simplicity, clarity and exactness in the conduct of life, or in every aspect of the conduct of life, as we do look for them in scientific explanation. We have no pressing need for satisfactory total explanations of our conduct and of our way of life. Our need is rather to construct and maintain a way of life of which we are not ashamed and which we shall not, on reflection, regret or despise, and which we respect. Our thinking generally is, and always ought to be, directed to this end, being practical and imaginative rather than an expression of theoretical curiosity. The repugnant aspect of utilitarianism is its ambition to explain everything, and to find a formula that will circumscribe permissible human concerns, once and for all.

There is a further—and last—possible misunderstanding of my thesis. If one stresses the unrationalized balancing of competing moral claims as characteristic of moral thinking, there is the risk that the word 'balance' will leave a too comfortable impression: as if one lives within morality, and within the moral conventions of a particular society, as within a stable building with secure foundations. In this century it is impossible to preserve this picture of stability. It has been obvious that respect for justice, and also any morality founded on concern for human welfare, are fragile constructions, liable to be toppled at any time by cruelty and fanaticism, and by the will to power. Alongside the balancing of conflicting moral claims, thinking about morality also includes thinking about how barriers against evil are most reliably maintained: that is, about how a standard of bare decency in social arrangements is to be maintained; for this standard is always under threat. This thinking about social evils is not generally a matter of the judicious balancing of competing moral claims, but rather of expressing and eliciting strong moral feelings. As morality is inextricably involved with conflict, so also it is inextricably involved with the control of destructive impulses. If morality were to be defined, which is unnecessary, it might be defined by reference to its central topics, and not by the alleged logical peculiarities of moral judgments, in the manner of Kant. It is a system of prohibitions and injunctions concerning justice in social relations, the control of violence and killings of all kinds, about war and peace, the regulation of kinship, the customs of friendship and family. My argument has been that it is for us natural to be unnatural in these spheres, following both reason and history, and consequently it is natural for us to be involved in repression and conflict: these are the costs of culture and of the balance between reason and memory.

Part II

Moral Conservatism

Chapter 7

Solidarity or Objectivity?

RICHARD RORTY

There are two principal ways in which reflective human beings try, by placing their lives in a larger context, to give sense to those lives. The first is by telling the story of their contribution to a community. This community may be the actual historical one in which they live, or another actual one, distant in time or place, or a quite imaginary one, consisting perhaps of a dozen heroes and heroines selected from history or fiction or both. The second way is to describe themselves as standing in immediate relation to a nonhuman reality. This relation is immediate in the sense that it does not derive from a relation between such a reality and their tribe, or their nation, or their imagined band of comrades. I shall say that stories of the former kind exemplify the desire for solidarity, and that stories of the latter kind exemplify the desire for objectivity. Insofar as a person is seeking solidarity, he or she does not ask about the relation between the practices of the chosen community and something outside that community. Insofar as he seeks objectivity, he distances himself from the actual persons around him not by thinking of himself as a member of some other real or imaginary group, but rather by attaching himself to something that can be described without reference to any particular human beings.

The tradition in Western culture that centers on the notion of the search for Truth, a tradition that runs from the Greek philosophers through the Enlightenment, is the clearest example of the attempt to find a sense in one's existence by turning away from solidarity to objectivity. The idea of Truth as something to be pursued for its own sake, not because it will be good for oneself, or for one's real or imaginary community, is the central theme of this tradition. It was perhaps the growing awareness by the Greeks of the sheer diversity of human communities that stimulated the emergence of

This paper is a revised version of a Howison Lecture given at the University of California at Berkeley in January 1983. A somewhat different version appeared in *Nanzan Review of American Studies*, vol. 6, 1984, and (in French translation) in *Critique*.

this ideal. A fear of parochialism, of being confined within the horizons of the group into which one happens to be born, a need to see it with the eyes of a stranger, helps produce the skeptical and ironic tone characteristic of Euripides and Socrates. Herodotus' willingness to take the barbarians seriously enough to describe their customs in detail may have been a necessary prelude to Plato's claim that the way to transcend skepticism is to envisage a common goal of humanity—a goal set by human nature rather than by Greek culture. The combination of Socratic alienation and Platonic hope gives rise to the idea of the intellectual as someone who is in touch with the nature of things, not by way of the opinions of his community, but in a more immediate way.

Plato developed the idea of such an intellectual by means of distinctions between knowledge and opinion, and between appearance and reality. Such distinctions conspire to produce the idea that rational inquiry should make visible a realm to which nonintellectuals have little access, and of whose very existence they may be doubtful. In the Enlightenment, this notion became concrete in the adoption of the Newtonian physical scientist as a model of the intellectual. To most thinkers of the eighteenth century, it seemed clear that the access to Nature which physical science had provided should now be followed by the establishment of social, political, and economic institutions that were in accordance with Nature. Ever since, liberal social thought has centered upon social reform as made possible by objective knowledge of what human beings are like—not knowledge of what Greeks or Frenchmen or Chinese are like, but of humanity as such. We are the heirs of this objectivist tradition, which centers on the assumption that we must step outside our community long enough to examine it in the light of something that transcends it, namely that which it has in common with every other actual and possible human community. This tradition dreams of an ultimate community which will have transcended the distinction between the natural and the social, which will exhibit a solidarity that is not parochial because it is the expression of an ahistorical human nature. Much of the rhetoric of contemporary intellectual life takes for granted that the goal of scientific inquiry into man is to understand "underlying structures," or, "culturally invariant factors," or, "biologically determined patterns."

Those who wish to ground solidarity in objectivity—call them "realists"—have to construe truth as correspondence to reality. So they must construct a metaphysics that has room for a special relation between beliefs and objects which will differentiate true from false beliefs. They also must argue that there are procedures of justification of belief which are natural and not merely local. So they must construct an epistemology that has room for a kind of justification that is not merely social but natural, springing from human nature itself, and made possible by a link between that part of nature and the rest of nature. On their view, the various procedures thought of as providing rational justification by one or another culture may or may not really *be* rational. For to be truly rational, procedures of justification *must* lead to the truth, to correspondence to reality, to the intrinsic nature of things.

By contrast, those who wish to reduce objectivity to solidarity—call them "pragmatists"—do not require either a metaphysics or an epistemology. They view truth as, in William James' phrase, what it is good for *us* to believe. So they do not need an account of a relation between beliefs and objects called "correspondence," nor an account of human cognitive abilities that ensures our species is capable of entering into that relation. They see the gap between truth and justification not as something to be bridged by isolating a natural and transcultural sort of rationality that can be used to criticize certain cultures and praise others, but simply as the gap between the actual good and the possible better. From a pragmatist point of view, to say that what is rational for us now to believe may not be *true*, is simply to say that somebody may come up with a better idea. It is to say there is always room for improved belief, since new evidence, or new hypotheses, or a whole new vocabulary, may come along.[1] For pragmatists, the desire for objectivity is not the desire to escape the limitations of one's community, but simply the desire for as much intersubjective agreement as possible, the desire to extend the reference of "us" as far as we can. Insofar as pragmatists make a distinction between knowledge and opinion, it is simply the distinction between topics on which such agreement is relatively easy to get and topics on which agreement is relatively hard to get.

"Relativism" is the traditional epithet applied to pragmatism by realists. Three different views are commonly referred to by this name. The first is the view that every belief is as good as every other. The second is the view that "true" is an equivocal term, having as many meanings as there are procedures of justification. The third is the view that there is nothing to be said about either truth or rationality apart from descriptions of the familiar procedures of justification that a given society—*ours*—uses in one or another area of inquiry. The pragmatist holds the ethnocentric third view. But he does not hold the self-refuting first view, nor the eccentric second view. He thinks his views are better than the realists, but he does not think that his views correspond to the nature of things. He thinks the very flexibility of the word "true"—the fact that it is merely an expression of commendation—insures its univocity. The term "true," on his account, means the same in all cultures, just as equally flexible terms like "here," "there," "good," "bad," "you," and "me" mean the same in all cultures. But the identity of meaning is, of course, compatible with diversity of reference, and with diversity of procedures for assigning the terms. So he feels free to use the term "true" as a general term of commendation in the same way as his realist opponent does—and in particular to use it to commend his own view.

However, it is not clear why "relativist" should be thought an appropriate term for the ethnocentric third view, the one which the pragmatist *does* hold. For the pragmatist is not holding a positive theory that says that something is relative to something else. He is, instead, making the purely *negative* point that we should drop the traditional distinction between knowledge and opinion, construed as the distinction between truth as correspondence to reality and truth as a commendatory term for well-justified beliefs. The reason the realist calls this negative claim "relativistic" is that he cannot believe that anybody would seriously deny that truth has an intrinsic nature. So when the pragmatist says there is nothing to be said about truth save that each of us will commend as true those beliefs he or she finds good to believe, the realist is inclined to interpret this as one more positive theory about the nature of truth: a theory according to which truth is simply the contemporary opinion of a chosen individual or group. Such a theory would, of course, be self-refuting. But the pragmatist does not have a theory of truth, much less a relativistic one. As a partisan of solidarity, his account of the value of cooperative human inquiry has only an ethical base, not an epistemological or metaphysical one. Not having *any* epistemology, *a fortiori* he does not have a relativistic one.

The question of whether truth or rationality has an intrinsic nature, of whether we ought to have a positive theory about either topic, is just the question of whether our self-description ought to be constructed around a relation to human nature or around a relation to a particular collection of human beings, whether we should desire objectivity or solidarity. It is hard to see how one could choose between these alternatives by looking more deeply into the nature of knowledge, or of man, or of nature. Indeed, the proposal that this issue might be so settled begs the question in favor of the realist, for it presupposes that knowledge, man, and nature *have* real essences which are relevant to the problem at hand. For the pragmatist, by contrast, knowledge is, like truth, simply a compliment paid to the beliefs we think so well justified that, for the moment, further justification is not needed. An inquiry into the nature of knowledge can, on his view, only be a socio-historical account of how various people have tried to reach agreement on what to believe.

This view, which I am calling "pragmatism," is almost, but not quite, the same as what Hilary Putnam, in his recent *Reason, Truth and History*, calls "the internalist conception of philosophy."[2] Putnam defines such a conception as one which gives up the attempt at a God's eye view of things, the attempt at contact with the nonhuman which I have been calling "the desire for objectivity." Unfortunately, he accompanies his defense of the antirealist views I am recommending with a polemic against a lot of the other people who hold these views—e.g., Kuhn, Feyerabend, Foucault, and myself. We are criticized as "relativists." Putnam presents internalism as a happy *via media* between realism and relativism. He speaks of "the plethora of relativisitic doctrines being marketed today"[3] and in particular of "the French philosophers" as holding "some fancy mixture of cultural relativism and structuralism."[4] But when it comes to criticizing these doctrines all that Putnam finds to attack is the so-called "incommensurability thesis": vis., "terms used in another culture cannot be equated in meaning or reference with any terms or expressions *we* possess."[5] He sensibly agrees with Donald Davidson in remarking that this thesis is self-refuting. Criticism of this thesis, however, is destructive of, at most, some incautious passages in some early writings by Feyerabend. Once this thesis is brushed aside, it is hard to see how Putnam himself differs from most of those he criticizes.

Putnam accepts the Davidsonian point that, as he puts it, "the whole justification of an interpretative scheme . . . is that it renders the behavior of others at least minimally reasonable by *our* lights."[6] It would seem natural to go on from this to say that we cannot get outside the range of those lights, that we cannot stand on neutral ground illuminated only by the natural light of reason. But Putnam draws back from this conclusion. He does so because he construes the claim that we cannot do so as the claim that the range of our thought is restricted by what he calls "institutionalized norms," publicly available criteria for settling all arguments, including philosophical arguments. He rightly says that there are no such criteria, arguing that the suggestion that there are is as self-refuting as the "incommensurability thesis." He is, I think, entirely right in saying that the notion that philosophy is or should become such an application of explicit criteria contradicts the very idea of philosophy.[7] One can gloss Putnam's point by saying that "philosophy" is precisely what a culture becomes capable of when it ceases to define itself in terms of explicit rules, and becomes sufficiently leisured and civilized to rely on inarticulate know-how, to substitute *phronesis* for codification, and conversation with foreigners for conquest of them.

But to say that we cannot refer every question to explicit criteria institutionalized by our society does not speak to the point the people whom Putnam calls "relativists" are making. One reason these people are pragmatists is precisely that they share Putnam's distrust of the positivistic idea that rationality is a matter of applying criteria.

Such a distrust is common, for example, to Kuhn, Mary Hesse, Wittgenstein, Michael Polanyi and Michael Oakeshott. Only someone who did think of rationality in this way would dream of suggesting that "true" means something different in different societies. For only such a person could imagine that there was anything to pick out to which one might make "true" relative. Only if one shares the logical positivists' idea that we all carry around things called "rules of language" that regulate what we say when, will one suggest that there is no way to break out of one's culture.

In the most original and powerful section of his book, Putnam argues that the notion that "rationality. . . is defined by the local cultural norms" is merely the demonic counterpart of positivism. It is, as he says, "a scientistic theory inspired by anthropology as positivism was a scientistic theory inspired by the exact sciences." By "scientism" Putnam means the notion that rationality consists in the application of critera.[8] Suppose we drop this notion, and accept Putnam's own Quinean picture of inquiry as the continual reweaving of a web of beliefs rather than as the application of criteria to cases. Then the notion of "local cultural norms" will lose its offensively parochial overtones. For now to say that we must work by our own lights, that we must be ethnocentric, is merely to say that beliefs suggested by another culture must be tested by trying to weave them together with beliefs we already have. It is a consequence of this holistic view of knowledge, a view *shared* by Putnam and those he criticizes as "relativists," that alternative cultures are not to be thought of on the model of alternative geometries. Alternative geometries are irreconcilable because they have axiomatic structures, and contradictory axioms. They are *designed* to be irreconcilable. Cultures are not so designed, and do not have axiomatic structures. To say that they have "institutionalized norms" is only to say, with Foucault, that knowledge is never separable from power—that one is likely to suffer if one does not hold certain beliefs at certain times and places. But such institutional backups for beliefs take the form of bureaucrats and policemen, not of "rules of language" and "criteria of rationality." To think otherwise is the Cartesian fallacy of seeing axioms where there are only shared habits, of viewing statements that summarize such practices as if they reported constraints enforcing such practices. Part of the force of Quine's and Davidson's attack on the distinction between the conceptual and the empirical is that the distinction between different cultures does not differ in kind from the distinction between different theories held by members of a single culture. The Tasmanian aborigines and the British colonists had trouble communicating, but this trouble was different only in extent from the difficulties in communication experienced by Gladstone and Disraeli. The trouble in all such cases is just the difficulty of explaining why other people disagree with us, of reweaving our beliefs to fit the fact of disagreement together with the other beliefs we hold. The same Quinean arguments that dispose of the positivists' distinction between analytic and synthetic truth dispose of the anthropologists' distinction between the intercultural and the intracultural.

On this holistic account of cultural norms, however, we do not need the notion of a universal transcultural rationality that Putnam invokes against those whom he calls "relativists." Just before the end of his book, Putnam says that once we drop the notion of a God's-eye point of view we realize that:

> We can only hope to produce a more rational *conception* of rationality or a better *conception* of morality if we operate from *within* our tradition (with its echoes of the Greek agora, of Newton, and so on, in the case of rationality, and with its echoes of scripture, of the philosophers, of the democratic revolutions, and so on . . . in the case of morality). We are invited to engage in a truly human dialogue.[9]

With this I entirely agree, and so, I take it, would Kuhn, Hesse, and most of the other so-called "relativists"—perhaps even Foucault. But Putnam then goes on to pose a further question:

> Does this dialogue have an ideal terminus? Is there a *true* conception of rationality, an ideal morality, even if all we ever have are our *conceptions* of these?

I do not see the point of this question. Putnam suggests that a negative answer—the view that "there is only the dialogue"—is just another form of self-refuting relativism. But, once again, I do not see how a claim that something does not exist can be construed as a claim that something is relative to something else. In the final sentence of his book, Putnam says that, "The very fact that we speak of our different conceptions as different conceptions of *rationality* posits a *Grenzbegriff*, a limited-concept of ideal truth." But what is such a posit supposed to do, except to say that from God's point of view the human race is heading in the right direction? Surely Putnam's "internalism" should forbid him to say anything like that. To say that *we* think we're heading in the right direction is just to say, with Kuhn, that we can, by hindsight, tell the story of the past as a story of progress. To say that we still have a long way to go, that our present views should not be cast in bronze, is too platitudinous to require support by positing limit-concepts. So it is hard to see what difference is made by the difference between saying "there is only the dialogue" and saying "there is also that to which the dialogue converges."

I would suggest that Putnam here, at the end of the day, slides back into the scientism he rightly condemns in others. For the root of scientism, defined as the view that rationality is a matter of applying criteria, is the desire for objectivity, the hope that what Putnam calls "human flourishing" has a transhistorical nature. I think that Feyerabend is right in suggesting that until we discard the metaphor of inquiry, and human activity generally, as converging rather than proliferating, as becoming more unified rather than more diverse, we shall never be free of the motives that once led us to posit gods. Positing *Grenzbegriffe* seems merely a way of telling ourselves that a nonexistent God would, if he did exist, be pleased with us. If we could ever be moved solely by the desire for solidarity, setting aside the desire for objectivity altogether, then we should think of human progress as making it possible for human beings to do more interesting things and be more interesting people, not as heading toward a place that has somehow been prepared for humanity in advance. Our self-image would employ images of making rather than finding, the images used by the Romantics to praise poets rather than the images used by the Greeks to praise mathematicians. Feyerabend seems to me right in trying to develop such a self-image for us, but his project seems misdescribed, by himself as well as by his critics, as "relativism."[10]

Those who follow Feyerabend in this direction are often thought of as necessarily enemies of the Enlightenment, as joining in the chorus that claims the traditional self-descriptions of the Western democracies are bankrupt, that they somehow have been shown to be "inadequate" or "self-deceptive." Part of the instinctive resistance to attempts by Marxists, Sartreans, Oakeshottians, Gadamerians and Foucauldians to reduce objectivity to solidarity is the fear that our traditional liberal habits and hopes will not survive the reduction. Such feelings are evident, for example, in Habermas' criticism of Gadamer's position as relativistic and potentially repressive, in the suspicion that Heidegger's attacks on realism are somehow linked to his Nazism, in the hunch that Marxist attempts to interpret values as class interests are usually just apologies for Leninist takeovers, and in the suggestion that Oakeshott's skepticism about rationalism in politics is merely an apology for the status quo.

I think that putting the issue in such moral and political terms, rather than in epistemological or metaphilosophical terms, makes clearer what is at stake. For now the question is not about how to define words like "truth" or "rationality" or "knowledge" or "philosophy," but about what self-image our society should have of itself. The ritual invocation of the "need to avoid relativism" is most comprehensible as an expression of the need to preserve certain habits of contemporary European life. These are the habits nurtured by the Enlightenment, and justified by it in terms of an appeal of Reason, conceived as a transcultural human ability to correspond to reality, a faculty whose possession and use is demonstrated by obedience to explicit criteria. So the real question about relativism is whether these same habits of intellectual, social, and political life can be justified by a conception of rationality as criterionless muddling through, and by a pragmatist conception of truth.

I think the answer to this question is that the pragmatist cannot justify these habits without circularity, but then neither can the realist. The pragmatists' justification of toleration, free inquiry, and the quest for undistorted communication can only take the form of a comparison between societies that exemplify these habits and those that do not, leading up to the suggestion that nobody who has experienced both would prefer the latter. It is exemplified by Winston Churchill's defense of democracy as the worst form of government imaginable, except for all the others that have been tried so far. Such justification is not by reference to a criterion, but by reference to various detailed practical advantages. It is circular only in that the terms of praise used to describe liberal societies will be drawn from the vocabulary of the liberal societies themselves. Such praise has to be in *some* vocabulary, after all, and the terms of praise current in primitive or theocratic or totalitarian societies will not produce the desired result. So the pragmatist admits that he has no ahistorical standpoint from which to endorse the habits of modern democracies he wishes to praise. These consequences are just what partisans of solidarity expect. But among partisans of objectivity they give rise, once again, to fears of the dilemma formed by ethnocentrism on the one hand and relativism on the other. Either we attach a special privilege to our own community, or we pretend an impossible tolerance for every other group.

I have been arguing that we pragmatists should grasp the ethnocentric horn of this dilemma. We should say that we must, in practice, privilege our own group, even though there can be no noncircular justification for doing so. We must insist that the fact that nothing is immune from criticism does not mean that we have a duty to justify everything. We Western liberal intellectuals should accept the fact that we have to start from where we are, and that this means there are lots of views we simply cannot take seriously. To use Neurath's familiar analogy, we can *understand* the revolutionary's suggestion that a sailable boat can't be made out of the planks which make up ours, and that we must simply abandon ship. But we cannot take his suggestion seriously. We cannot take it as a rule for action, so it is not a live option. For some people, to be sure, the option *is* live. These are the people who have always hoped to become a New Being, who have hoped to be converted rather than persuaded. But we—the liberal Rawlsian searchers for consensus, the heirs of Socrates, the people who wish to link their days dialectically each to each—cannot do so. Our community—the community of the liberal intellectuals of the secular modern West—wants to be able to give a *post factum* account of any change of view. We want to be able, so to speak, to justify ourselves to our earlier selves. This preference is not built into us by human nature. It is just the way *we* live now.[11]

This lonely provincialism, this admission that we are just the historical moment that we are, not the representatives of something ahistorical, is what makes traditional Kantian liberals like Rawls draw back from pragmatism.[12] "Relativism," by contrast, is merely a red herring. The realist is, once again, projecting his own habits of thought upon the pragmatist when he charges him with relativism. For the realist thinks that the whole point of philosophical thought is to detach oneself from any particular community and look down at it from a more universal standpoint. When he hears the pragmatist repudiating the desire for such a standpoint he cannot quite believe it. He thinks that everyone, deep down inside, *must* want such detachment. So he attributes to the pragmatist a perverse form of his own attempted detachment, and sees him as an ironic, sneering aesthete who refuses to take the choice between communities seriously, a mere "relativist." But the pragmatist, dominated by the desire for solidarity, can only be criticized for taking his own community *too* seriously. He can only be criticized for ethnocentrism, not for relativism. To be ethnocentric is to divide the human race into the people to whom one must justify one's beliefs and the others. The first group—one's *ethnos*—comprises those who share enough of one's beliefs to make fruitful conversation possible. In this sense, everybody is ethnocentric when engaged in actual debate, no matter how much realist rhetoric about objectivity he produces in his study.[13]

What is disturbing about the pragmatist's picture is not that it is relativistic but that it takes away two sorts of metaphysical comfort to which our intellectual tradition has become accustomed. One is the thought that membership in our biological species carries with it certain "rights," a notion that does not seem to make sense unless the biological similarities entail the possession of something non-biological, something that links our species to a nonhuman reality and thus gives the species moral dignity. This picture of rights as biologically transmitted is so basic to the political discourse of the Western democracies that we are troubled by any suggestion that "human nature" is not a useful moral concept. The second comfort is provided by the thought that our community cannot wholly die. The picture of a common human nature oriented toward correspondence to reality as it is in itself comforts us with the thought that even if our civilization is destroyed, even if all memory of our political or intellectual or artistic community is erased, the race is fated to recapture the virtues and the insights and the achievements that were the glory of that community. The notion of human nature as an inner structure that leads all members of the species to converge to the same point, to recognize the same theories, virtues, and works of art as worthy of honor, assures us that even if the Persians had won, the arts and sciences of the Greeks would sooner or later have appeared elsewhere. It assures us that even if the Orwellian bureaucrats of terror rule for a thousand years the achievements of the Western democracies will someday be duplicated by our remote descendents. It assures us that "man will prevail," that something reasonably like *our* world-view, *our* virtues, *our* art, will bob up again whenever human beings are left alone to cultivate their inner natures. The comfort of the realist picture is the comfort of saying not simply that there is a place prepared for our race in our advance, but also that we now know quite a bit about what that place looks like. The inevitable ethnocentrism to which we are all condemned is thus as much a part of the realist's comfortable view as of the pragmatists' uncomfortable one.

The pragmatist gives up the first sort of comfort because he thinks that to say that certain people have certain rights is merely to say that we should treat them in certain ways. It is not to give a *reason* for treating them in those ways. As to the second sort of comfort, he suspects that the hope that something resembling *us* will inherit the earth is impossible to eradicate, as impossible as eradicating the hope of surviving our individual deaths through some satisfying transfiguration. But he does not want to turn this hope into a theory of the nature of man. He wants solidarity to be our *only* comfort, and to be seen not to require metaphysical support.

My suggestion that the desire for objectivity is in part a disguised form of the fear of the death of our community echoes Nietzsche's charge that the philosophical tradition that stems from Plato is an attempt to avoid facing up to contingency, to escape from time and chance. Nietzsche thought that realism was to be condemned not only by arguments from its theoretical incoherence, the sort of argument we find in Putnam and Davidson, but also on practical, pragmatic, grounds. Nietzsche thought that the test of human character was the ability to live with the thought that there was no convergence. He wanted us to be able to think of truth as:

> a mobile army of metaphors, metonyms, and anthromorphisms—
> in short a sum of human relations, which have been enhanced,
> transposed, and embellished poetically and rhetorically and which
> after long use seem firm, canonical, and obligatory to a people.[14]

Nietzsche hoped that eventually there might be human beings who could and did think of truth in this way, but who still liked themselves, who saw themselves as *good* people for whom solidarity was *enough*.[15]

I think that pragmatism's attack on the various structure-content distinctions that buttress the realist's notion of objectivity can best be seen as an attempt to let us think of truth in this Nietzschean way, as entirely a matter of solidarity. That is why I think we need to say, despite Putnam, that "there is only the dialogue," only *us*, and to throw out the last residues of the notion of "trans-cultural rationality." But this should not lead us to repudiate, as Nietzsche sometimes did, the elements in our movable host which embody the ideas of Socratic conversation, Christian fellowship, and Enlightenment science. Nietzsche ran together his diagnosis of philosophical realism as an expression of fear and resentment with his own resentful idiosyncratic idealizations of silence, solitude, and violence. Post-Nietzschean thinkers like Adorno and Heidegger and Foucault have run together Nietzsche's criticisms of the metaphysical tradition on the one hand with his criticisms of bourgeois civility, of Christian love, and of the nineteenth century's hope that science would make the world a better place to live, on the other. I do not think there is any interesting connection between these two sets of criticisms. Pragmatism seems to me, as I have said, a philosophy of solidarity rather than of despair. From this point of view, Socrates's turn away from the gods, Christianity's turn from an Omnipotent Creator to the man who suffered on the Cross, and the Baconian turn from science as contemplation of eternal truth to science as instrument of social progress, can be seen as so many preparations for the act of social faith that is suggested by a Nietzschean view of truth.[16]

The best argument we partisans of solidarity have against the realistic partisans of objectivity is Nietzsche's argument that the traditional Western metaphysico-epistemological way of firming up our habits simply isn't working anymore. It isn't doing its job. It has become as transparent a device as the postulation of deities who turn out, by a happy coincidence, to have chosen *us* as their people. So the pragmatist suggestion that we substitute a "merely" ethical foundation for our sense of community—or, better, that we think of our sense of community as having no foundation except shared hope and the trust created by such sharing—is put forward on practical grounds. It is *not* put forward as a corollary of a metaphysical claim that the objects in the world contain no intrinsically action-guiding properties, nor of an epistemological claim that we lack a faculty of moral sense, nor of a semantical claim that truth is reducible to justification. It is a suggestion about how we might think of ourselves in order to avoid the kind of resentful belatedness—characteristic of the bad side of Nietzsche—which now characterizes much of high culture. This resentment arises from the realization, which I referred to at the beginning of this essay, that the Enlightenment's search for objectivity has often gone sour.

The rhetoric of scientific objectivity, pressed too hard and taken too seriously, has led us to people like B. F. Skinner on the one hand and people like Althusser on the other—two equally pointless fantasies, both produced by the attempt to be "scientific" about our moral and political lives. Reaction against scientism led to attacks on natural science as a sort of false god. But there is nothing wrong with science, there is only something wrong with the attempt to divinize it, the attempt characteristic of realistic philosophy. This reaction has also led to attacks on liberal social thought of the type common to Mill and Dewey and Rawls as a mere ideological superstructure, one which obscures the realities of our situation and represses attempts to change that situation. But there is nothing wrong with liberal democracy, nor with the philosophers who have tried to enlarge its scope. There is only something wrong with the attempt to see their efforts as failures to achieve something they were not trying to achieve—a demonstration of the "objective" superiority of our way of life over all other alternatives. There is, in short, nothing wrong with the hopes of the Enlightenment, the hopes that created the Western democracies. The value of the ideals of the Enlightenment is, for us pragmatists, just the value of some of the institutions and practices they have created. In this essay I have sought to distinguish these institutions and practices from the philosophical justifications for them provided by partisans of objectivity, and to suggest an alternative justification.

NOTES

1. This attitude toward truth, in which the consensus of a community rather than a relation to a nonhuman reality is taken as central, is associated not only with the American pragmatic tradition but with the work of Popper and Habermas. Habermas' criticisms of lingering positivist elements in Popper parallel those made by Deweyan holists of the early logical empiricists. It is important to see, however, that the pragmatist notion of truth common to James and Dewey is not dependent upon either Peirce's notion of an "ideal end of inquiry" nor on Habermas' notion of an "ideally free community." For criticism of these notions, which in my view are insufficiently ethnocentric, see my "Pragmatism, Davidson, and Truth," Ernest LePore, ed., *Truth and Interpretation* (Oxford: Blackwell, 1986), and "Habermas and Lyotard on Postmodernity" in *Praxis International*, 4 (1984).

2. Hilary Putnam, *Reason, Truth, and History* (Cambridge: Cambridge University Press, 1981), 49–50.

3. Ibid., 119.

4. Ibid., x.

5. Ibid., 114.

6. Ibid., 119. See Davidson's "On the Very Idea of a Conceptual Scheme," in his *Inquiries into Truth and Interpretation* (Oxford: Oxford University Press, 1984) for a more complete and systematic presentation of this point.

7. Putnam, 113.

8. Ibid., 126.

9. Ibid., 216.

10. See, e.g., Paul Feyerabend, *Science in a Free Society* (London: New Left Books, 1978), 9, where Feyerabend identifies his own view with "relativism (in the old and simple sense of Protagoras)." This identification is accompanied by the claim that " 'Objectively' there is not much to choose between anti-semitism and humanitarianism." I think Feyerabend would have served himself better by saying that the scare-quoted word "objectively" should simply be dropped from use, together with the traditional philosophical distinctions between scheme and content (see the Davidson essay cited in note 6 above) which buttress the subjective-objective distinction, than by saying that we may keep the word and use it to say the sort of thing Protagoras said. What Feyerabend is really against is the correspondence theory of truth, not the idea that some views cohere better than others.

11. This quest for consensus is opposed to the sort of quest for authenticity that wishes to free itself from the opinion of our community. See, for example, Vincent Descombes' account of Deleuze in *Modern French Philosophy* (Cambridge: Cambridge University Press, 1980), 153: "Even if philosophy is essentially demystificatory, philosophers often fail to produce authentic critiques; they defend order, authority, institutions, 'decency,' everything in which the ordinary person believes." On the pragmatist or ethnocentric view I am suggesting, all that critique can or should do is play off elements in "what the ordinary person believes" against other elements. To attempt to do more than this is to fantasize rather than to converse. Fantasy may, to be sure, be an incentive to more fruitful conversation, but when it no longer fulfills this function it does not deserve the name of "critique."

12. In *A Theory of Justice* Rawls seemed to be trying to retain the authority of Kantian "practical reason" by imagining a social contract devised by choosers "behind a veil of ignorance"—using the "rational self-interest" of such choosers as a touchstone for the ahistorical validity of certain social institutions. Much of the criticism to which that book was subjected, e.g., by Micheal Sandel in his *Liberalism and the Limits of Justice* (Cambridge: Cambridge University Press, 1982), has centered on the claim that one cannot escape history in this way. In the meantime, however, Rawls has put forward

a meta-ethical view which drops the claim to ahistorical validity. (See his "Kantian Constructivism in Moral Theory," *Journal of Philosophy*, Volume 77, 1980, and his "Justice as Fairness—Political not Metaphysical," *Philosophy and Public Affairs*, Volume 14, No. 3, 1985). Concurrently, T. M. Scanlon has urged that the essence of a "contractualist" account of moral motivation is better understood as the desire to justify one's action to others than in terms of "rational self-interest." See Scanlon, "Contractualism and Utilitarianism" in A. Sen and B. Williams, eds., *Utilitarianism and Beyond* (Cambridge: Cambridge University Press, 1982). Scanlon's emendation of Rawls leads in the same direction as Rawls' later work, since Scanlon's use of the notion of "justification to others on grounds they could not reasonably reject" chimes with the "constructivist" view that what counts for social philosophy is what can be justified to a particular historical community, not to "humanity in general." On my view, the frequent remark that Rawls' rational choosers look remarkably like twentieth-century American liberals is perfectly just, but not a criticism of Rawls. It is merely a frank recognition of the ethnocentrism which is essential to serious, nonfantastical, thought. I defend this view in "Postmodernist Bourgeois Liberalism," *Journal of Philosophy*, Volume 80, 1983.

13. In an important paper called "The Truth in Relativism," included in his *Moral Luck* (Cambridge: Cambridge University Press, 1981), Bernard Williams makes a similar point in terms of a distinction between "genuine confrontation" and "notional confrontation." The latter is the sort of confrontation that occurs, asymmetrically, between us and primitive tribespeople. The belief-systems of such people do not present, as Williams puts it, "real options" for us, for we cannot imagine going over to their view without "self-deception or paranoia." These are the people whose beliefs on certain topics overlap so little with ours that their inability to agree with us raises no doubt in our minds about the correctness of our own beliefs. Williams' use of "real option" and "notional confrontation" seems to me very enlightening, but I think he turns these notions to purposes they will not serve. Williams wants to defend ethical relativism, defined as the claim that when ethical confrontations are merely notional "questions of appraisal do not genuinely arise." He thinks they *do* arise in connection with notional confrontations between, e.g., Einsteinian and Amazonian cosmologies. (See Williams, 142.) This distinction between ethics and physics seems to me an awkward result to which Williams is driven by his unfortunate attempt to find *something* true in relativism, an attempt that is a corollary of his attempt to be "realistic" about physics. On my (Davidsonian) view, there is no point in distinguishing between true sentences that are "made true by reality" and true sentences that are "made true by us," because the whole idea of "truth-makers" needs to be dropped. So I would hold that there is *no* truth in relativism, but this much truth in ethnocentrism: we cannot justify our beliefs (in physics, ethics, or any other area) to everybody, but only to those whose beliefs overlap ours to some appropriate extent. (This is not a theoretical

problem about "untranslatability," but simply a practical problem about the limitations of argument; it is not that we live in different worlds than the Nazis or the Amazonians, but that conversion from or to their point of view, though possible, will not be a matter of inference from previously shared premises.)

14. Nietzsche, "On Truth and Lie in an Extra-Moral Sense," in *The Viking Portable Nietzsche*, ed. and trans., Walter Kaufmann, 46–47.

15. See Sabina Lovibond, *Realism and Imagination in Ethics* (Minneapolis: University of Minnesota Press, 1983), 158: "An adherent of Wittgenstein's view of language should equate that goal with the establishment of a language-game in which we could participate ingenuously, while retaining our awareness of it as a specific historical formation. A community in which such a language-game was played would be one . . . whose members understood their own form of life and yet were not embarrassed by it."

16. See Hans Blumenberg, *The Legitimation of Modernity* (Cambridge, Mass.: MIT Press, 1982), for a story about the history of European thought which, unlike the stories told by Nietzsche and Heidegger, sees the Enlightenment as a definitive step forward. For Blumenberg, the attitude of "self-assertion," the kind of attitude that stems from a Baconian view of the nature and purpose of science, needs to be distinguished from "self-foundation," the Cartesian project of grounding such inquiry upon ahistorical criteria of rationality. Blumenberg remarks, pregnantly, that the "historicist" criticism of the optimism of the Enlightenment, criticism which began with the Romantics' turn back to the Middle Ages, undermines self-foundation but not self-assertion.

Chapter 8

The Tower of Babel

MICHAEL OAKESHOTT

I

The project of finding a short cut to heaven is as old as the human race. It is represented in the mythology of many peoples, and it is recognized always as an impious but not ignoble enterprise. The story of the Titans is, perhaps, the most complicated of the myths which portray this *folie de grandeur*, but the story of the Tower of Babel is the most profound. We may imagine the Titans drawing back after the first unsuccessful assault to hear one of their number suggest that their program was too ambitious, that perhaps they were trying to do too much and to do it too quickly. But the builders of the Tower, whose top was to reach to heaven, were permitted no such conference; their enterprise involved them in the babblings of men who speak, but do not speak the same language. Like all profound myths, this represents a project the fascination of which is not confined to the childhood of the race, but is one which the circumstances of human life constantly suggest and one which no failure can deprive of its attraction. It indicates also the consequences of such an enterprise. I interpret it as follows.

The pursuit of perfection as the crow flies is an activity both impious and unavoidable in human life. It involves the penalties of impiety (the anger of the gods and social isolation), and its reward is not that of achievement but that of having made the attempt. It is an activity, therefore, suitable for individuals, but not for societies. For an individual who is impelled to engage in it, the reward may exceed both the penalty and the inevitable defeat. The penitent may hope, or even expect, to fall back, a wounded hero, into the arms of an understanding and forgiving society. And even the impenitent can be reconciled with himself in the powerful necessity of his impulse, though, like Prometheus, he must suffer for it. For a society, on the other hand, the penalty is a chaos of conflicting ideals, the disruption of a common life, and the reward is the renown which attaches to monumental folly. *A mesure que l'humanité se perfectionne l'homme se dégrade.* Or, to interpret the myth in a more light-hearted fashion: human life is a gamble; but while the individual must be allowed to bet according to his inclination (on the favorite or on an outsider), society should always back the field. Let us consider the matter in application to our own civilization.

The activity with which we are concerned is what is called moral activity, that is, activity which may be either good or bad. The moral life is human affection and behavior determined, not by nature, but by art. It is conduct to which there is an alternative. This alternative need not be consciously before the mind; moral conduct does not necessarily involve the reflective choice of a particular action. Nor does it require that each occasion shall find a man without a disposition, or even without predetermination, to act in a certain way: a man's affections and conduct may be seen to spring from his character without thereby ceasing to be moral. The freedom without which moral conduct is impossible is freedom from a natural necessity which binds *all* men to act alike. This does not carry us very far. It identifies moral behavior as the exercise of an acquired skill (though the skill need not have been self-consciously acquired), but it does not distinguish it from other kinds of art—from cookery or from carpentry. However, it carries us far enough for my purpose, which is to consider the *form* of the moral life, and in particular the form of the moral life of contemporary Western civilization.

In any manifestation of the moral life, form and content are, of course, inseparable. Nevertheless, neither can be said to determine the other; and in considering the form we shall be considering an abstraction which, in principle, is indifferent to any particular content, and indifferent also to any particular ethical theory. The practical question, What kinds of human enterprise should be designated right and wrong? and the philosophical question, What is the ultimate nature of moral criteria? are both outside what we are to consider. We are concerned only with the shape of the moral life. And our concern must be philosophical and historical, rather than practical, because neither a society nor an individual is normally given the opportunity of making an express choice of the form of a moral life.

The moral life of our society discloses a form neither simple nor homogeneous. Indeed, the form of our morality appears to be a mixture of two ideal extremes, a mixture the character of which derives from the predominance of one extreme over the other. I am not convinced of the necessary ideality of the extremes; it is perhaps possible that one, if not both, could exist as an actual form of the moral life. But even if this is doubtful, each can certainly exist with so little modification from the other that it is permissible to begin by regarding them as possible forms of morality. Let us consider the two forms which, either separately or in combination, compose the form of the moral life of the Western world.

II

In the first of these forms, the moral life is *a habit of affection and behavior;* not a habit of reflective *thought,* but a habit of *affection* and *conduct.* The current situations of a normal life are met, not by consciously applying to ourselves a rule of behavior, nor by conduct recognized as the expression of a moral ideal, but by acting in accordance with a certain habit of behavior. The moral life in this form does not spring from the consciousness of possible alternative ways of behaving and a choice, determined by an opinion, a rule or an ideal, from among these alternatives; conduct is as nearly as possible without reflection. And consequently, most of the current situations of life do not appear as occasions calling for judgment, or as problems requiring solutions; there is no weighing up of alternatives or reflection on consequences, no uncertainty, no battle of scruples. There is, on the occasion, nothing more than the unreflective following of a tradition of conduct in which we have been brought up. And such moral habit will disclose itself as often in *not* doing, in the taste which dictates abstention from certain actions, as in performances. It should, of course, be understood that I am not here describing a form of the moral life that assumes the existence of a moral sense or of moral intuition, nor a form of the moral life presupposing a moral theory that attributes authority to conscience. Indeed, no specific theory of the source of authority is involved in this form of the moral life. Nor am I describing a merely primitive form of morality, that is, the morality of a society unaccustomed to reflective thought. I am describing the form moral action takes (because it can take no other) in all the emergencies of life when time and opportunity for reflection are lacking, and I am supposing that what is true of the emergencies of life is true of most of the occasions when human conduct is free from natural necessity.

Every form of the moral life (because it is affection and behavior determined by art) depends upon education. And the character of each form is reflected in the kind of education required to nurture and maintain it. From what sort of education will this first form of the moral life spring?

We acquire habits of conduct, not by constructing a way of living upon rules or precepts learned by heart and subsequently practiced, but by living with people who habitually behave in a certain manner: we acquire habits of conduct in the same way as we acquire our native language. There is no point in a child's life at which he can be said to begin to learn the language habitually spoken in his hearing; and there is no point in his life at which he can be said to begin to learn habits of behavior from the people constantly about him. No doubt, in both cases, what is learnt (or some of it) can be formulated in rules and precepts; but in neither case do we, in this kind of education, learn by learning rules and precepts. What we learn here is what may be learned without the formulation of its rules. And not only may a command of language and behavior be achieved without our becoming aware of the rules, but also, if we have acquired a knowledge of the rules, this sort of command of language and behavior is impossible until we have forgotten them as rules and are no longer tempted to turn speech and action into the applications of rules to a situation. Further, the education by means of which we acquire habits of affection and behavior is not only coeval with conscious life, but it is carried on, in practice and observation, without pause in every moment of our waking life, and perhaps even in our dreams; what is begun as imitation continues as selective conformity to a rich variety of customary behavior. This sort of education is not compulsory; it is inevitable. And lastly (if education in general is making oneself at home in the natural and civilized worlds), this is not a separable part of education. One may set apart an hour in which to learn mathematics and devote another to the Catechism, but it is impossible to engage in any activity whatever without contributing to this kind of moral education, and it is impossible to enjoy this kind of moral education in an hour set aside for its study. There are, of course, many things that cannot be learned in this sort of education. We may learn in this manner to play a game, and we may learn to play it without breaking the rules, but we cannot acquire a knowledge of the rules themselves without formulating them or having them formulated for us. And further, without a knowledge of the rules we can never know for certain whether or not we are observing them, nor shall we be able to explain why the referee has blown his whistle. Or, to change the metaphor, from this sort of education can spring the ability never to write a false line of poetry, but it will give us neither the ability to scan nor a knowledge of the names of the various metric forms.

It is not difficult, then, to understand the sort of moral education by means of which habits of affection and behavior may be acquired;

it is the sort of education that gives the power to act appropriately and without hesitation, doubt or difficulty, but does not give the ability to explain our actions in abstract terms, or defend them as emanations of moral principles. Moreover, this education must be considered to have failed its purpose if it provides a range of behavior insufficient to meet all situations without the necessity of calling upon reflection, or if it does not make the habit of behavior sufficiently compelling to remove hesitation. But it must not be considered to have failed merely because it leaves us ignorant of moral rules and moral ideals. And a man may be said to have acquired most thoroughly what this kind of moral education can teach him when his moral dispositions are inseverably connected with his *amour-propre*, when the spring of his conduct is not an attachment to an ideal or a felt duty to obey a rule, but his self-esteem, and when to act wrongly is felt as diminution of his self-esteem.

Now, it will be observed that this is a form of morality that gives remarkable stability to the moral life from the point of view either of an individual or of a society; it is not in its nature to countenance large or sudden changes in the kinds of behavior it desiderates. Parts of a moral life in this form may collapse, but since the habits of conduct that compose it are never recognized as a system, the collapse does not readily spread to the whole. And being without a perceived rigid framework distinct from the modes of behavior themselves (a framework, for example, of abstract moral ideals), it is not subject to the kind of collapse that springs from the detection of some flaw or incoherence in a system of moral ideals. Intellectual error with regard to moral ideas or opinions does not compromise a moral life firmly based upon a habit of conduct. In short, the stability that belongs to this form of the moral life derives from its elasticity and its ability to suffer change without disruption. First, there is in it nothing that is absolutely fixed. Just as in a language there may be certain constructions that are simply bad grammar, but in all the important ranges of expression the language is malleable by the writer who uses it and he cannot go wrong unless he deserts its genius, so in this form of the moral life, the more thorough our education the more certain will be our taste and the more extensive our range of behavior within the tradition. Custom is always adaptable and susceptible to the *nuance* of the situation. This may appear a paradoxical assertion; custom, we have been taught, is blind. It is, however, an insidious piece of misobservation; custom is not blind, it is only "blind as a bat." And anyone who has studied a tradition of customary behavior (or a tradition of any other sort) knows that both rigidity and instability are foreign to its character. And secondly, this form of the moral life is capable of change as well as of local variation. Indeed, no traditional way of behavior, no traditional skill, ever remains fixed; its history is one of continuous change. It is true that the change it admits is neither great nor sudden; but then, revolutionary change is usually the product of the eventual overthrow of an aversion from change, and is characteristic of something that has few internal resources of change. And the appearance of changelessness in a morality of traditional behavior is an illusion that springs from the erroneous belief that the only significant change is that which is either induced by selfconscious activity or is, at least, observed on the occasion. The sort of change that belongs to this form of the moral life is analogous to the change to which a living language is subject: nothing is more habitual or customary than our ways of speech, and nothing is more continuously invaded by change. Like prices in a free market, habits of moral conduct show no revolutionary changes because they are never at rest. But it should be observed, also, that because the internal movement characteristic of this form of the moral life does not spring from reflection upon moral principles, and represents only an unselfconscious exploitation of the genius of the tradition of moral conduct, it does not amount to moral self-criticism. And, consequently, a moral life of this kind, if it degenerates into superstition, or if crisis supervenes, has little power of recovery. Its defense is solely its resistance to the conditions productive of crisis.

One further point should, perhaps, be noticed: the place and character of the moral eccentric in this form of the moral life, when it is considered as the form of the moral life of a society. The moral eccentric is not, of course, excluded by this form of morality. (The want of moral sensibility, the hollowness of moral character, which seems often to inhere in people whose morality is predominantly one of custom, is improperly attributed to the customary form of their morality; its cause lies elsewhere.) We sometimes think that deviation from a customary morality must always take place under the direction of a formulated moral ideal. But this is not so. There is a freedom and inventiveness at the heart of every traditional way of life, and deviation may be an expression of that freedom, springing from a sensitiveness to the tradition itself and remaining faithful to the traditional form. Generally speaking, no doubt, the inspiration of deviation from moral habit is perfectionist, but it is not necessarily consciously perfectionist. It is not, in essence, rebellious, and may be likened to the sort of innovation introduced into a plastic art by the fortuitous appearance in an individual of a specially high degree of manual skill, or to the sort of change a great stylist may make in a language. Although in any particular instance deviation may lead the individual eccentric astray, and although it is not something that can profitably be imitated, moral eccentricity is of value to a society whose morality is one of habit of behavior (regardless of the direction it may take) so long as it remains the activity of the individual and is not permitted to disrupt the communal life. In a morality of an habitual way of behavior, then, the influence of the moral eccentric may be powerful but is necessarily oblique, and the attitude of society toward him is necessarily ambivalent. He is admired but not copied, reverenced but not followed, welcomed but ostracized.

III

The second form of the moral life we are to consider may be regarded as in many respects the opposite of the first. In it activity is determined, not by a habit of behavior, but by *the reflective application of a moral criterion*. It appears in two common varieties: as *the self-conscious pursuit of moral ideals*, and as *the reflective observance of moral rules*. But it is what these varieties have in common that is important, because it is this, and not what distinguishes them from one another, that divides them from the first form of morality.

This is a form of the moral life in which a special value is attributed to self-consciousness, individual or social; not only is the rule or the ideal the product of reflective thought, but the application of the rule or the ideal to the situation is also a reflective activity. Normally the rule or the ideal is determined first and in the abstract; that is, the first task in constructing an art of behavior in this form is to express moral aspirations in words—in a rule of life or in a system of abstract ideals. This task of verbal expression need not begin with a moral *de omnibus dubitandum*; but its aim is not only to set out the desirable ends of conduct, but also to set them out clearly and unambiguously and to reveal their relations to one another. Secondly, a man who would enjoy this form of the moral life must be certain of his ability to defend these formulated aspirations against criticism. For, having been brought into the open, they will henceforth be liable to attack. His third task will be to translate them into behavior, to apply them to the current situations of life as they arise. In this form of the moral life, then, action will spring from a judgment concerning the rule or end to be applied and the determination to apply it. The situations of living should, ideally, appear as problems to be solved, for it is only in this form that they will receive the attention they call for. And there will be a resistance to the urgency of action; it will appear more important to have the right moral ideal, than to act. The application of a rule or an ideal to a situation can never be easy; both ideal and situation will usually require interpretation, and a rule of life (unless the life has been simplified by the drastic reduction of the variety of situations which are allowed to appear) will always be found wanting unless it is supplemented with an elaborate casuistry or hermeneutic. It is true that moral ideals and moral rules may become so familiar that they take on the character of an habitual or traditional way of *thinking* about behavior. It is true also that long familiarity with our ideals may have enabled us to express them more concretely in a system of specific rights and duties, handy in application. And further, a moral ideal may find its expression in a type of human character— such as the character of the gentleman—and conduct become the imaginative application of the ideal character to the situation. But these qualifications carry us only part of the way: they may remove the necessity for *ad hoc* reflection on the rules and ideals themselves, but they leave us still with the problem of interpreting the situation and the task of translating the ideal, the right or the duty into behavior. For the right or the duty is always to observe a rule or realize an end, and not to behave in a certain concrete manner. Indeed, it is not desired, in this form of the moral life, that tradition should carry us all the way; its distinctive virtue is to be subjecting behavior to a continuous corrective analysis and criticism.

This form of the moral life, not less than the other, depends upon education, but upon an education of an appropriately different sort. In order to acquire the necessary knowledge of moral ideals or of a rule of life, we need something more than the observation and practice of behavior itself. We require, first, an intellectual training in the detection and appreciation of the moral ideals themselves, a training in which the ideals are separated and detached from the necessarily imperfect expression they find in particular actions. We require, secondly, training in the art of the intellectual management of these ideals. And thirdly, we require training in the application of ideals to concrete situations, in the art of translation and in the art of selecting appropriate means for achieving the ends which our education has inculcated. Such an education may be made compulsory in a society, but if so it is only because it is not inevitable. It is true that, as Spinoza says,[1] a substitute for a perfectly trained moral judgment may be found in committing a rule of life to memory and following it implicitly. But, though this is as far as some pupils will get, it cannot be considered to be the aim of this moral education. If it is to achieve its purpose, this education must carry us far beyond the acquisition of a moral technique; and it must be considered to have failed in its purpose if it it has not given both ability to determine behavior by a self-conscious choice and an understanding of the ideal grounds of the choice made. Nobody can fully share this form of the moral life who is not something of a philosopher and something of a self-analyst: its aim is moral behavior springing from the communally cultivated reflective capacities of each individual.

Now, a moral life in which everyone who shares it knows at each moment exactly what he is doing and why, should be well protected against degeneration into superstition and should, moreover, give remarkable confidence to those who practice it. Nevertheless, it has its dangers, both from the point of view of an individual and from that of a society. The confidence that belongs to it is mainly a confidence in respect of the moral ideals themselves, or of the moral rule. The education in the ideals or in the rule must be expected to be the most successful part of this moral education; the art of applying the ideals is more difficult both to teach and to learn. And together with the certainty about how to *think* about moral ideals, must be expected to go a proportionate uncertainty about how to *act*. The constant analysis of behavior tends to undermine, not only prejudice in moral habit, but moral habit itself, and moral reflection may come to inhibit moral sensibility.

Further, a morality that takes the form of the self-conscious pursuit of moral ideals is one which, at every moment, calls upon those who practice it to determine their behavior by reference to a vision of perfection. This is not so much the case when the guide is a moral rule, because the rule is not represented as perfection and constitutes a mediation, a cushion, between the behavior it demands on each occasion and the complete moral response to the situation. But when the guide of conduct is a moral ideal we are never suffered to escape from perfection. Constantly, indeed on all occasions, the society is called upon to seek virtue as the crow flies. It may even be said that the moral life, in this form, demands an hyperoptic moral vision and encourages intense moral emulation among those who enjoy it, the moral eccentric being recognized, not as a vicarious sufferer for the stability of a society, but as a leader and a guide. And the unhappy society, with an ear for every call, certain always about what it ought to *think* (though it will never for long be the same thing), in action shies and plunges like a distracted animal.

Again, a morality of ideals has little power of self-modification; its stability springs from its inelasticity and its imperviousness to change. It will, of course, respond to interpretation, but the limits of that response are close and severe. It has a great capacity to resist change, but when that resistance is broken down, what takes place is not change but revolution—rejection and replacement. Moreover, every moral ideal is potentially an obsession; the pursuit of moral ideals is an idolatry in which particular objects are recognized as 'gods'. This potentiality may be held in check by more profound reflection, by an intellectual grasp of the whole system that gives place and proportion to each moral ideal; but such a grasp is rarely achieved. Too often the excessive pursuit of one ideal leads to the exclusion of others, perhaps all others; in our eagerness to realize justice we come to forget charity, and a passion for righteousness has made many a man hard and merciless. There is, indeed, no ideal the pursuit of which will not lead to disillusion; *chagrin* waits at the end for all who take this path. Every admirable ideal has its opposite, no less admirable. Liberty or order, justice or charity, spontaneity or deliberateness, principle or circumstance, self or others, these are the kinds of dilemmas with which this form of the moral life is always confronting us, making us see double by directing our attention always to abstract extremes, none of which is wholly desirable. It is a form of the moral life that puts upon those who share it, not only the task of translating moral ideals into appropriate forms of conduct, but also the distracting intellectual burden of removing the verbal conflict of ideals before moral behavior is possible. These conflicting ideals are, of course, reconciled in all amiable characters (that is, when they no longer appear as ideals), but that is not enough; a verbal and theoretical reconciliation is required. In short, this is a form of the moral life that is dangerous in an individual and disastrous in a society. For an individual it is a gamble which may have its reward when undertaken within the limits of a society which is not itself engaged in the gamble; for a society it is mere folly.

IV

This brief characterization of what appear to be two forms of the moral life, while perhaps establishing their distinction or even their opposition, will have made us more doubtful about their capability of independent existence. Neither, taken alone, recommends itself convincingly as a likely form of the moral life, in an individual or in a society; the one is all habit, the other all reflection. And the more closely we examine them, the more certain we become that they are, not forms of the moral life at all, but ideal extremes. And when we turn to consider what sort of a form of the moral life they offer in combination, we may perhaps enjoy the not illusory confidence that we are approaching more nearly to concrete possibility, or even historical reality.

In a mixture in which the first of these extremes is dominant, the moral life may be expected to be immune from a confusion between behavior and the pursuit of an ideal. Action will retain its primacy, and, whenever it is called for, will spring from habit of behavior. Conduct itself will never become problematical, inhibited by the hesitations of ideal speculation or the felt necessity of bringing philosophic talent and the fruits of philosophic education to bear upon the situation. The confidence in action, which belongs to the well-natured customary moral life, will remain unshaken. And the coherence of the moral life will not wait upon the abstract unity that the reflective relation of values can give it. But, in addition, this mixed form of the moral life may be supposed to enjoy the advantages that spring from a reflective morality—the power to criticize, to reform and to explain itself, and the power to propagate itself beyond the range of the custom of a society. It will enjoy also the appropriate intellectual confidence in its moral standards and purposes. And it will enjoy all this without the danger of moral criticism usurping the place of a habit of moral behavior, or of moral speculation bringing disintegration to moral life. The education in moral habit will be supplemented, but not weakened, by the education in moral ideology. And in a society, that enjoyed this form of the moral life, both habit and ideology might be the common possession of all its members, or moral speculation might in fact be confined to the few, while the morality of the many remained one of the habit of behavior. But, in any case, the internal resources of movement of this form of morality would be supplied by both its components: to the potential individual eccentricity that belongs to a traditional morality would be added the more consciously rebellious eccentricity, which has its roots in the more precisely followed perfectionism of a morality of ideals. In short, this form of the moral life will offer to a society advantages similar to those of a religion that has taken to itself a theology (though not necessarily a popular theology) but without losing its character as a way of living.

On the other hand, a morality whose form is a mixture in which the second of our extremes is dominant will, I think, suffer from a permanent tension between its component parts. Taking charge, the

morality of the self-conscious pursuit of ideals will have a disinte-
grating effect upon habit of behavior. When action is called for,
speculation or criticism will supervene. Behavior itself will tend to
become problematical, seeking its self-confidence in the coherence
of an ideology. The pursuit of perfection will get in the way of a
stable and flexible moral tradition, the naive coherence of which will
be prized less than the unity that springs from self-conscious analysis
and synthesis. It will seem more important to have an intellectually
defensible moral ideology than a ready habit of moral behavior. And
it will come to be assumed that a morality that is not easily trans-
ferable to another society, that lacks an obvious universality, is (for
that reason) inadequate for the needs of the society of its origin.
The society will wait upon its self-appointed moral teachers, pursuing
the extremes they recommend and at a loss when they are silent.
The distinguished and inspiring visiting preacher, who nevertheless
is a stranger to the way we live, will displace the priest, the father
of his parish. In a moral life constantly or periodically suffering the
ravages of the armies of conflicting ideals, or (when these for the
time have passed) falling into the hands of censors and inspectors,
the cultivation of a habit of moral behavior will have as little
opportunity as the cultivation of the land when the farmer is confused
and distracted by academic critics and political directors. Indeed, in
such a mixture (where habit of behavior is subordinate to the pursuit
of ideals) each of the components is unavoidably playing a role
foreign to its character; as in a literature in which criticism has
usurped the place of poetry, or in a religious life in which the pursuit
of theology offers itself as an alternative to the practice of piety.

These, however, must be counted incidental, though grave, im-
perfections in this mixture of extremes in the moral life; the radical
defect of this form is the radical defect of its dominant extreme—
its denial of the poetic character of all human activity. A prosaic
tradition of thought has accustomed us to the assumption that moral
activity, when analyzed, will be found to consist in the translation
of an idea of what ought to be into a practical reality, the transformation of an ideal into a concrete existence. And we are accustomed,
even, to think of poetry in these terms; first, a 'heart's desire' (an
idea) and then its expression, its translation into words. Nevertheless,
I think this view is mistaken; it is the superimposition upon art and
moral activity generally of an inappropriate didactic form. A poem
is not the translation into words of a state of mind. What the poet
says and what he wants to say are not two things, the one succeeding
and embodying the other, they are the same thing; he does not
know what he wants to say until he has said it. And the 'corrections'

he may make to his first attempt are not efforts to make words correspond more closely to an already formulated idea or to images already fully formed in his mind, they are renewed efforts to formulate the idea, to conceive the image. Nothing exists in advance of the poem itself, except perhaps the poetic passion. And what is true of poetry is true also, I think, of all human moral activity. Moral ideals are not, in the first place, the products of reflective thought, the verbal expressions of unrealized ideas, which are then translated (with varying degrees of accuracy) into human behavior; they are the products of human behavior, of human practical activity, to which reflective thought gives subsequent, partial and abstract expression in words. What is good, or right, or what is considered to be reasonable behavior may exist in advance of the situation, but only in the generalized form of the possibilities of behavior determined by art and not by nature. That is to say, the capital of moral ideals upon which a morality of the pursuit of moral ideals goes into business has always been accumulated by a morality of habitual behavior, and appears in the form of abstract ideas only because (for the purposes of subscription) it has been transformed by reflective thought into a currency of ideas.[2] This view of the matter does not, of course, deprive moral ideals of their power as critics of human habits, it does not denigrate the activity of reflective thought in giving this verbal expression to the principles of behavior; there is no doubt whatever that a morality in which reflection has no part is defective. But it suggests that a morality of the pursuit of moral ideals, or a morality in which this is dominant, is not what it appears at first sight to be, is not something that can stand on its own feet. In such a morality, that which has power to rescue from superstition is given the task of generating human behavior—a task which, in fact, it cannot perform. And it is only to be expected that a morality of this sort will be subject to sudden and ignominious collapse. In the life of an individual this collapse need not necessarily be fatal; in the life of a society it is likely to be irretrievable. For a society is a common way of life; and not only is it true that a society may perish of a disease that is not necessarily fatal even to those of its members who suffer from it, but it is also true that what is corrupting in the society may not be corrupting in its members.

V

The reader, knowing as much as I about the form of the moral life of contemporary Christendom, will not need to be told where all this is leading. If what I have said is not wide of the mark, it may perhaps be agreed that the form of our morality is that of a mixture in which the morality of the self-conscious pursuit of moral ideals is dominant. The moral energy of our civilization has for many centuries been applied mainly (though not, of course, exclusively) to building a Tower of Babel; and in a world dizzy with moral ideals we know less about how to behave in public and in private than ever before. Like the fool, our eyes have been on the ends of the earth. Having lost the tread of Ariadne, we have put our confidence in a plan of the labyrinth, and have given our attention to interpreters of the plan. Lacking habits of moral behavior, we have fallen back upon moral opinions as a substitute; but, as we all know, when we reflect upon what we are doing we too often conclude that it is wrong. Like lonely men who, to gain reassurance, exaggerate the talents of their few friends, we exaggerate the significance of our moral ideals to fill in the hollowness of our moral life. It is a pitiless wedding we have celebrated with our shadowy ideal of conduct. No doubt our present moral distraction (which is now several centuries old) springs partly from doubts we have in respect of the ideals themselves; all the effort of analysis and criticism has not yet suc- ceeded in establishing a single one of them unquestionably. But this is not the root of the matter. The truth is that a morality in this form, regardless of the quality of the ideals, breeds nothing but distraction and moral instability. Perhaps it is a partial appreciation of this that has led some societies to give an artificial stability to their moral ideals. A few of these ideals are selected, those few are turned into an authoritative canon, which is then made a guide to legislation or even a ground for the violent persecution of eccentricity. A moral ideology is established and maintained because this appears the only means of winning the necessary moral stability for the society. But in fact it is no remedy; it merely covers up the corruption of consciousness, the moral distraction inherent in morality as the self-conscious pursuit of moral ideals. However, it serves to illustrate the truth that the one kind of society that must of necessity be the enemy of profitable moral eccentricity is the society whose moral organization springs from the pursuit of ideals; for the moral life of such a society is itself nothing better than an arbitrary selection of moral eccentricities.

Now, I am not contending that our morality is wholly enclosed in the form of the self-conscious pursuit of moral ideals. Indeed, my view is that this is an ideal extreme in moral form and not, by itself, a possible form of morality at all. I am suggesting that the form of our moral life is dominated by this extreme, and that our moral life consequently suffers the internal tension inherent in this form. Certainly we possess habits of moral behavior, but too often our self-conscious pursuit of ideals hinders us from enjoying them. Self-consciousness is asked to be creative, and habit is given the role of critic; what should be subordinate has come to rule, and its rule is a misrule. Sometimes the tension appears on the surface, and on these occasions we are aware that something is wrong. A man who fails to practice what he preaches does not greatly disturb us; we know that preaching is in terms of moral ideals and that no man can practice them perfectly. This is merely the minor tension between ideal and achievement. But when a man preaches 'social justice' (or indeed any other ideal whatsoever) and at the same time is obviously without a habit of ordinary decent behavior (a habit that belongs to our morality but has fortunately never been idealized), the tension I speak of makes its appearance. And the fact that we are still able to recognize it is evidence that we are not wholly at the mercy of a morality of abstract ideals. Nevertheless, I do not think that anyone who has considered the matter will be disposed to deny we are for the most part dominated by this morality. It is not our fault; we have been given little or no choice in the matter. It is, however, our misfortune. And it may be relevant, in conclusion, to consider briefly how it has come about.

On this subject, the history of European morals, I have nothing new to say; I can only direct attention to what is already well-known. The form of contemporary western European morality has come to us from the distant past. It was determined in the first four centuries of the Christian era, that momentous period of our history when so much of our intellectual and emotional outlook began to emerge. It would, of course, be absurd to suggest that European morality sprang from some new species of seed first sown in that period; what, if anything, was new at that time was the mixture of seed which was at the disposal of those generations, to be sown, cultivated and sown once more until its characteristic fruit became fixed. It was an age of moral change. In that Greco-Roman world the old habits of moral behavior had lost their vitality. There were, no doubt, men who were good neighbors, faithful friends and pious citizens, whose confidence in the customs that determined their conduct was still unshaken; but, in general, the impetus of moral habit of behavior seems to have been spent—illustrating, perhaps, the defect of a form of morality too securely insulated from the criticism of ideals. It was, in consequence, an age of intense moral self-consciousness, an age of moral reformers who, unavoidably, preached a morality of the pursuit of ideals and taught a variety of dogmatic moral ideologies. The intellectual energy of the time was directed toward the determination of an ideal, and the moral energy toward the translation of that ideal into practice.[3] Moral self-consciousness itself became a virtue;[4] genuine morality was identified with the 'practice of philosophy'.[5] And it was thought that for the achievement of a good life it was necessary that a man should submit to an artificial moral training, a moral gymnastic, ἀσχησιζ; learning and discipline must be added to 'nature'. The age, of course, was able to distinguish between a man who attained to a merely intellectual appreciation of moral ideals and one who was successful in the enterprise of translating ideal into conduct, but it was common ground that the moral life was to be achieved only, as Philo said, "by reading, by meditation and by the calling to mind of noble ideals." In short, what the Greco-Roman world of this period had to offer was a morality in which the self-conscious pursuit of moral ideals was pre-eminent.

And our inheritance from that other great source of our moral inspiration, from early Christianity, was of a similar character. Indeed it is not an inheritance which in this matter can be securely separated from that of the ancient world as a whole. In the earliest days, to be a Christian was to be a member of a community animated by a faith and sustained by a hope—faith in a person and hope for a coming event. The morality of these communities was a custom of behavior appropriate to the character of the faith and to the nature of the expectation. It was a way of living distinguished in its place and time by the absence from it of a formulated moral ideal; and it was a way of living departure from which alone involved the penalty of exclusion from the community. And further, it was a way of living that admitted, but did not demand, extremes of behavior, counsels of perfection. The nearest thing to a moral ideal known to these communities was the ideal of charity; the nearest thing to a moral rule was the precept to love God and one's neighbor. It was a morality that found its characteristic verbal expression in the phrase, τούζ τρδποζ κμρίομ, the custom of the Lord. But over these earliest Christian communities, in the course of two centuries, there came a great change. The habit of moral behavior was converted into the self-conscious pursuit of formulated moral ideals—a conversion parallel to the change from faith in a person to belief in a collection of abstract propositions, a creed. This change sprang from a variety of sources; from a change in the circumstances of the Christian's life, from the pressure of the alien intellectual world in which the Christian was set down, from the desire to give a reason for the hope that animated him, from the necessity of translating the Christian way of life into a form in which it could be appreciated by those who had never shared the original inspiration and who, having to learn their Christianity as a foreign language, needed a grammar. The urge to speculate, to abstract and to define, which overtook Christianity as a religion, infected also Christianity as a way of moral life. But, whatever was the impulse of the change, it appears that by the middle of the third century there existed a Christian morality in the familiar form of the self-conscious pursuit of moral ideals, and by the time of St. Ambrose the *form* of this morality had become indistinguishable from that of the morality of the surrounding world, a morality of virtues and vices and of the translation of ideals into actions. A Christian morality in the form of a way of life did not, of course, perish, and it has never completely disappeared. But from this time in the history of Christendom a Christian habit of moral behavior (which had sprung from the circumstances of Christian life) was swamped by a Christian moral ideology, and the perception of the poetic character of human conduct was lost.

I do not wish to suggest that either the self-conscious morality of the Greco-Roman world at the beginning of our era, or the change that overtook Christian morality in the second and third centuries, was avoidable. The one was merely the filling of the vacuum left by the collapse of a traditional morality, and as for the other—perhaps, in order to convert the world, a morality must be reduced to the easily translatable prose of a moral ideal, must be defined and made intellectually coherent, even though the price is a loss of spontaneity and confidence and the approach of the danger of obsession. The fact, however, remains that the moral inheritance of western Europe, both from the classical culture of the ancient world and from Christianity, was not the gift of a morality of habitual behavior, but of a moral ideology. It is true that, in the course of centuries, this moral form went some way toward being reconverted into a morality of habit of behavior. Such a conversion is certainly possible when moral ideals become familiar and, finding expression in customs and institutions that exert a direct pressure upon conduct, cease to be mere ideals. And it is true, also, that the invading barbarians contributed a morality of custom rather than of idea. Nevertheless, modern European morality has never been able to divest itself of the form in which it first emerged. And having once committed the indiscretion of formulating itself in the abstract terms of moral ideals, it was only to be expected that its critics (who have never for long been silent) should seize upon these, and that in defending them against attack they should become rigid and exaggerated. Every significant attack upon Christian morality (that of Nietzsche, for example) has been mistaken for an attack upon the particular moral ideals of Christian life, whereas whatever force it possessed derived from the fact that the object of attack was a morality of ideals that had never succeeded in becoming a morality of habit of behavior.

The history of European morals, then, is in part the history of the maintenance and extension of a morality whose form has, from the beginning, been dominated by the pursuit of moral ideals. In so far as this is an unhappy form of morality, prone to obsession and at war with itself, it is a misfortune to be deplored; in so far as it cannot now readily be avoided, it is a misfortune to be made the best of. And if a morality of ideals is now all, or at least the best, of what we have, it might seem an injudicious moment to dwell upon its defects. But in order to make the best of an unavoidable situation, we need to know its defects as well as feel its necessity. And what at the present time stands between us and the opportunity (such as it is) of surmounting our misfortune is not our sense of the difficulty of doing so, but an erroneous inference we have drawn from our situation—the belief, which has slowly settled upon us, encouraged by almost all the intellectual tendencies of recent centuries, that it is no misfortune at all, but a situation to be welcomed. For the remarkable thing about contemporary European morality is not merely that its form is dominated by the self-conscious pursuit of ideals, but that this form is generally thought to be better and higher than any other. A morality of habit of behavior is dismissed as primitive and obsolete; the pursuit of moral ideals (whatever discontent there may be with the ideals themselves) is identified with moral enlightenment. And further, it is prized (and has been particularly prized on this account since the seventeenth century) because it appears to hold out the possibility of that most sought-after consummation—a 'scientific' morality. It is to be feared, however, that in both these appearances we are sadly deceived. The pursuit of moral ideals has proved itself (as might be expected) an untrustworthy form of morality, the spring neither of a practical nor of a scientific moral life.

The predicament of Western morals, as I read it, is first that our moral life has come to be dominated by the pursuit of ideals, a dominance ruinous to a settled habit of behavior; and, secondly, that we have come to think of this dominance as a benefit for which we should be grateful or an achievement of which we should be proud. And the only purpose to be served by this investigation of our predicament is to disclose the corrupt consciousness, the self-deception that reconciles us to our misfortune.

NOTES

1. *Ethica*, V, x.

2. For example, Jên (consideration of others) in the Confucian morality was an abstraction from the filial piety and respect for elders which constitute the ancient Chinese habit of moral behavior. The activity of the Sages, who (according to Chuang Tzu) *invented* goodness, duty and the rules and ideals of moral conduct, was one in which a concrete morality of habitual behavior was sifted and refined; but, like too critical anthologists, they threw out the imperfect approximations of their material and what remained was not the reflection of a literature but merely a collection of masterpieces.

3. Epictetus, *Diss.*, i, 4 and 30.

4. *Ibid.*, 2, 10.

5. *Dio Chrysostom*, ii, 239.

Chapter 9

Freedom and Custom

ROGER SCRUTON

1. There is a certain attitude that makes freedom the main business of political thought and civil liberty the aim of government. I shall use the word 'liberalism' to refer to this attitude, in the hope that established usage will condone my description. And I shall explore and criticize two aspects of liberal thought: first, the concept of freedom in which it is based; secondly, the attack upon what Mill (liberalism's most eloquent exponent) called the "despotism of custom." My conclusions will be tentative; but I should like to suggest that, properly understood, freedom and custom may require each other. Moreover to describe them as *opposites* is to make it impossible to see how either could be valued by a rational being, or why any politician should concern himself with their support or propagation.

2. I will not consider any particular liberal thinker in detail, partly because liberal thinkers tend to be rather difficult to pin down on the issue that concerns me, that of their underlying assumptions about human nature. My method will be to start from a very simplified version of the liberal idea of freedom, and then impose upon it the kind of complexity which alone can endow it with value. In the course of this the definition of freedom will be seen to move precisely toward, and not away from, a conception of customary usage. For the strategy to be at all persuasive I must begin from an idea of freedom that is stripped of all the qualifications that liberal thinkers normally provide for it. Those qualifications usually smuggle in the unexamined beliefs about human nature that I wish to question.

3. Here, then, is the simplified idea of freedom: a man is free to the extent that he is able to obtain what he desires. This is intended not as an exposition of the metaphysical idea of 'free will', but as a definition of political freedom, or rather, of that kind of freedom that can be thought to be advanced or hindered by political arrangements. According to this idea, freedom is measurable. If we assume from the start that it is also valuable (perhaps, even, that it is the sole value that can be politically *pursued*), then we are likely to define the ideal state in liberal terms, as the system of constraints

necessary to maximize freedom. Since the nineteenth century the dominant concept used to define those constraints has been that of 'harm'. I do not think that this concept can be made to do the work that liberal thinkers require from it: it stands in need of a theory of human nature that will describe as fully as possible the peculiar ways in which men can be harmed. (For men are a very special kind of thing.) To some extent, however, such a theory is implied in the doctrine—variously expounded by Mill, Sidgwick and Hart—that 'harm' is an interference with 'interests', and that the only interests that can be taken into consideration in the political sphere are those founded in 'rights'. The concept of a right can be assumed to be prior to that of political liberty only by assuming one of the standard doctrines of liberal thought: that there are 'natural' rights, and in that doctrine a whole theory of human nature is contained. Until it is fully expressed and defended, however, it would be wrong to think that we have given a serious justification either for constraint or for its opposite.

Notice that the above way of justifying political constraint is very different from, although it might eventually support, the constitutionalist theories inspired by Montesquieu. These tend to show why and how the *powers* of institutions and individuals might be politically limited. This procedure seems at first sight to lay less emphasis on the concept of liberty. It merely assumes that every man has reason to be protected against power. It might be true, however, that this reason cannot be expounded without recourse to an ideal of political freedom, together with the theory of human nature that gives support to it.

Rather than criticize either of those over-arching political theories I shall concentrate, instead, on the original idea of freedom, since it seems to me that the principal defects of liberal theories of the state are already contained in that idea.

4. First, I should like to make some distinctions among desires. Desires may be fleeting or enduring: and I take it that there is a sense in which a merely fleeting desire is less involved in the personality of the agent than an enduring desire, so that the agent normally suffers less through its frustration.

There is also a distinction between a serious desire and a mere velleity. This is related to, but not identical with, the first distinction. A velleity is a desire that persists only until obstructed: that is, it has minimal motivating power, enough only to overcome the general friction of agency, and not enough to set itself against a resistant world.

It seems to me that a political arrangement that sought to encourage and satisfy fleeting desires and mere velleities, but which did this by creating conditions that hindered the fulfillment of genuine agency, would be an arrangement that deprived us of something that could reasonably be called our 'freedom'. Extremes of pamperedness, where no desire transgresses the limits of the fleeting, and all desires are fulfilled, are not states of freedom. Or if they are, then it becomes puzzling that anyone should think freedom to be a value.

5. Let us consider then only enduring and serious desires. There are still many important distinctions to be drawn. For example, we can distinguish the mild from the intense (a distinction of motivating power), the calm from the urgent (a distinction of a less quantitative kind, concerning the ability of a desire to conceal itself until its time has come), the shallow from the profound. The last difference is not truly quantitative at all, and it may be thought, therefore, by those liberal theories that depend upon the measurement of one desire against another, that it does not exist, or is reducible to some other distinction that fits more readily into the liberal picture. (The same thought is common also to those who describe human and political matters in terms of preference theory, the theory of games, and other intriguing simplifications.) But I shall argue that it is a real distinction, and an important one, since it concerns the relation of the desire to the self of the agent. An example might make the distinction clearer: a desire to seduce someone with whom I have become casually acquainted may be intense, urgent, and also calculating. Suppose the desire is not fulfilled, and on the next day is either forgotten or cast over with a veil or irony. This I should call a shallow desire. By contrast, I may wish to seduce, or rather, unite myself with, someone whom I have long known and respected. This desire is not urgent, nor is it intense in the sense of determining my action against all normal opposition. And yet it persists, I return to it, and as the years pass and I see it unfulfilled, I feel part of myself dwindling away in sadness or incoherence. This I should call a profound desire. It is possible that some people do not have profound desires; it is extremely unlikely that there are people whose desires are not sometimes intense, urgent or domineering.

The distinction is related to two others: that between the spasmodic and the persistent, and that between the long term and the short term. The latter distinction (commented on by Kenny, and in another way by Nagel) deserves some mention here. I can desire to do this, here, now. Or I can desire something for my future without wanting it now. It is plausible to suggest that certain beings—notably those with no concept of the future—can respond to the promptings of the first kind of desire while remaining forever unacquainted with the second.

6. Two of those distinctions interest me in the context of the present discussion: that between the profound and the shallow, and that between the long term and the short term. In neither case, it must be said, is the distinction to be elucidated in terms of the concept of intention, although of course an account of human agency that failed to consider the idea of intention is unlikely to generate a theory of political freedom. I can imagine a theory that said that an urgent desire is distinguished by the fact that it is (or, according to your theory of intention, is accompanied by or realized in) a present intention, the calm desire by the like presence of an intention for the future. But in neither case, it seems to me, need there be any intention at all. I may, out of moral or religious scruples, intend not to satisfy a desire, however urgent. Similarly, while it is natural to associate long-term desires with planning, deliberation, and so again with intention, this reference to intention is neither sufficient nor necessary to distinguish the long-term from the short-term desire. I may, for example, have a long-term desire one day to redeem my wasted life by a noble gesture; and yet self-knowledge might at the same time remind me of the impossibility of achieving this, and so (by a well-known law) remove the possibility of intending it.

7. Nevertheless, the introduction of the concept of intention makes it possible to make a first serious attack on the primitive notion of freedom from which I began. Among all the many desires that circulate within me, there are some that correspond to intentions and some that do not. The first carry a peculiar personal endorsement, the nature of which it is part of our business to discern. A political order that obstructs only those desires a man has no intention to fulfill clearly removes less of his freedom than one that obstructs his intentions while leaving other desires to fulfill themselves at will. Indeed, it is hard to see how the agent *himself* can see the first state as interfering in his freedom in any way whatever. (Here we see the beginning of a complication, long familiar to Marxists and their forebears: that between the first- and third-person view of freedom. Are we aiming at a state in which people cannot *feel* the constraint on their freedom, or a state in which the constraint is not there? Is it more desirable to be really free although perpetually deluded into thinking oneself in bondage, or really in bondage and deluded into thinking oneself free? To put it in Leibnizian terms: would it matter

if freedom were no more than a 'well-founded phenomenon'? I return to this question below.)

Given such considerations, it seems odd to think that the concept of desire will be sufficient alone to generate an idea of political freedom.

8. A second difficulty for our original definition derives from the fact that we can distinguish desires, not merely in terms of their motivational character, but in terms of their satisfaction. It is a necessary truth that desire seeks its own satisfaction. But it is not a necessary truth that the state that constitutes the satisfaction be desired under the description that would be applied to it by someone who is in it. For example, I may desire to drink, but not to be in the state of having drunk, a bottle of wine. As my knowledge of myself and the world increases, this disparity between my desires to have and my desires to hold becomes steadily greater.

The disparity to which I refer is no easy matter to understand. It has at least the following aspects, or 'moments'. (The Hegelian term suggests itself, since in an important sense each stands to the next as anticipation and as necessary condition, while the full complexity of the tendency they exhibit can be understood only from the final, 'realized' stage.)

(a) I may desire to have something and find that I desire not to keep it when obtained, an experience from which I may or may not learn. (Learning here involves acquiring practical knowledge, specifically, that disposition of character known as temperance.)

(b) I may desire to have something and find that the satisfaction of that desire leaves me restless and unhappy. Here we see the divergence between the idea of the satisfaction of a desire and that of the satisfaction of the person who experiences it.

(c) I may desire to have something I discover to be undesirable, not just in the sense of wanting to be rid of it, but in the sense of ascribing to it a negative value. By an almost inevitable transition, the idea of value has entered my reflections on the object of desire. It is difficult to see how this long-term view of things, which involves comparison between past desire and present satisfaction, could long forbear the thought that some states of being are more worthwhile than others.

(d) I may desire something while *at the same time* realizing that
it leads to my personal dissatisfaction, and thinking it to be
undesirable. I may again learn to overcome such desires, and
the disposition involved in this is wisdom.

Reflecting on such features we may notice the following: first,
self-consciousness has a central role in the make-up of the desire to
hold what I have obtained. Secondly, the concept of value is inseparable from some of the thoughts upon which such a desire depends.
Thirdly, there is the beginnings of a distinction, made from the
agent's point of view, between satisfaction of desire and satisfaction
of self. I cannot argue the point here, but it seems to me that these
three phenomena come and go together.

9. The distinction between desire and intention (see section 6)
is integral to the notion of a self-conscious being. And it is the
freedom of the self-conscious being that concerns us, since only such
a being is a *zoon politikon*. Drawing on the conclusions implicit in
the last section, we find ourselves obliged to consider how we would
describe the freedom of a being who has, not only desires and
intentions, but also a conception of his own satisfaction, and a
conception of the desirable (of the value of the object of desire). It
then becomes increasingly difficult to confine ourselves within a
definition that refers freedom to the satisfaction of desire alone.
Consider the following two political arrangements:

In the first, human beings are given every opportunity to satisfy
each desire as it arises, whatever its profundity, and whatever the
state that results from it. Yet the members of the community live in
such circumstances that none of their desires leads to personal satisfaction or to a sense of the value of holding what they need struggle
so little to have (cf. Huxley's *Brave New World*).

In the second, many desires are impossible to fulfill. But all
those fields in which the expression and development of human
energy is permitted involve desires for things considered desirable
by those who are motivated by them, and which bring the satisfaction
of the person in addition to the satisfaction of desire.

If you said that the first of these is a state of political freedom,
the second a state of enslavement, then you would find it impossible
to say why men should value freedom and not servitude, and your
political philosophy (if you are a liberal) would be at an end. But
of course there is something absurd about calling the first state
described above a state of freedom, since it is one in which all true
decision-making is eroded. There is no room now for deliberation,
and a man might as well give himself up to the vagaries of every

impulse. Intentions wither, and so too does the sense of oneself as an agent.

10. That last idea is one that I should like to try to clarify. For we now find ourselves at the point where the true challenge to liberalism must be offered, and the idea of agency is integral to that challenge. All kinds of beings have desires and satisfactions, but not all of them have intentions or values or self-consciousness. Yet our sense of ourselves as agents is intimately connected with those three features. How, then, can we specify the conditions of our freedom and not take them into consideration? So our final amendment to the first idea of freedom will have to read like this: political freedom consists in the absence of obstacles to those desires which are profound, long term, satisfying to the self, consonant with personal values and able to issue in consistent intentional activity, together with any 'lesser' desires which can be shown not to conflict with them. Some such view was once expressed by D. H. Lawrence:

> All that matters is that men and women should do what they really want to do. Though here [i.e. in questions of sex and marriage] we must remember that man has a double set of desires, the shallow and the profound, the personal, superficial, temporary desires, and the inner, impersonal, great desires that are fulfilled in long periods of time. The desires of the moment are easy to recognize, but the others, the deeper ones, are difficult. It is the business of our chief thinkers to tell us of our deeper desires, not to keep shrilling our little desires into our ears (A propos of *Lady Chatterly's Lover* [London, 1931], 52–53).

It is natural that this kind of challenge to the original liberal position should be raised by the problem of sexual relations, and I shall mention the problem again. But I should like to remove from Lawrence's remark the element of atavism: the distinction we are pursuing is not that between the personal and the impersonal. On the contrary: if we represent it in that way then we shall lose what I shall argue to be essential to any account of political values—the first person viewpoint of the agent. The distinctions towards which I have gestured indicate that some desires belong more deeply to the agent than others; but it is those that belong, and not those which pass him by, that are significant. Those—the profound, long term, self-satisfying, and so on—I shall call collectively the 'primary' desires of the agent. It is the constraints on primary desires that will hurt, and which the agent will seek to overthrow; and it is in terms of such desires that the true 'harm' of a self-conscious being should be defined.

But now we have a far deeper question than that of the acceptability of the definition of freedom. Suppose we accept it, or some modified version of it. It would still seem impossible really to understand the conditions of political freedom if we do not also understand the conditions that generate or permit the formation of primary desires. It could be (for all that Mill and his progeny have said) that the uninstructed political agent, acting out of liberal impulses, and armed with some experiment in living which he seeks to protect from the opprobrium of the multitude, will, in furthering the cause of liberty, bring about the conditions that make primary desires impossible. It could be, as Bradley once argued, that the ethic of tolerance voids the world of all sense of a distinction between what is desirable and what is not. It could also be that, from a third-person point of view, liberal society is, as some Marxists say it is, simply a congeries of fetishistic impulse, allowing satisfaction to every desire only because every desire is an artificial product of its own remorseless negation of true human nature.

11. Both those speculations are intemperate, and as much in need of philosophical support as the practices they disfavor. But whichever way we now turn, it is clear that we can no longer avoid the question of 'true human nature'. In particular, we must say something about its relation to the three features of 'primary' desires that I emphasized: self-consciousness, self-satisfaction, and the sense of the desirable. In due course, I shall consider one small part of the vast issue concerning the real distinction (if there is one) between beast and man. I shall reflect on a central feature of self-consciousness, which I shall call the 'sense of my identity through time', and it is worth anticipating later discussion by indicating already why I should single out such a feature for consideration.

The sense of identity through time is necessary for the formation of long-term desires: I must believe that I shall exist in the future if such desires are to be possible. It is also necessary for the formation of intentions, as is obvious. It is required for the existence of profound desires, since such desires arise out of, and also go to constitute, the image of myself as having a 'life' in which I may be fulfilled or frustrated. It is—if Kant's argument in the "Transcendental Deduction" has force—a necessary ingredient in self-consciousness as such. Finally, it is integral to our idea of the desirable, since we must see the desirable as that which we shall be pleased to keep, and not just as that which we wish to obtain; such a thought is impossible without the sense of identity through time.

Notice that I have spoken of a 'sense'. In fact the logical relations to which I have referred argue only that certain states of mind involved in agency require the *belief* in my continuity through time. Nevertheless, I do not think that it is a mere phenomenological luxury to describe this belief as a kind of sense. This is not merely because of the ineliminable indexical component in the belief. It is also because the belief so transforms my motivation as to be active in all that I perceive, suffer and do. It would be impossible to remove it and to think that anything of my experience would remain unaltered. In this respect, if in no other, Kant was surely right to speak of time as the "form" of inner sense.

12. The mention of Kant leads me to consider a deep metaphysical stratagem, which is available to the liberal, and which we must explore as a preliminary to considering the sense of identity through time. This stratagem was adopted by Kant in giving expression to the particular political liberalism that appealed to him, and versions of it reappear in modern liberal writings—notably in the work of Rawls.

I have introduced a distinction between desire and intention, together with certain conceptions that have some intimate connection with the concept of the self. Kant, in his moral philosophy, and in that small part of his philosophy that could be described as political, fastened on to those intuitive conceptions, and the distinction associated with them, and distilled from them, as it were, a metaphysical essence. The picture is this: when a man is motivated by the desire to do something, we often find it plausible to say that he is acted on by the desire, as though the desire were some force of which he is the (perhaps entirely passive) victim. It is most plausible to say this in the case of those desires that are intense, urgent, and have some animal component (by which I mean a component which it would make sense to attribute to a creature without self-consciousness). We might even speak of a man being *overcome* by a desire; this expression suggests that the agency of a man lies elsewhere than in his desires, since we can describe his desires as though they were external forces that he may fail to combat.

By contrast it never makes sense to say that a man is overcome by an intention, or even that intentions act on or through him, in the manner of desires. On the contrary, he *himself* acts through his intentions. They are the manifestation of his agency, and when, for example, someone intends to do what he desires not to do, or desires to do what he does not intend, we do not think of him as a kind of battlefield, in which warring forces gather—intentions on the one side, and desire on the other. We think of *him* as standing in opposition to his desires. In other words, we regard the person (or self) as governed by a principle of agency which is intrinsic to it, and not reducible to any motivating force.

If we take those intuitive observations and exaggerate them to the point of near implausibility, and if we combine our exaggeration with the intuition that a central feature of self-consciousness is the sense of identity through time, then we arrive at the following picture. The self is a temporally extended autonomous agent, acting on the world through intention (or 'will'). This will aims at the satisfaction, not of desire, but of the self, and its guiding principle is value. But, being autonomous—that is, motivated by nothing outside itself—it must be the originator of that principle. The will creates, out of its sovereign autonomy, the values that direct it. By contrast, desires act on the self externally, and belong to another part, what Kant called the "pathological" part, of man. They neither create values nor enact them. They are forces that constrain the will much as the will is constrained by any other aspect of nature.

From this picture we now derive a new sophisticated version of the liberal theory. Freedom is freedom not of desire but of the will. Political freedom consists in the absence of constraint upon our 'autonomy'. A society is free to the extent that it is possible for an individual to be self-commanded in the peculiar manner of the rational agent. If we combine this with the view of Kant, that the autonomous will envisages and (where possible) creates that Kingdom of Ends in which all wills act in harmony, it follows that nothing further need be said about the constraints that will maximize political freedom.

13. Kant claimed that the autonomous self will bind itself by a universal law. This law claims to be, and, in the event of full autonomy, actually is, universally valid, since it is recommended on the basis of reason alone. Take away that idea of objectivity and the result is not far from the existentialist concept of authenticity: I exist as an agent to the extent that I determine my actions; self-determination requires me to free myself from the arbitrary sway of all laws and impulses that are not self-imposed. But what I will for myself is unique to me. It is indeed my individuality (the point of view that is uniquely mine), so that I cannot be bound by a universal law without ceasing to be myself.

This gives rise to the most metaphysical of all expressions of the liberal theory of freedom. But since the background metaphysics is founded in a real sense that human freedom is different in kind from the freedom of an animal, it is ultimately of greater philosophical interest than the theories offered by Mill. It provides, I think, the master-thought of many recent liberal philosophies.

I have day-to-day desires and predilections, and these demand satisfaction. But they have value to me only if I see them as arising in harmony with what I 'choose to be'. What I choose to be is a thing with a 'life' of its own, and with a 'style' of life that realizes its autonomy. True political freedom is, primarily, the freedom for existential choice, and only secondarily the freedom to satisfy desire. (If you like, it is freedom to satisfy those desires that express the autonomy of the agent.) It is essential to Rawls' theory of justice, for example, that his 'model-conception' of the individual in the original position is that of a Kantian moral agent. But Rawls' Kantian agent is concerned to protect his capacity for 'authentic' choice, and recognizes the possibility that his values may in the end be divergent from those of the community that surrounds him.

The following picture may now emerge as a possible liberal doctrine: I have desires that, however urgent, may go unfulfilled without any sense of injury to myself, ranging from the desire for a beer while driving across a lonely moor, to the urgent desire to make love to someone who rejects me. I have other desires that are so deeply connected with my sense of myself that I must inevitably regard their violation as a violation of right. It is a violation of right because it is a trespass upon my existence. Consider an interdiction that prevents, for no reason connected with the interest of the parties, marriage between two people who wish to marry. Or an interdiction which prevents me, for no reason connected with my interest, from pursuing the career I have chosen, and for which I am suited, and for which I have prepared myself. Or the edict that arbitrarily transports me from my homeland to some inhospitable place, and scatters my children abroad. The indignities genuinely resented in those countries described as totalitarian seem to have this character, of radical and arbitrary interference with a man's desire to be what he really is. The doctrine might then go on to define political freedom as the political ability to satisfy that desire.

14. But without the metaphysical doctrine of the autonomous, self-creating and self-commanding will, all this can only be a metaphor and, if we are persuaded by it, this must be because we guess at some way of rewriting the doctrine that will remove its well-

known and intolerable conclusion—the commitment to a transcendental self that acts in a world to which it is metaphysically impeded from belonging. The best way to rewrite the doctrine is in terms of the distinction among desires that I earlier referred to. In the course of that rewriting we will find that the notion of political freedom leads us to look with some favor upon customary constraint.

First let us reject, what I think modern philosophers have given us many good reasons to reject, the Kantian idea that the will can be wholly separated from desire and assigned to a different subject from the subject of desire. My desires are as much *mine* as are my intentions, and while it is true that I can sometimes speak of them as though they were forces *acting* on me, this is possible only sometimes and for special reasons. If I thought of *all* my desires in that way then I should be incapable of deliberation, and my capacity to form intentions would vanish.

If we reject the absolute Kantian view of the distinction between desire and intention then we reject much. In particular, we reject the possibility of forming in any coherent way the existentialist doctrine of man as self-created. But we can still reconstruct another distinction that might provide the grounds for a definition of freedom. This is the distinction (now a matter of degree) between desires that belong to the self and desires that do not.

15. This reconstruction will depend on our being clear about the methodological significance of the first person case. Much of the attraction of liberalism lies in the fact that it intends to describe a state of political freedom that can be seen to be such by the individual agent. Anti-liberal theories sometimes begin from a doctrine of the 'real interests' of the subject, while adopting a wholly third-personal stance toward the social world—the stance not of participant but of observer. It may then seem quite arbitrary whether the real interests of the subject should also be recognized by him as desirable. A doctrine of political freedom that said that a state is free provided men could pursue only their real interests within it, if combined with a theory of human nature that makes a man's 'real interests' things he does not, or perhaps even cannot, value, is clearly not a doctrine of freedom. Suppose it were argued that his own death is always the 'real interest' of a Jew (as it is now sometimes argued that death is the real interest of the deformed fetus); or suppose it were argued that the renunciation of all rights of ownership, all claims of personal and local allegiance, all self-aggrandizement and personal pride, were the real interest of every man. Both those doctrines have been used to perpetuate tyranny, and the second is

often preached in England. Their repellent aspect derives from the fact that the real interest of the victim is described in such a way that, from his own point of view, he cannot (in normal circumstances) desire it.

It might be thought that what is wrong with that tyrannical account of freedom is the assertion that political freedom should make possible *only* the pursuit of real interests. But it seems to me that, if you have the conception of a real interest, you cannot think that you give people true freedom by allowing equal expression to those desires which do, and those which do not satisfy it, unless you also think that there could not possibly be a conflict between the two kinds of desire. The real interest of something is that which is in accordance with its nature, and which fulfills it according to that nature. (It is a 'need'.) A thing that deviates from its real interest deviates from its nature and hence from itself. And it would be impossible to see why we should value freedom if it meant *simply* the indefinite license to diverge from our nature.

The real problem is not with the idea of a real interest, but with the conception of human nature with which it was conjoined. It is an essential feature of human nature that we have a first-person perspective on our actions. It is part of our real interest that we should be able to do that which, from our own point of view, we can see to be desirable. The idea that, if you oppose liberalism, you must do so in the name of tyranny, seems to me almost always to be founded on the mistaken view that liberalism alone can give a first-person perspective on political freedom—that is, that liberalism alone can show why the *agent* should desire to be free.

16. At the heart of our first person perspective on the world there is, I have suggested, a peculiar sense of our continuity through time. This sense is most vividly manifest in our ability to have long-term desires and ambitions for ourselves, and to separate in our deliberations those desires which, when gratified, gratify only themselves, from those desires which contribute to our fulfillment. It is in terms of this sense of our continuity through time that the Kantian doctrine of autonomy can be reconstructed, and with it the thought that underlies the original definition of freedom. But we find that, as this reconstruction proceeds, the liberal ideal of freedom ceases to be persuasive. For it seeks to derive the constraints that are licensed by freedom from the idea of the autonomous agent, without recognizing that there must be constraints that make the autonomous agent possible. These constraints must be understood independently. It seems to me that there are such constraints. There are disciplines

that foster the first-person view of action, together with the primary desires that constitute our true autonomy. These are not things we *choose* from a state of autonomy, but things that generate our autonomy precisely because they are not chosen. In normal circumstances custom is one of them.

I have supposed that our reconstruction of the Kantian autonomy will be in terms of primary desires. It is those we can think of as being definitive of what we are, rather than of what happens to us. To reach the state from which the desirability of freedom can be perceived, a being must acquire primary desires. It is often said that the world of the autonomous being (the being with primary desires) is a different world from the world of the animal. And yet the transition from animal to free being does not involve any change in the world, only a change in intentionality (in how the world is seen). This change comes about when a being begins to see his extension in time from the present to the final moment and to envisage what it would be like then to *have* been the person that he now is. All the primary desires that I mentioned earlier are bound up with the pressure to see ourselves in that way. Our autonomous being is therefore constrained by whatever is necessary to bring about such a picture of one's life.

The first thing that is necessary is the capacity to envisage the future, and to envisage oneself as part of that future. The 'free' being must also contemplate his place in the future in such a way as to incorporate it into present deliberations, both under the aspect of value and under that of desire. There are many ways in which this might be done, and I cannot see that we can give an *a priori* argument for the superiority of one way over another. But I should like to emphasize the fact that all the obvious ways in which this moral education is acquired involve reference precisely to the kind of constraint that custom introduces into our lives. The agent who surveys the future in the light of present values must have some sense that his mode of action toward the world in the future, and the world itself, will still be comprehensible to him. If it were the case that custom were mere repetition, blindly and mechanically performed, then it would, of course, be absurd to suggest that custom could play a part in developing that sense. But custom is an intentional activity; a customary act contains within itself the reason for its performance; it looks backwards to how things have been and forwards to how things will be, while representing the present as consonant with past and future. It is against the background of custom that primary desires acquire their force and vitality.

18. As I say, I can give no conclusive *a priori* argument in favor of that position. But I believe that it suffices to shift the onus of proof. The habitual liberal assumption is that the onus lies always on the other side: that the liberal defense of freedom is sufficiently complete in itself to challenge all-comers to refute it. On the contrary, I have argued that the liberal conception of freedom *presupposes* an idea of autonomy. And it is simply a natural assumption to make, that an autonomous being does not leap into existence like Athena from the head of Zeus. On the contrary, he may be the product of an elaborate education that already contains and imposes the constraints the liberal wished to use his concept of freedom to test. In other words, the liberal definition of political freedom presupposes a theory of human nature, one consequence of which may be that constraint on human conduct can be justified without referring to that definition. The concept of freedom cannot, then, be the single master concept in political thought, nor the aim of freedom the single constituent of political practice.

But let me add a few points that will shift the onus further, by removing what I take to be the prevailing prejudices against custom. These prejudices seem generally to exemplify three things: a confusion between custom and habit, a failure to understand tradition and its place in human conduct, and an inaccurate perception of the nature of social institutions.

19. *The confusion between custom and habit.* A habit is an activity that is repeated, but which embodies within itself no reason for its repetition that is accessible to the agent. It is something one does without knowing why. (Of course it may be that there are reasons for acquiring habits, and it may also be true that without habits the development of primary desires is impeded.) If habit seems like a form of bondage it is because its value is usually apparent only from the third-person point of view. Thus, in the theory of evolution, or functionalist theories of social behavior, the habits of animals and people are shown to be useful to them, even when they connote no gratification, or none beyond that involved in instinct, or appetite. Even though customs are not themselves chosen, to act out of custom is to act intentionally, and in such a way as to create a link between oneself and others. The customary action is the one for which the answer to the question, "Why are you doing that?" is "It is what is done." In that answer many things are embodied: the thought of a community of rational agents who act alike; the thought that their acting alike is reasonable; an indifference to time, and a consequent sense of what it would be like to act likewise at any other time. In

this way customary activity effects two important results in the consciousness of the rational being. It reassures him of the existence of a public world, in which the validity of certain forms of action is recognized or at least recognizable. And it enables him to project his activities forward into the future, by laying hold of the continuity through which to experience that future as safe. (Consider here the customs of common courtesy.) It is hardly surprising that there is a peculiar pleasure in the customary act, or that people are genuinely attached to customs. One can regret a habit, and try unsuccessfully to break with it. But one cannot try to break with a custom unless one is being *forced* to comply.

Now there are people who imagine that custom has an inevitable 'despotic' power—people like Mill, or the Shelley of *The Revolt of Islam*. But is it not more plausible to suppose that a sense of the public validity of action, and a sense of the safety of the future (of the future as a place where one exists still knowing what to do), are normal preconditions for the development of primary desires? If so, then custom can be seen as a normal step on the way to autonomy.

Custom is often associated (notably, of course, by Yeats) with ceremony. This is perhaps for the following reason. Ceremony takes a particular occasion of personal significance—a birthday, a feast day, a marriage, a death—and represents it as an instance of a universal. The ceremony contains a significance that transcends the present moment, and an intimation of values that are shared. But this value in ceremony is a value for the participant: it consists in the temporary saturation of his first-person perspective with a sense of the permanence of the social world. That is a very special case of custom providing the facilities for our primary desires. It is surely no accident that these desires (in particular, those involving erotic love) require ceremonial enactment.

20. *The misconception of tradition.* Tradition provides one of the ways in which men acquire the sense of their continuity. Custom is the simplest case of tradition, but tradition is habitually misrepresented by liberal thinkers, probably on account of the mistaken argument that to belong to a tradition is to be unthinkingly subservient to the authority of the past. This view neglects the role of consciousness in the exercise of traditional forms of behavior. Consider marriage. The reason for marrying lies in the past: not just the past relations of the couple involved, but the past history of sexual union. This is the way in which the bond between the sexes has been cemented; it is familiar, accepted, and associated with settled expectations. It enables the participants to envisage what they are

doing in becoming attached to each other. By enacting this tradition the agent sees a greater significance in his act than the desire that propelled him towards it. His future becomes present to him, and he knows himself as part of that future. In this way the marriage bond clarifies the agent's responsibility toward the world. There is a *prima facie* case for thinking that the existence of such traditions and the enormous constraints implicit in them is precisely what is required for the full development and exercise of primary desires.

It is of the essence of a tradition that it is alive, that it grows, develops and declines, in obedience to the inner determination of its nature. A tradition exploits the freedom of its participants: they grow into it, but adapt it through their participation. A model for this kind of development is provided by the tradition of common law, which is neither a habit, nor merely a custom, and still less a body of rules. It is a developing way of seeing the social world, and redefines the place of the individual in that world by responding to and influencing his own self-image.

21. *The inaccurate perception of social institutions.* If we consider that, because men are free by nature, their freedom does not need to be acquired, then not only do we commit an evident logical fallacy; we naturally begin to think of institutions in a single, highly distorted way. They become not the precondition but the outcome of human freedom. (Or, if they are not the outcome of freedom, they are then dismissed as local tyrannies.) It is characteristic of liberal thought to see all institutions on the model of what lawyers call 'voluntary associations'—even the institutions that constitute the state. (Hence the connection of liberal ideas of freedom with the politics of the 'social contract' and 'tacit consent'.) But the legal reality of most serious institutions cannot be accommodated by the idea of a voluntary association, as has been recognized since Roman times. In a similar way the moral reality of those institutions, which are involved in the formation of the autonomous being, cannot be considered as derived from autonomous choice. An institution that forms the character of the autonomous being must also have a soul or character of its own. Consider the university: the institution provides us with the reasons we have for remaining in it. We could hardly have understood those reasons had the institution not arisen (in the long and mysterious way in which such institutions arise). There is a deep question of political philosophy as to how such non-contractual associations can be considered legitimate. But they exist, and are a natural offshoot of the requirement of formative experiences in the history of the autonomous agent. These facts are evident to reflection.

All institutions require custom if they are to endure. Were custom to be constantly broken down, then it is reasonable to suppose that no noncontractual institution could even be *formed*. The state is such an institution. If we concede that *any* political constraint is required for the creation of an autonomous being, then the state is necessary. So custom is necessary too.

22. I have given a few, partly empirical, partly *a priori*, reasons for thinking that custom and its associated forms of conduct are necessary for the formation of the 'primary' desires that form the basis of our autonomy. It is only such desires that political freedom should be concerned to foster, since it is only then that freedom can be considered to be a value. Custom is not, then, the enemy of freedom, but its necessary precondition. The business of government is not the generation of abstract civil liberty, but the founding of the institutions that make liberty possible. Without a background of customary usage the activity of government would be impossible.

Of course, a sophisticated liberal, armed with a philosophical theory of human nature, might very well accept what I have said. But the theory of human nature is certainly not there in Mill. Had it been there then it may have awoken him to the fact that freedom is not the only political value. If we look back on the liberal attack on custom we can see a reason why it avoided the theoretical commitment that would have given it cogency. In attacking custom the liberal was attacking the freedom of the majority, by tearing down the institutions through which their self-identity is formed. If people react now to the self-assertiveness—indeed the self-righteousness—of *On Liberty*, it is partly because they feel the aggression that underlies Mill's simplification of the human world. But could a liberal of Mill's persuasion really tolerate the political void that the acceptance of his doctrine generates? I doubt it, for, just as his idea of freedom is parasitic on deeper assumptions about human nature that he prefers not to explore, so is his lifestyle parasitic on a social order that he fails (such is the self-involvement of his nature) to support or condone.

Chapter 10

The Diversity of Goods

CHARLES TAYLOR

I

What did utilitarianism have going for it? A lot of things undoubtedly: its seeming compatibility with scientific thought; its this-worldly humanist focus, its concern with suffering. But one of the powerful background factors behind much of this appeal was *epistemological*. A utilitarian ethic seemed to be able to fit the canons of rational validation as these were understood in the intellectual culture nourished by the epistemological revolution of the seventeenth century and the scientific outlook that partly sprang from it.

In the utilitarian perspective, one validated an ethical position by hard evidence. You count the consequences for human happiness of one or another course, and you go with the one with the highest favorable total. What counts as human happiness was thought to be something conceptually unproblematic, a scientifically establishable domain of facts like others. One could abandon all the metaphysical or theological factors—commands of God, natural rights, virtues— which made ethical questions scientifically undecidable. Bluntly, we could calculate.

Ultimately, I should like to argue that this is but another example of the baleful effect of the classical epistemological model, common to Cartesians and empiricists, which has had such a distorting effect on the theoretical self-understanding of moderns. This is something which is above all visible in the sciences of man, but I think it has wreaked as great havoc in ethical theory.

The distortive effect comes in that we tend to start formulating our meta-theory of a given domain with an already formed model of valid reasoning, all the more dogmatically held because we are oblivious to the alternatives. This model then makes us quite incapable of seeing how reason does and can really function in the domain, to the degree that it does not fit the model. We cut and chop the reality of, in this case, ethical thought to fit the Procrustean bed of our model of validation. Then, since meta-theory and theory cannot be isolated from one another, the distortive conception begins to shape our ethical thought itself.

A parallel process, I should like to argue, has been visible in the sciences of man, with similar stultifying effects on the practice of students of human behavior. The best, most insightful, practice of history, sociology, psychology is either devalued or misunderstood, and as a consequence we find masses of researchers engaging in what very often turns out to be futile exercises, of no scientific value whatever, sustained only by the institutional inertia of a professionalized discipline. The history of behaviorism stands as a warning of the virtual immortality that can be attained by such institutionalized futility.

In the case of ethics, two patterns of thought have especially benefited from the influence of the underlying model of validation. One is utilitarianism, which as I have just mentioned seemed to offer calculation over verifiable empirical quantities in the place of metaphysical distinctions. The other is various species of formalism. Kant is the originator of one of the most influential variants, without himself having fallen victim, I believe, to the narrowing consequences that usually follow the adoption of a formalism.

Formalisms, like utilitarianism, have the apparent value that they would allow us to ignore the problematic distinctions between different qualities of action or modes of life, which play such a large part in our actual moral decisions, feelings of admiration, remorse, etc., but which are so hard to justify when others controvert them. They offer the hope of deciding ethical questions without having to determine which of a number of rival languages of moral virtue and vice, of the admirable and the contemptible, of unconditional versus conditional obligation, are valid. You could finesse all this, if you could determine the cases where a maxim of action would be unrealizable if everyone adopted it, or where its universal realization was something you could not possibly desire; or if you could determine what actions you could approve no matter whose standpoint you adopted of those persons affected; or if you could circumscribe the principles that would be adopted by free rational agents in certain paradigm circumstances.

Of course, all these formulae for ethical decision repose on some substantive moral insights; otherwise they would not seem even plausible candidates as models of *ethical* reasoning. Behind these Kant-derived formulae stands one of the most fundamental insights of modern Western civilization, the universal attribution of moral personality: in fundamental ethical matters, everyone ought to count, and all ought to count in the same way. Within this outlook, one absolute requirement of ethical thinking is that we respect other human agents as subjects of practical reasoning on the same footing as ourselves.

In a sense, this principle is historically parochial. This is not the way the average Greek in ancient times, for instance, looked on his Thracian slave. But, in a sense, it also corresponds to something very deep in human moral reasoning. All moral reasoning is carried on within a community; and it is essential to the very existence of this community that each accord the other interlocutors this status as moral agents. The Greek who may not have accorded it to his Thracian slave most certainly did to his compatriots. That was part and parcel of there being recognized issues of justice between them. What modern civilization has done, partly under the influence of Stoic natural law and Christianity, has been to lift all the parochial restrictions that surrounded this recognition of moral personality in earlier civilizations.

The modern insight, therefore, flows very naturally from one of the basic preconditions of moral thinking itself, along with the view— overwhelmingly plausible, to us moderns—that there is no defensible distinction to be made in this regard between different classes of human beings. This has become so widespread that even discrimination and domination is in fact justified on universalist grounds. (Even South Africa has an official ideology of *apartheid*, which can allow theoretically for the peoples concerned to be not unequal, but just different.)

So we seem on very safe ground in adopting a decision procedure that can be shown to flow from this principle. Indeed, this seems to be a moral principle of a quite different order from the various contested languages of moral praise, condemnation, aspiration or aversion, which distinguish rival conceptions of virtue and paradigm modes of life. We might even talk ourselves into believing that it is not a moral principle in any substantive contestable sense at all, but some kind of limiting principle of moral reasoning. Thus we might say with Richard Hare, for example, that in applying this kind of decision procedure we are following not moral intuitions, but rather our linguistic intuitions concerning the use of the word 'moral'.

Classical utilitarianism itself incorporated this universal principle in the procedural demand that in calculating the best course, the happiness of each agent count for one, and of no agent for more than one. Here again one of the fundamental issues of modern thought is decided by what looks like a formal principle, and utilitarianism itself got a great deal of its *prima facie* plausibility from the strength of the same principle. If everyone counts as a moral agent, then what they desire and aim at ought to count, and the right course of action should be what satisfies all, or the largest number possible. At least this chain of reasoning can appear plausible.

But clear reasoning ought to demand that we counteract this tendency to slip over our deepest moral convictions unexamined. They look like formal principles only because they are so foundational to the moral thinking of our civilization. We should strive to formulate the underlying moral insights just as clearly and expressly as we do all others.

When we do so, of course, we shall find that they stand in need of justification like the others. This points us to one of the motives for construing them as formal principles. For those who despair of reason as the arbiter of moral disputes (and the epistemological tradition has tended to induce this despair in many), making the fundamental insights into a formal principle has seemed a way of avoiding a moral scepticism which was both implausible and distasteful.

But, I want to argue, the price of this formalism, as also of the utilitarian reduction, has been a severe distortion of our understanding of our moral thinking. One of the big illusions which grows from either of these reductions is the belief that there is a single consistent domain of the 'moral', that there is one set of considerations, or mode of calculation, which determines what we ought 'morally' to do. The unity of the moral is a question that is conceptually decided from the first on the grounds that moral reasoning just is equivalent to calculating consequences for human happiness, or determining the universal applicability of maxims, or something of the sort.

But once we shake ourselves clear from the formalist illusion, of the utilitarian reduction—and this means resisting the blandishments of its underlying model of rational validation—we can see that the boundaries of the moral are an open question; indeed, the very appropriateness of a single term here can be an issue.

We could easily decide—a view which I would defend—that the universal attribution of moral personality is valid, and lays obligations on us that we cannot ignore; but that there are also other moral ideals and goals—e.g., of less than universal solidarity, or of personal excellence—that cannot be easily coordinated with universalism, and can even enter into conflict with it. To decide *a priori* what the bounds of the moral are is just to obfuscate the question whether and to what degree this is so, and to make it incapable of being coherently stated.

II

I should like to concentrate here on a particular aspect of moral language and moral thinking that gets obscured by the epistemologically motivated reduction and homogenization of the moral we find in both utilitarianism and formalism. These are the qualitative distinctions we make between different actions, or feelings, or modes of life, as being in some way morally higher or lower, noble or base, admirable or contemptible. It is these languages of qualitative contrast that get marginalized, or even expunged altogether, by the utilitarian or formalist reductions. I want to argue, in opposition to this, that they are central to our moral thinking and ineradicable from it.

Some example might help here of such qualitative distinctions commonly subscribed to. For some people, personal integrity is a central goal: what matters is that one's life express what one truly senses as important, admirable, noble, desirable. The temptations to be avoided here are those of conformity to established standards that are not really one's own, or of dishonesty with oneself concerning one's own convictions or affinities. The chief threat to integrity is a lack of courage in face of social demands, or in face of what one has been brought up to see as the unthinkable. This is a recognizable type of moral outlook.

We can see a very different type if we look at a Christian model of *agapê*, such as one sees, for example, with Mother Theresa. The aim here is to associate oneself with, to become in a sense a channel of, God's love for men, which is seen as having the power to heal the divisions among men and take them beyond what they usually recognize as the limits to their love for one another. The obstacles to this are seen as various forms of refusal of God's *agapê*, either through a sense of self-sufficiency, or despair. This outlook understands human moral transformation in terms of images of healing, such as one sees in the New Testament narratives.

A very different, yet historically related, modern view centers on the goal of liberation. This sees the dignity of human beings as consisting in their directing their own lives, in their deciding for themselves the conditions of their own existence, as against falling prey to the domination of others, or to impersonal natural or social mechanisms which they fail to understand, and therefore cannot control or transform. The inner obstacles to this are ignorance, or lack of courage, or falsely self-depreciatory images of the self; but these are connected with external obstacles in many variants of modern liberation theory. This is particularly so of the last: self-depreciating images are seen as inculcated by others who benefit from the structures of domination in which subject groups are encased. Fanon has made this kind of analysis very familiar for the colonial context, and his categories have been transposed to a host of others, especially to that of women's liberation.

Let us look briefly at one other such language, that of rationality, as this is understood, for instance, by utilitarians. We have here the model of a human being who is clairvoyant about his goals, and capable of objectifying and understanding himself and the world that surrounds him. He can get a clear grasp of the mechanisms at work in self and world, and can thus direct his action clear-sightedly and deliberately. To do this he must resist the temptations offered by the various comforting illusions that make the self or the world so much more attractive than they really are in the cold light of science. He must fight off the self-indulgence that consists of giving oneself a picture of the world that is satisfying to one's *amour propre*, or one's sense of drama, or one's craving for meaning, or any of these metaphysical temptations. The rational man has the courage of austerity; he is marked by his ability to adopt an objective stance to things.

I introduce these four examples to give some intuitive basis to an otherwise abstract discussion. But I did not have to look far. These moral outlooks are very familiar to us from our own moral reasoning and sensibility, or those of people we know (and sometimes of people we love to hate). I am sure that some of the details of my formulation will jar with just about any reader. But that is not surprising. Formulating these views is a very difficult job. Like all self-interpretive activity, it is open to potentially endless dispute. This is, indeed, part of the reason why these outlooks have fallen under the epistemological cloud and therefore have tended to be excluded from the formalist and utilitarian meta-ethical pictures. But one or some of these, or others like them, underlie much of our deciding what to do, our moral admirations, condemnations, contempts, and so on.

Another thing that is evident straight off is how different the examples are from each other. I mean not only are they based on very different pictures of man, human possibility and the human condition; but they frequently lead to incompatible prescriptions in our lives—incompatible with each other, and also with the utilitarian calculation that unquestionably plays some part in the moral reasoning of most moderns. (The modern dispute about utilitarianism is not about whether it occupies some of the space of moral reason, but whether it fills the whole space.) It could be doubted whether giving comfort to the dying is the highest util-producing activity possible in contemporary Calcutta. But, from another point of view, the dying are in an extremity that makes calculation irrelevant.

But, nevertheless, many people find themselves drawn by more than one of these views, and are faced with the job of somehow making them compatible in their lives. This is where the question can arise whether all the demands we might consider moral and recognize as valid can be coherently combined. This question naturally raises another one, whether it is really appropriate to talk of a single type of demand called "moral." This is the more problematic when we reflect that we all recognize other qualitative distinctions we would not class right off as moral, or perhaps even on reflection would refuse the title to; for instance, being 'cool' or being macho, or others of this sort. So the question of drawing a line around the moral becomes a difficult one. And it may even come to appear as an uninteresting verbal one in the last analysis. The really important question may turn out to be how we combine in our lives two or three or four difficult goals, or virtues, or standards, which we feel we cannot repudiate but which seem to demand incompatible things of us. Which of these we dignify with the term 'moral', or whether we so designate all of them, may end up appearing a mere question of labeling—unless, that is, it confuses us into thinking there is in principle only one set of goals or standards that can be accorded ultimate significance. In certain contexts, it might help clarity to drop the word, at least provisionally, until we get over the baleful effects of reductive thinking on our meta-ethical views.

III

Before going on to examine further the implications of this for social theory, it will be useful to look more closely at these languages of qualitative contrast. What I am gesturing at with the term 'qualitative contrast' is the sense that one way of acting or living is higher than others, or in other cases that a certain way of living is debased. It is essential to the kind of moral view just exemplified that this kind of contrast be made. Some ways of living and acting have a special status, they stand out above others; while, in certain cases, others are seen as despicable.

This contrast is essential. We should be distorting these views if we tried to construe the difference between higher and lower as a mere difference of degree in the attainment of some common good, as utilitarian theory would have us do. Integrity, charity, liberation, and the like stand out as worthy of pursuit in a special way, incommensurable with other goals we might have, such as the pursuit of wealth, or comfort, or the approval of those who surround us. Indeed, for those who hold to such views of the good, we ought to be ready to sacrifice some of these lesser goods for the higher.

Moreover, the agent's being sensible of this distinction is an essential condition of his realizing the good concerned. For our recognizing the higher value of integrity, or charity, or rationality, and so on, is an essential part of our being rational, charitable, having integrity and so on. True, we recognize such a thing as unconscious virtue, which we ascribe to people who are good but quite without a sense of their superiority over others. This lack of self-congratulation we consider itself to be a virtue, as the deprecatory expression 'holier than thou' implies. But the absence of self-conscious superiority does not mean an absence of sensitivity to the higher goal. The saintly person is not 'holier than thou', but he is necessarily moved by the demands of charity in a special way, moved to recognize that there is something special here; in this particular case, he has a sense of awe before the power of God, or of wonder at the greatness of man as seen by God. And a similar point could be made for the other examples: an essential part of achieving liberation is sensing the greatness of liberated humanity—and consequently being sensible of the degradation of the dominated victim; an essential part of integrity is the recognition that it represents a demand on us of a special type, and so on.

Another way of making this point is to say that motivation enters into the definition of the higher activity or way of being in all these cases. The aspiration to achieve one of these goods is also an aspiration to be motivated in a certain way, or to have certain motivations win out in oneself. This is why we can speak of these aspirations as involving second-order motivations (as I have tried to do elsewhere, following Harry Frankfurt).[1]

We can articulate the contrast or incommensurability involved here in a number of ways. One way of saying it is via the notion of obligation. Ordinary goals, for instance for wealth or comfort, are goals that a person may have or not. If he does, then there are a number of instrumental things that he ought to do—hypothetically, in Kant's sense—to attain them. But if he lacks these goals, no criticism attaches to him for neglecting to pursue them. By contrast, it is in the nature of what I have called a higher goal that it is one we *should* have. Those who lack them are not just free of some additional instrumental obligations that weigh with the rest of us; they are open to censure. For those who subscribe to integrity, the person who cares not a whit for it is morally insensitive, or lacks courage, or is morally coarse. A higher goal is one from which one cannot detach oneself just by expressing a sincere lack of interest, because to recognize something as a higher goal is to recognize it as one that men ought to follow. This is, of course, the distinction that Kant drew between hypothetical and categorical imperatives.

Or rather, I should say that it is a closely related distinction. For Kant the boundary between the categorical and the hypothetical was meant to mark the line between the moral and the non-moral. But there are languages of qualitative contrast that we are quite ready to recognize as non-moral, even bearing in mind the fuzzy boundaries of the domain that this word picks out. We often apply such languages in what we call the aesthetic domain. If I see something especially magnificent in the music of Mozart as against some of his humdrum contemporaries, then I will judge you as insensitive in some way if you rate them on a par. The word 'insensitive' here is a word of deprecation. This is a difference one *should* be sensible of, in my view.

Of course, I would not speak of this as a *moral* condemnation, but condemnation it would be nevertheless. I do not react to this difference as I do to differences of taste, which correspond to no such incommensurability, for example whether you like the symphonies of Bruckner or not.

The criterion for incommensurability I am offering here is therefore not the same as Kant's for the moral. But, as I have already indicated, I do not think that a line can be drawn neatly and unproblematically around the moral. Of course, if someone professes to see no distinction between his concern for the flowers in his garden and that for the lives of refugees faced with starvation, so that he proposes to act in both cases just to the degree that he feels interested at the time, we are rightly alarmed, and take this more seriously than the failure to appreciate Mozart over Boieldieu. We feel more justified in intervening here, and remonstrating with him, even forcing him to act, or subjecting him to some social or other penalty for non-acting. We feel, in other words, that the obligation here is 'categorical' in the stronger sense that licenses our intervention even against his will.

But the boundary here is necessarily fuzzier and very much open to dispute. Whereas the weaker sense of 'categorical' that could apply to the distinction I am drawing above turns on the question whether a declared lack of interest in a certain good simply neutralizes it for you, or whether on the contrary, it redounds to your condemnation, shows you up as being blind, or coarse, or insensitive, or cowardly, or brutalized, too self-absorbed, or in some way subject to censure. This, I would like to argue, is a relatively firm boundary—although the languages in which we draw it, each of us according to his own outlook, are very much in dispute between us—but it does not mark the moral from the non-moral. The languages of qualitative contrast embrace more than the moral.

A second way in which we can articulate this contrast is through the notions of admiration and contempt. People who exhibit higher goods to a signal degree are objects of our admiration; and those who fail are sometimes objects of our contempt. These emotions are bound up with our sense that there are higher and lower goals and activities. I would like to claim that if we did not mark these contrasts, if we did not have a sense of the incommensurably higher, then these emotions would have no place in our lives.

In the end, we can find ourselves experiencing very mitigated admiration for feats we barely consider worthy of special consideration. I have a sort of admiration, mixed with tolerant amusement, for the person who has just downed twenty-two pancakes to win the eating contest. But that is because I see some kind of victory over self in the name of something which resembles a self-ideal. He wanted to be first, and he was willing to go to great lengths for it; and that goal at least stands out from that of being an average person, living just like everybody else. It is only because I see the feat in these terms, which are rather a caricature than an example of a higher aspiration, that the feeling of admiration can get even a mitigated grip on this case.

But we also find ourselves admiring people where there is no victory over self, where there is no recognizable achievement in the ordinary sense at all. We can admire people who are very beautiful, or have a striking grace or personal style, even though we may recognize that it is none of their doing. But we do so only because the aura of something higher, some magic quality contrasting with the ordinary and the humdrum, surrounds such people. The reasons why this should be so go very deep into the human psyche and the human form of life, and we find them hard to understand, but a special aura of this kind contributes often to what we call the 'charisma' of public figures (a word that conveys just this sense of a gift from on high, something we have not done for ourselves). Those who consider this kind of aura irrational, who resist the sense of something higher here, are precisely those who refuse their admiration to the 'charismatic', or to 'beautiful people'. Or at least they are those who claim to do so; for sometimes one senses that they are fighting a losing battle with their own feelings on this score.

In this way, admiration and contempt are bound up with our sense of the qualitative contrasts in our lives, of there being modes of life, activities, feeling, qualities, that are incommensurably higher. Where these are moral qualities, we can speak of moral admiration. These emotions provide one of the ways that we articulate this sense of the higher in our lives.

A third way we do so is in the experience we can call very loosely 'awe'. I mentioned above that a sensibility to the higher good is part of its realization. The sense that a good occupies a special place, that it is higher, is the sense that it somehow commands our respect. This is why there is a dimension of human emotion, which we can all recognize, and which Kant again tried to articulate with his notion of the *Achtung* which we feel before the moral law. Once again, I propose to extend a Kantian analysis beyond the case of the unambiguously moral. Just as our admiration for the virtuosi of some higher goal extends to other contexts than the moral, so our sense of the incommensurable value of the goal does. For this sense, as a term of art translating Kant's *Achtung*, I propose 'awe'.

IV

It is this dimension of qualitative contrast in our moral sensibility and thinking that gets short shrift in the utilitarian and formalist reductions. One of the main points of utilitarianism was to do away with this and reduce all judgments of ethical preference to quantitative form in a single dimension. In a different way, formalisms manage to reduce these contrasts to irrelevance; ethical reasoning can finesse them through a procedure of determining what is right that takes no account of them, or allows them in merely as subjective preferences, and therefore is not called upon to judge their substantive merits.

Now my argument was that a big part of the motivation for both reductions was epistemological; that they seemed to allow for a mode of ethical reasoning that fitted widely held canons of validation. We can now see better why this was so.

It is partly because these languages of contrast are so hard to validate once they come into dispute. If someone does not see that integrity is a goal one should seek, or that liberation is alone consistent with the dignity of man, how do you go about demonstrating this? But this is not the whole story. That argument is difficult in this area does not mean that it is impossible, that there is no such thing as a rationally induced conviction. That so many who have opted for utilitarianism or formalism can jump to this latter conclusion as far as higher goals are concerned is due to two underlying considerations that are rarely spelled out.

The first is that the ethical views couched in languages of contrast seem to differ in contestability from those that underlie utilitarianism and formalism. No one seems very ready to challenge the view that, other things being equal, it is better that men's desires be fulfilled than that they be frustrated, that they be happy rather than miserable. Counter-utilitarians challenge rather whether the entire range of ethical issues can be put in these terms, whether there are not other goals that can conflict with happiness, whose claims have to be adjudicated together with utility. Again, as we saw, formalistic theories get their plausibility from the fact that they are grounded on certain moral intuitions which are almost unchallenged in modern society, based as they are in certain preconditions of moral discourse itself combined with a thesis about the racial homogeneity of humanity, which it is pretty hard to challenge in a scientific, deparochialized and historically sensitive contemporary culture.

The premises of these forms of moral reasoning can therefore easily appear to be of a quite different provenance from those that deal with qualitative contrast. Against these latter, we can allow ourselves to slip into ethical skepticism while exempting the former, either on the grounds that they are somehow self-evident, or even that they are not based on ethical insight at all but on something firmer, like the logic of our language.

But, in fact, these claims to firmer foundation are illusory. What is really going on is that some forms of ethical reasoning are being privileged over others because in our civilization they come less into dispute or look easier to defend. This has all the rationality of the drunk in the well-known story (which the reader may forgive me for repeating) who was looking for his latch key late one night under a street lamp. A passerby, trying to be helpful, asked him where he had dropped it. "Over there," answered the drunk, pointing to a dark corner. "Then why are you looking for it here?" "Because there's so much more light here," replied the drunk.

In a similar way, we have been maneuvred into a restrictive definition of ethics, which takes account of some of the goods we seek, for example utility, and universal respect for moral personality, while excluding others, viz. the virtues and goals like those mentioned above, largely on the grounds that the former are subject to less embarrassing dispute.

This may seem a little too dismissive of the traditions of reductive meta-ethics, because in fact there is a second range of considerations that have motivated the differential treatment of languages of contrast. That is that they seem to have no place in a naturalist account of man.

The goal of a naturalist account of man comes in the wake of the scientific revolution of the seventeenth century. It is the aim of explaining human beings like other objects in nature. But a part of the practice of the successful natural science of modern times consists in its eschewing what we might call subject-related properties. By this I mean properties that things bear only insofar as they are objects of experience of subjects. The classical example of these in the seventeenth-century discussion were the so-called secondary properties, like color or felt temperature. The aim was to account for what happens invoking only properties that the things concerned possessed absolutely, as one might put it (following Bernard Williams' use in his discussion of a related issue),[2] properties, that is, that they would possess even if (even when) they are not experienced.

How can one follow this practice in a science of animate beings, that is of beings who exhibit motivated action? Presumably, one can understand motivated action in terms of a tendency of the beings concerned to realize certain consummations in certain conditions. As long as these consummations are characterized absolutely, the demands of a naturalistic science of animate subjects seem to be met. Hence we get a demand which is widely recognized as a requirement of materialism in modern times: that we explain human behavior in terms of goals whose consummations can be characterized in physical terms. This is what, for example, for many Marxists establishes the claim that their theory is a materialist one: that it identifies as predominant the aim of getting the means of life (which presumably could ultimately be defined in physical terms).

But without being taken as far as materialism, the requirement of absoluteness can serve to discredit languages of qualitative contrast. For these designate different possible human activities and modes of life as higher and lower. And these are plainly subject-related notions. In the context of a naturalist explanation, one goal may be identified as more strongly desired than others, for example if the subject concerned gave it higher priority. But there is no place for the notion of a higher goal, which in the very logic of the contrast must be distinguishable from the strongest motive—else the term would have no function in moral discourse at all.

For those who cleave to naturalism, the languages of contrast must be suspect. They correspond to nothing in reality, which we may interpret as what we need to invoke in our bottom line explanatory language of human behavior. They appear, therefore, to designate purely subjective factors. They express the way we feel, not the way things are. But then this gives a rational basis to ethical skepticism, to the view that there is no rational way of arbitrating between rival outlooks expressed in such languages of contrast. This seems to give a strong intellectual basis to downgrading ethical reasoning, at least that cast in contrastive languages. For those who are impressed by naturalist considerations, but still want to salvage some valid form of ethical reasoning, utilitarianism or formalism seem attractive.[3]

But this ground for skepticism is faulty. It leaves undefended the premise that our accounts of man should be naturalistic in just this sense. Purging subject-related properties makes a lot of sense in an account of inanimate things. It cannot be taken as *a priori* self-evident that it will be similarly helpful in an account of human beings. We would have to establish *a posteriori* that such an absolute account of human life was possible and illuminating before we could draw conclusions about what is real, or know even how to set up the distinction objective/subjective.

In fact, though there is no place to examine the record here, it does not seem that absolute accounts offer a very plausible avenue. Put in other terms, it may well be that much of human behavior will be understandable and explicable only in a language that characterizes motivation in a fashion that marks qualitative contrasts and is therefore not morally neutral. In this it will be like what we recognize today as the best example of clairvoyant self-understanding by those who have most conquered their illusions. If a science that describes consummations in exclusively physical terms cannot fill the bill, and if we, therefore, have to take account of the significances of things for agents, how can we know *a priori* that the best account available of such significances will not require some use of languages of qualitative contrast? It seems to me rather likely that it will.

In the absence of some demonstration of the validity of naturalism of this kind, the utilitarian and formalist reductions are clearly arbitrary. For they have little foundation in our ethical sensibility and practice. Even utilitarians and formalists make use of languages of contrast in their lives, decisions, admirations, and contempts. One can see that in my fourth example above. 'Rational' as used by most utilitarians is a term in a qualitative contrast; it is the basis of moral admiration and contempt; it is a goal worthy of respect. The fact that it finds no place in their own meta-theory says a lot about the value of this theory.

V

Once we get over the epistemologically induced reductions of the ethical, the problems of moral reasoning appear in a quite different light. I just have space here to mention some of the consequences for social theory.

An obviously relevant point is that we come to recognize that the ethical is not a homogeneous domain, with a single kind of good, based on a single kind of consideration. We have already noted at least three kinds of consideration that are morally relevant. The first is captured by the notion of utility, that what produces happiness is preferable to its opposite. The second is what I called the universal attribution of moral personality. These can combine to produce modern utilitarianism, as a theory that lays on us the obligation of universal benevolence in the form of the maximization of general happiness. But the second principle is also the source of moral imperatives that conflict with utilitarianism; and this in notorious ways, for example demanding that we put equal distribution before the goal of maximizing utility. Then, thirdly, there are the variety of goals that we express in languages of qualitative contrast, which are, of course, very different from each other.

The goods we recognize as moral which means at least as laying the most important demands on us, overriding all lesser ones, are therefore diverse. But the habit of treating the moral as a single domain is not just gratuitous or based on a mere mistake. The domain of ultimately important goods has a sort of prescriptive unity. Each of us has to answer all these demands in the course of a single life, and this means that we have to find some way of assessing their relative validity, or putting them in an order of priority. A single coherent order of goods is rather like an idea of reason in the Kantian sense, something we always try to define without ever managing to achieve it definitively.

The plurality of goods ought to be evident in modern society, if we could set aside the blinkers that our reductive meta-ethics imposes on us. Certainly we reason often about social policies in terms of utility. And we also take into account considerations of just distribution, as also of the rights of individuals, which are grounded on the principle of universal moral personality. But there are also considerations of the contrastive kind that play an important role. For instance, modern Western societies are all citizen republics, or strive to be. Their conception of the good is partly shaped by the tradition of civic humanism. The citizen republic is to be valued not just as a guarantee of general utility, or as a bulwark of rights. It may even endanger these in certain circumstances. We value it also because we generally hold that the form of life in which men govern themselves, and decide their own fate through common deliberation, is higher than one in which they live as subjects of even an enlightened despotism.

But just as the demands of utility and rights may diverge, so those of the citizen republic may conflict with both. For instance, the citizen republic requires a certain sense of community, and what is needed to foster this may go against the demands of maximum utility. Or it may threaten to enter into conflict with some of the rights of minorities. And there is a standing divergence between the demands of international equality and those of democratic self-rule in advanced Western societies. Democratic electorates in these societies will probably never agree to the amount of redistribution consistent with redressing the past wrongs of imperialism, or meeting in full the present requirements of universal human solidarity. Only despotic regimes, like Cuba and the DDR, bleed themselves for the Third World—not necessarily for the best of motives, of course.

It ought to be clear from this that no single-consideration procedure, be it that of utilitarianism, or a theory of justice based on an ideal contract, can do justice to the diversity of goods we have to weigh together in normative political thinking. Such one-factor functions appeal to our epistemological squeamishness, which makes us dislike contrastive languages. And they may even have a positive appeal of the same kind in so far as they seem to offer the prospect of exact calculation of policy, through counting utils, or rational-choice theory. But this kind of exactness is bogus. In fact, they only have a semblance of validity through leaving out all that they cannot calculate.

The other strong support for single-factor theory comes from the radical side. Radical theories, such as Marxism, offer an answer to the demand for a unified theory—which we saw is a demand we cannot totally repudiate, at least as a goal—by revolutionary doctrines that propose sweeping away the plurality of goods now recognized in the name of one central goal that will subsume what is valuable in all of them. Thus the classless society will allegedly make unnecessary the entrenching of individual rights, or the safeguarding of 'bourgeois' civic spirit. It will provide an unconstrained community, in which the good of each will be the goal of all, and maximum utility a by-product of free collaboration, and so on.

But Marxism at least does not make the error of holding that all the goods we now seek can be reduced to some common coinage. At least it proposes to bring about unity through radical change. In the absence of such change, commensurability cannot be achieved. Indeed, it is of the essence of languages of contrast that they show our goals to be incommensurable.

If this is so, then there is no way of saving single-consideration theory however we try to reformulate it. Some might hope for instance to salvage at least the consequentialism out of utilitarianism: we would give up the narrow view that all that is worth valuing is states of happiness, but we would still try to evaluate different courses of action purely in terms of their consequences, hoping to state everything worth considering in our consequence-descriptions.

But unless the term 'consequentialism' is to be taken so widely as to lose all meaning, it has to contrast with other forms of deliberation, for instance, one in which it matters whether I act in a certain way and not just what consequences I bring about. To put it differently, a non-consequentialist deliberation is one that values actions in ways that cannot be understood as a function of the consequences they have. Let us call this valuing actions intrinsically.

The attempt to reconstruct ethical and political thinking in consequentialist terms would, in fact, be another *a priori* fiat determining the domain of the good on irrelevant grounds. Not as narrow as utilitarianism, perhaps, it would still legislate certain goods out of existence. For some languages of contrast involve intrinsic evaluation: the language of integrity, for instance. I have integrity to the degree to which my actions and statements are true expressions of what is really of importance to me. It is their intrinsic character as revelations or expressions that count, not their consequences. And the same objection would hold against a consequentialist social choice function. We may value our society for the way it makes integrity possible in its public life and social relations, or criticize a society for making it impossible. It may also be the case, of course, that we value the integrity for its effects on stability, or republican institutions, or something of the kind. But this cannot be all. It will certainly matter to us intrinsically as well as consequentially.

A consequentialist theory, even one which had gone beyond utilitarianism, would still be a Procrustes bed. It would once again make it impossible for us to get all the facets of our moral and political thinking in focus. And it might induce us to think that we could ignore certain demands because they fail to fit into our favored mode of calculation. A meta-ethics of this kind stultifies thought.

Our political thinking needs to free itself both from the dead hand of the epistemological tradition, and the utopian monism of radical thought, in order to take account of the real diversity of goods that we recognize.

NOTES

1. Cf. Volume I chapter I of my *Philosophical Papers* and Harry Frankfurt, "Freedom of the will and the concept of a person," *Journal of Philosophy* 67: 1 (1971), 5–20.

2. Bernard Williams, *Descartes: The Project of Pure Enquiry* (Harmondsworth, 1978).

3. For a naturalist attack on the objectivity of value, see J. L. Mackie, *Ethics: Inventing Right and Wrong* (Harmondsworth, 1977).

Chapter 11

Epistemological Crises, Dramatic Narrative and the Philosophy of Science

ALASDAIR MACINTYRE

I

What is an epistemological crisis? Consider, first, the situation of ordinary agents who are thrown into such crises. Someone who has believed that he was highly valued by his employers and colleagues is suddenly fired; someone proposed for membership of a club whose members were all, so he believed, close friends is blackballed. Or someone falls in love and needs to know what the loved one *really* feels; someone falls out of love and needs to know how he or she can possibly have been so mistaken in the other. For all such persons the relationship of *seems* to *is* becomes crucial. It is in such situations that ordinary agents who have never learned anything about academic philosophy are apt to rediscover for themselves versions of the other-minds problem and the problem of the justification of induction. They discover, that is, that there is a problem about the rational justification of inferences from premises about the behavior of other people to conclusions about their thoughts, feelings, and attitudes and of inferences from premises about how individuals have acted in the past to conclusions expressed as generalizations about their behavior—generalizations that would enable us to make reasonably reliable predications about their future behavior. What they took to be evidence pointing unambiguously in some one direction now turns out to have been equally susceptible of rival interpretations. Such a discovery is often paralyzing, and were we, all of us, all of the time to have to reckon with the multiplicity of possible interpretations open to us, social life as we know it could scarcely continue. For social life is sustained by the assumption that we are, by and large, able to construe each others' behavior—that error, deception, self-deception, irony and ambiguity, although omnipresent in social life, are not so pervasive as to render reliable reasoning and reasonable action impossible. But can this assumption in any way be vindicated?

Consider what it is to share a culture. It is to share schemata that are at one and the same time constitutive of and normative for intelligible action by myself and are also means for my interpretations of the actions of others. My ability to understand what you are doing and my ability to act intelligibly (both to myself and to others) are one and the same ability. It is true that I cannot master these schemata without also acquiring the means to deceive, to make more or less elaborate jokes, to exercise irony and utilize ambiguity, but it is also, and even more importantly, true that my ability to conduct any successful transactions depends on my presenting myself to most people most of the time in unambiguous, unironical, undeceiving, intelligible ways. It is these schemata that enable inferences to be made from premises about past behavior to conclusions about future behavior and present inner attitudes. They are not, of course, empirical generalizations; they are prescriptions for interpretation. But while it is they that normally preserve us from the pressure of the other-minds problem and the problem of induction, it is precisely they that can in certain circumstances thrust those very problems upon us.

For it is not only that an individual may rely on the schemata that have hitherto informed all his interpretations of social life and find that he or she has been led into radical error or deception, so that for the first time the schemata are put in question—perhaps for the first time they also in this moment become visible to the individual who employs them—but it is also the case that the individual may come to recognize the possibility of systematically different possibilities of interpretation, of the existence of alternative and rival schemata, which yield mutually incompatible accounts of what is going on around him. Just this is the form of epistemological crisis encountered by ordinary agents, and it is striking that there is not a single account of it anywhere in the literature of academic philosophy. Perhaps this is an important symptom of the condition of that discipline. But happily we do possess one classic study of such crises. It is Shakespeare's *Hamlet*.

Hamlet arrives back from Wittenberg with too many schemata available for interpreting the events at Elsinore of which already he is a part. There is the revenge schema of the Norse sagas; there is the renaissance courtier's schema; there is a Machiavellian schema about competition for power. But he not only has the problem of which schema to apply; he also has the other ordinary agents' problem: whom now to believe? His mother? Rosencrantz and Guildenstern? His father's ghost? Until he has adopted some schema he does not know what to treat as evidence; until he knows what to treat as evidence he cannot tell which schema to adopt. Trapped in this epistemological circularity the general form of his problem is "what is going on here?" Thus Hamlet's problem is close to that of the literary critics who have asked, "What is going on in Hamlet?" And it is close to that of directors who have asked "What should be cut and what should be included in my production so that the audience may understand what is going on in *Hamlet?*"

The resemblance between Hamlet's problem and that of the critics and directors is worth noticing; for it suggests that both are asking a question that could equally well be formulated as "what is going on in *Hamlet?*" or "how ought the narrative of these events to be constructed?" Hamlet's problems arise because the dramatic narrative of his family and of the kingdom of Denmark through which he identified his own place in society and his relationships to others has been disrupted by radical interpretative doubts. His task is to reconstitute, to rewrite that narrative, reversing his understanding of past events in the light of present responses to his probing. This probing is informed by two ideals, truth and intelligibility, and the pursuit of both is not always easily coherent. The discovery of an hitherto unsuspected truth is just what may disrupt an hitherto intelligible account. And, of course, while Hamlet tries to discover a true and intelligible narrative of the events involving his parents and Claudius, Gertrude and Claudius are trying to discover a true and intelligible narrative of Hamlet's investigation. To be unable to render oneself intelligible is to risk being taken to be mad—is, if carried far enough, to be mad. And madness or death may always be the outcomes that prevent the resolution of an epistemological crisis, for an epistemological crisis is always a crisis in human relationships.

When an epistemological crisis is resolved, it is by the construction of a new narrative, which enables the agent to understand *both* how he or she could intelligibly have held his or her original beliefs *and* how he or she could have been so drastically misled by them. The narrative in terms of which he or she at first understood and ordered experiences is itself made into the subject of an enlarged narrative. The agent has come to understand how the criteria of truth and understanding must be reformulated. He has had to become epistemologically self-conscious and at a certain point he may have come to acknowledge two conclusions: the first is that his new forms of understanding may themselves, in turn, come to be put in question at any time; the second is that, because in such crises the criteria of truth, intelligibility and rationality may always themselves be put in question—as they are in *Hamlet*—we are never in a position to claim that now we possess the truth or now we are fully rational. The most that we can claim is that this is the best account anyone has been able to give so far, and that our beliefs about what the marks of 'a best account so far' are will themselves change in what are, at present, unpredictable ways.

Philosophers have often been prepared to acknowledge this historical character in respect of scientific theories; but they have usually wanted to exempt their own thinking from the same historicity. So, of course, have writers of dramatic narrative; *Hamlet* is unique among plays in its openness to reinterpretation. Consider, by contrast, Jane Austen's procedure in *Emma*. Emma insists on viewing her protege, Harriet, as a character in an eighteenth-century romance. She endows her, deceiving both herself and Harriet, with the conventional qualities of the heroine of such a romance. Harriet's parentage is not known; Emma converts her into the foundling heroine of aristocratic birth so common in such romances. And she designs for Harriet precisely the happy ending of such a romance, marriage to a superior being. By the end of *Emma* Jane Austen has provided Emma with some understanding of what it was in herself that had led her not to perceive the untruthfulness of her interpretation of the world in terms of romance. *Emma* has become a narrative about narrative. But Emma, although she experiences moral reversal, has only a minor epistemological crisis, if only because the standpoint which she now, through the agency of Mr. Knightly, has come to adopt, is presented as though it were one from which *the* world as it is can be viewed. False interpretation has been replaced not by a more adequate interpretation, which itself, in turn, may one day be transcended, but simply by the truth. We, of course, can see that Jane Austen is merely replacing one interpretation by another, but Jane Austen herself fails to recognise this and so has to deprive Emma of this recognition too.

Philosophers have customarily been Emmas and not Hamlets, except that in one respect they have often been even less perceptive than Emma. For Emma it becomes clear that her movement toward the truth necessarily had a moral dimension. Neither Plato nor Kant would have demurred. But the history of epistemology, like the history of ethics itself, is usually written as though it were not a moral narrative, that is, in fact as though it were not a narrative.

For narrative requires an evaluative framework in which good or bad character helps to produce unfortunate or happy outcomes.

One further aspect of narratives and their role in epistemological crises remains to be noticed. I have suggested that epistemological progress consists in the construction and reconstruction of more adequate narratives and forms of narrative and that epistemological crises are occasions for such reconstruction. But if this were really the case then two kinds of questions would need to be answered. The first would be of the form: how does this progress begin? What are the narratives from which we set out? The second would be of the form: how comes it, then, that narrative is not only given so little place by thinkers from Descartes onwards, but has so often before and after been treated as a merely aesthetic form? The answers to these questions are not entirely unconnected.

We begin from myth, not only from the myths of primitive peoples, but from those myths or fairy stories that are essential to a well-ordered childhood. Bruno Bettelheim has written "Before and well into the oedipal period (roughly, the ages between three and six or seven), the child's experience of the world is chaotic. . . . During and because of the oedipal struggles, the outside world comes to hold more meaning for the child and he begins to try to make some sense of it. . . . As a child listens to a fairy tale, he gets ideas about how he may create order out of the chaos that is his inner life."[1] It is from fairy tales, so Bettelheim argues, that the child learns how to engage himself with and perceive an order in social reality; and the child who is deprived of the right kind of fairy tale at the right age later on is apt to have to adopt strategies to evade a reality he has not learned how to interpret or to handle.

"The child asks himself, 'Who am I? Where did I come from? How did the world come into being? Who created man and all the animals? What is the purpose of life?'. . . . He wonders who or what brings adversity upon him and what can protect him against it. Are there benevolent powers in addition to his parents? *Are* his parents benevolent powers? How should he form himself, and why? Is there hope for him, though he may have done wrong? Why did all this happen to him? What will it mean to his future?"[2] The child originally requires answers that are true to his own experience, but of course the child comes to learn the inadequacy of that experience. Bettelheim points out that the young child told by adults that the world is a globe suspended in space and spinning at incredible speeds may feel bound to repeat what they say, but would find it immensely more plausible to be told that the earth is held up by a giant. But in time the young child learns that what the adults told him is indeed true. And such a child may well become a Descartes, one who feels that all narratives are misleading fables when compared with what he now takes to be the solid truth of physics.

Yet to raise the question of truth need not entail rejecting myth or story as the appropriate and perhaps the only appropriate form in which certain truths can be told. The child may become not a Descartes, but a Vico or a Hamann who writes a story about how he had to escape from the hold that the stories of his childhood and the stories of the childhood of the human race originally had upon him in order to discover how stories can be true stories. Such a narrative will be itself a history of epistemological transitions and this narrative may well be brought to a point at which questions are thrust upon the narrator which make it impossible for him to continue to use it as an instrument of interpretation. Just this, of course, happens to Descartes, who having abjured history as a means to truth, recounts to us his own history as the medium through which the search for truth is to be carried on. For Descartes and for others this moment is when an epistemological crisis occurs. And all those questions the child has asked of the teller of fairy tales arise in a new adult form. Philosophy is now set the same task that had once been set for myth.

II

Descartes's description of his own epistemological crisis has, of course, been uniquely influential. Yet Descartes radically misdescribes his own crisis and thus has proved a highly misleading guide to the nature of epistemological crises in general. The agent who is plunged into an epistemological crisis knows something very important: that a schema of interpretation he has trusted so far has broken down irremediably in certain highly specific ways. So it is with Hamlet. Descartes, however, starts from the assumption that he knows nothing whatsoever until he can discover a presuppositionless first principle on which all else can be founded. Hamlet's doubts are formulated against a background of what he takes to be—rightly—well-founded beliefs; Descartes's doubt is intended to lack any such background. It is to be contextless doubt. Hence also that tradition of philosophical teaching arises that presupposes Cartesian doubts can be entertained by anyone at any place or time. But, of course, someone who really believed that he knew nothing would not even know how to begin on a course of radical doubt; for he would have no conception of what his task might be, of what it would be to settle his doubts and to acquire well-founded beliefs. Conversely, anyone who knows enough to know *that* does indeed possess a set of extensive epistemological beliefs, which he is not putting in doubt at all.

Descartes's failure is complex. First of all, he does not recognise that among the features of the universe that he is not putting in doubt is his own capacity not only to use the French and the Latin languages, but even to express the same thought in both languages; and as a consequence he does not put in doubt what he has inherited in and with these languages, namely, a way of ordering both thought and the world expressed in a set of meanings. These meanings have a history; seventeenth-century Latin bears the marks of having been the language of scholasticism, just as scholasticism was itself marked by the influence of twelfth-and thirteenth-century Latin. It was perhaps because the presence of his languages was invisible to the Descartes of the *Discours* and the *Meditationes* that he did not notice either what Gilson pointed out in detail, how much of what he took to be the spontaneous reflections of his own mind was, in fact, a repetition of sentences and phrases from his school textbooks. Even the *Cogito* is to be found in Saint Augustine.

What thus goes unrecognised by Descartes is the presence not only of languages, but of a tradition—a tradition that he took himself to have successfully disowned. It was from this tradition that he inherited his epistemological ideals. For at the core of this tradition was a conception of knowledge as analogous to vision: the mind's eye beholds its objects by the light of reason. At the same time this tradition wishes to contrast sharply knowledge and sense-experience, including visual experience. Hence there is metaphorical incoherence at the heart of every theory of knowledge in this Platonic and Augustinian tradition, an incoherence that Descartes unconsciously reproduces. Thus Descartes also cannot recognise that he is responding not only to the timeless demands of skepticism, but to a highly specific crisis in one particular social and intellectual tradition.

One of the signs that a tradition is in crisis is that its accustomed ways for relating *seems* and *is* begining to break down. Thus the pressures of skepticism become more urgent and attempts to do the impossible, to refute skepticism once and for all, become projects of central importance to the culture and not mere private academic enterprises. Just this happens in the late middle ages and the sixteenth century. Inherited modes of ordering experience reveal too many rival possibilities of interpretation. It is no accident that there are a multiplicity of rival interpretations of both the thought and the lives of such figures as Luther and Machiavelli in a way that there are not for such equally rich and complex figures as Abelard and Aquinas. Ambiguity, the possibility of alternative interpretations, becomes a central feature of human character and activity. *Hamlet* is Shakespeare's brilliant mirror to the age, and the difference between Shakespeare's account of epistemological crises and Descartes's is now clear. For Shakespeare invites us to reflect on the crisis of the self as a crisis in the tradition that has formed the self; Descartes by his attitude to history and to fable has cut himself off from the possibility of recognising himself; he has invented an unhistorical self-endorsed, self-consciousness and tries to describe his epistemological crisis in terms of it. Small wonder that he misdescribes it.

Consider by contrast Galileo. When Galileo entered the scientific scene, he was confronted by much more than the conflict between the Ptolemaic and Copernican astronomies. The Ptolemaic system was itself inconsistent both with the widely accepted Platonic requirements for a true astronomy and with the perhaps even more widely accepted principles of Aristotelian physics. These latter were, in turn, inconsistent with the findings over two centuries about motion of scholars at Oxford, Paris and Padua. Not surprisingly, instrumentalism flourished as a philosophy of science and Osiander's instrumentalist reading of Copernicus was no more than the counterpart to earlier instrumentalist interpretations of the Ptolemaic system. Instrumentalism, like attempts to refute skepticism, is characteristically a sign of a tradition in crisis.

Galileo resolves the crisis by a threefold strategy. He rejects instrumentalism; he reconciles astronomy and mechanics; and he redefines the place of experiment in natural science. The old mythological empiricist view of Galileo saw him as appealing to the facts against Ptolemy and Aristotle; what he actually did was to give a new account of what an appeal to the facts had to be. Wherein lies the superiority of Galileo to his predecessors? The answer is that he, for the first time, enables the work of all his predecessors to be evaluated by a common set of standards. The contributions of Plato, Aristotle, the scholars at Merton College, Oxford, and at Padua, the work of Copernicus himself at last all fall into place. Or, to put matters in another and equivalent way: the history of late medieval science can finally be cast into a coherent narrative. Galileo's work implies a rewriting of the narrative that constitutes the scientific tradition. For it now became retrospectively possible to identify those anomalies that had been genuine counterexamples to received theories from those anomalies that could justifiably be dealt with by ad hoc explanatory devices or even ignored. It also became retrospectively possible to see how the various elements of various theories had fared in their encounters with other theories and with observations and experiments, and to understand how the form in which they had survived bore the marks of those encounters. A theory always bears the marks of its passage through time and the theories with which Galileo had to deal were no exception.

Let me cast the point I am trying to make about Galileo in a way which, at first sight, is perhaps paradoxical. We are apt to suppose that because Galileo was a peculiarly great scientist, therefore he has his own peculiar place in the history of science. I am suggesting instead that it is because of his peculiarly important place in the history of science that he is accounted a particularly great scientist. The criterion of a successful theory is that it enable us to understand its predecessors in a newly intelligible way. It, at one and the same time, enables us to understand precisely why its predecessors have to be rejected or modified and also why, without and before its illumination, past theory could have remained credible. It introduces new standards for evaluating the past. It recasts the narrative that constitutes the continuous reconstruction of the scientific tradition.

This connection between narrative and tradition has hitherto gone almost unnoticed, perhaps because tradition has usually been taken seriously only by conservative social theorists. Yet those features of tradition that emerge as important when the connection between tradition and narrative is understood are ones conservative theorists are unlikely to attend to. For what constitutes a tradition is a conflict of interpretations of that tradition, a conflict which itself has a history susceptible of rival interpretations. If I am a Jew, I have to recognise that the tradition of Judaism is partly constituted by a continuous argument over what it means to be a Jew. Suppose I am an American: the tradition is one partly constituted by continuous argument over what it means to be an American and partly by continuous argument over what it means to have rejected tradition. If I am an historian, I must acknowledge that the tradition of historiography is partly, but centrally, constituted by arguments about what history is and ought to be, from Hume and Gibbon to Namier and Edward Thompson. Notice that all three kinds of tradition—religious, political, intellectual—involve epistemological debate as a necessary feature of their conflicts. For it is not merely that different participants in a tradition disagree; they also disagree as to how to characterize their disagreements and as to how to resolve them. They disagree as to what constitutes appropriate reasoning, decisive evidence, conclusive proof.

A tradition then not only embodies the narrative of an argument, but is only to be recovered by an argumentative retelling of that narrative which will itself be in conflict with other argumentative retellings. Every tradition therefore is always in danger of lapsing into incoherence and when a tradition does so lapse it sometimes can only be recovered by a revolutionary reconstitution. Precisely such a reconstitution of a tradition that had lapsed into incoherence was the work of Galileo.

It will now be obvious why I introduced the notion of tradition by alluding negatively to the viewpoint of conservative theorists. For they, from Burke onwards, have wanted to counterpose tradition and reason and tradition and revolution. Not reason, but prejudice; not revolution, but inherited precedent; these are Burke's key oppositions. Yet if the present arguments are correct it is traditions that are the bearers of reason, and traditions at certain periods actually require and need revolutions for their continuance. Burke saw the French Revolution as merely the negative overthrow of all that France had been and many French conservatives have agreed with him, but later thinkers as different as Peguy and Hilaire Belloc were able retrospectively to see the great revolution as reconstituting a more ancient France, so that Jeanne D'Arc and Danton belong within the same single, if immensely complex, tradition.

Conflict arises, of course, not only within, but between traditions and such a conflict tests the resources of each contending tradition. It is yet another mark of a degenerate tradition that it has contrived a set of epistemological defenses that enable it to avoid being put in question or at least to avoid recognising that it is being put in question by rival traditions. This is, for example, part of the degeneracy of modern astrology, of some types of psychoanalytic thought, and of liberal Protestantism. Although, therefore, any feature of any tradition, any theory, any practice, any belief can always under certain conditions be put in question, the practice of putting in question, whether within a tradition or between traditions, itself always requires the context of a tradition. Doubting is a more complex activity than some skeptics have realized. To say to oneself or to someone else "Doubt all your beliefs here and now" without reference to historical or autobiographical context is not meaningless; but it is an invitation not to philosophy, but to mental breakdown, or rather to philosophy as a means of mental breakdown. Descartes concealed from himself, as we have seen, an unacknowledged background of beliefs that rendered what he was doing intelligible and sane to himself and to others. But suppose he had put that background in question too—what would have happened to him then?

We are not without clues, for we do have the record of the approach to breakdown in the life of one great philosopher. "For I have already shown," wrote Hume,

> that the understanding, when it acts alone, and according to its most general principles, entirely subverts itself, and leaves not the lowest degree of evidence in any proposition, either in philosophy or common life. . . . The *intense* view of these manifold contradictions and imperfections in human reason has so wrought upon me, and heated my brain, that I am ready to reject all belief and reasoning, and can look upon no opinion even as more probable or likely than another. Where am I, or what? From what causes do I derive my existence, and to what condition shall I return? Whose favour shall I court, and whose anger must I dread? What beings surround me? And on whom have I any influence? I am confronted with all these questions, and begin to fancy myself in the most deplorable condition imaginable, inviron'd with the deepest darkness and utterly depriv'd of the use of every member and faculty.[3]

We may note three remarkable features of Hume's cry of pain. First, like Descartes, he has set a standard for the foundations of his beliefs that could not be met; hence all beliefs founder equally. He has not asked if he can find good reasons for preferring in respect of the best criteria of reason and truth available some among others of the limited range of possibilities of belief that actually confront him in his particular cultural situation. Secondly, he is in consequence thrust back without any answers or possibility of answers upon just that range of questions that, according to Bettelheim, underlie the whole narrative enterprise in early childhood. There is indeed the most surprising and illuminating correspondence between the questions Bettelheim ascribes to the child and the questions framed by the adult, but desperate, Hume. For Hume by his radical skepticism has lost any means of making himself—or others—intelligible to himself, let alone, to others. His very skepticism itself becomes unintelligible.

There is perhaps a possible world in which 'empiricism' would have become the name of a mental illness, while 'paranoia' would be the name of a well-accredited theory of knowledge. For in this world empiricists would be consistent and unrelenting—unlike Hume—and they would thus lack any means to order their experience of other people or of nature. Even a knowledge of formal logic would not help them; for until they knew how to order their experiences they would possess neither sentences to formalize nor reasons for choosing one way of formalizing them rather than another. Their world would indeed be reduced to that chaos Bettelheim perceives in the child at the beginning of the oedipal phase. Empiricism would lead not to sophistication, but to regression. Paranoia by contrast would provide considerable resources for living in the world. The empiricist maxims, "Believe only what can be based upon sense-experience" or Occam's razor, would leave us bereft of all generalizations and therefore of all attitudes toward the future (or the past). They would isolate us in a contentless present. But the paranoid maxims, "Interpret everything that happens as an outcome of envious malice" and "Everyone and everything will let you down" receive continuous confirmation for those who adopt them. Hume cannot answer the question, "What beings surround me?" But Kafka knew the answer to this very well, "In fact the clock has certain personal relationships to me, like many things in the room, save that now, particularly since I gave notice—or rather since I was given notice. . .—they seem to be beginning to turn their backs on me, above all the calendar . . . Lately it is as if it had been metamorphosed. Either it is absolutely uncommunicative—for example, you want its advice, you go up to it, but the only thing it says is 'Feast of the Reformation'—which probably has a deeper significance, but who can discover it?—or, on the contrary, it is nastily ironic."[4]

So in this possible world they will speak of Hume's Disease and of Kafka's Theory of Knowledge. Yet is this possible world so different from that which we inhabit? What leads us to segregate at least some types of mental from ordinary, sane behavior is that they presuppose and embody ways of interpreting the natural and social world that are radically discordant with our customary and, as we take it, justified modes of interpretation. That is, certain types of mental illness seem to presuppose rival theories of knowledge. Conversely every theory of knowledge offers us schemata for accepting some interpretations of the natural and social world rather than others. As Hamlet discovered earlier, the categories of psychiatry and of epistemology must be to some extent interdefinable.

III

What I have been trying to sketch are a number of conceptual connections that link such notions as those of an epistemological crisis, a narrative, a tradition, natural science, skepticism and madness.

There is one group of recent controversies in which the connections between these concepts has itself become a central issue. I refer, of course, to the debates that originated from the confrontation between Thomas Kuhn's philosophy of science and the views of those philosophers of science who in one way or another are the heirs of Sir Karl Popper. It is not surprising, therefore, that the positions I have taken should imply conclusions about those controversies, conclusions which are not quite the same as those of any of the major participants. Yet it is perhaps because the concepts I have examined—such as those on epistemological crisis and of the relationship of conflict to tradition—have provided the largely unexamined background to the recent debates that their classification may, in fact, help to resolve some of the issues. In particular I shall want to argue that the positions of some of the most heated antagonists—notably Thomas Kuhn and Imre Lakatos—can be seen to converge once they are emended in ways toward which the protagonists themselves have moved in their successive reformulations of their positions.

One very striking new conclusion will, however, also emerge. For I shall want to reinforce my thesis that dramatic narrative is the crucial form for the understanding of human action and I shall want to argue that natural science can be a rational form of inquiry if and only if the writing of a true dramatic narrative—that is, of history understood in a particular way—can be a rational activity. Scientific reason turns out to be subordinate to, and intelligible only in terms of, historical reason. And if this is true of the natural sciences, *a fortiori* it will be true also of the social sciences.

It is therefore sad that social scientists have all too often treated the work of writers such as Kuhn and Lakatos as it stood. Kuhn's writing in particular has been invoked time and again—for a period of ten years or so, a ritual obeisance toward Kuhn seems almost to have been required in presidential addressess to the American Political Science Association—to license the theoretical failures of social science. But while Kuhn's work uncriticized—or for that matter Popper or Lakatos uncriticized—represent a threat to our understanding, Kuhn's work criticized provides an illuminating application for the ideas I have been defending.

My criticisms of Kuhn will fall into three parts. In the first I shall suggest that his earlier formulations of his position are much more radically flawed than he himself has acknowledged. I shall then argue that it is his failure to recognise the true character of the flaws in his earlier formulations that leads to the weakness of his later revisions. Finally I shall suggest a more adequate form of revision.

What Kuhn originally presented was an account of epistemological crises in natural science, which is essentially the same as the Cartesian account of epistemological crises in philosophy. This account was superimposed on a view of natural science that seems largely indebted to the writings of Michael Polanyi. (Kuhn nowhere acknowledges any such debt.) What Polanyi had shown is that all justification takes place within a social tradition and that the pressures of such a tradition enforce often unrecognised rules by means of which discrepant pieces of evidence or difficult questions are often put on one side with the tacit assent of the scientific community. Polanyi is the Burke of the philosophy of science and I mean this analogy with political and moral philosophy to be taken with great seriousness. For all my earlier criticisms of Burke now become relevant to the criticism of Polanyi. Polanyi, like Burke, understands tradition as essentially conservative and essentially unitary. (Paul Feyerabend— at first sight so different from Polanyi—agrees with Polanyi in his understanding of tradition. It is just because he so understands the scientific tradition that he rejects it and has turned himself into the Emerson of the philosophy of science; not "Every man his own Jesus," but "Every man his own Galileo.") He does not see the omnipresence of conflict—sometimes latent—within living traditions. It is because of this that anyone who took Polanyi's view would find it very difficult to explain how a transition might be made from one tradition to another or how a tradition that had lapsed into incoherence might be reconstructed. Since reason operates only *within* traditions and communities according to Polanyi, such a transition or a reconstruction could not be a work of reason. It would have to be a leap in the dark of some kind.

Polanyi never carried his argument to this point. But what is a major difficulty in Polanyi's position was presented by Kuhn as though it were a discovery. Kuhn did, of course, recognize very fully how a scientific tradition may lapse into incoherence. And he must have (with Feyerabend) the fullest credit for recognizing in an original way the significance and character of incommensurability. But the conclusions he draws, namely that "proponents of competing paradigms must fail to make complete contact with each other's viewpoints" and that the transition from one paradigm to another requires a "conversion experience" do not follow from his premises concerning incommensurability. These last are threefold: adherents of rival paradigms during a scientific revolution disagree about what set of problems provide the test for a successful paradigm in that particular scientific situation; their theories embody very different concepts; and they "see different things when they look from the same point in the same direction." Kuhn concludes that "just because it is a transition between incommensurables" the transition cannot be made step by step; and he uses the expression "gestalt switch" as well as "conversion experience." What is important is that Kuhn's account of the transition requires an additional premise. It is not just that the adherents of rival paradigms disagree, but that *every* relevant area of rationality is invaded by that disagreement. It is not just that threefold incommensurability is present, but rationality apparently cannot be present in any other form. Now this additional premise would indeed follow from Polanyi's position and if Kuhn's position is understood as presupposing something like Polanyi's then Kuhn's earlier formulations of his positions become all too intelligible; and so do the accusations of irrationalism by his critics, accusations Kuhn professes not to understand.

What follows from the position thus formulated? It is that scientific revolutions are epistemological crises understood in a Cartesian way. Everything is put in question simultaneously. There is no rational continuity between the situation at the time immediately preceding the crisis and any situation following it. To such a crisis the language of evangelical conversion would indeed be appropriate. We might indeed begin to speak with the voice of Pascal, lamenting that the highest achievement of reason is to learn what reason cannot achieve. But of course, as we have already seen, the Cartesian view of epistemological crises is false; it can never be the case that everything is put in question simultaneously. That would, indeed, lead to large and unintelligible lacunas not only in the history of practices, such as those of the natural sciences, but also in the personal biographies of scientists.

Moreover Kuhn does not distinguish between two kinds of transition experience. The experience that he is describing seems to be that of the person who having been thoroughly educated into practices defined and informed by one paradigm has to make the transition to a form of scientific practice defined and informed by some radically different paradigm. Of this kind of person what Kuhn asserts may well on occasion be true. But such a scientist is always being invited to make a transition that has already been made by others; the very characterization of his situation presupposes that the new paradigm is already operative while the old still retains some power. But what of the very different type of transition made by those scientists who first invented or discovered the new paradigm? Here Kuhn's divergences from Polanyi ought to have saved him from his original Polanyi-derived conclusion. For Kuhn does recognize very fully and insightfully how traditions lapse into incoherence. What some, at least, of those who are educated into such a tradition may come to recognize is the gap between its *own* epistemological ideals and its actual practices. Of those who recognize this some may tend towards skepticism and some toward instrumentalism. Just this, as we have already seen, characterized late medieval and six- teenth-century science. What the scientific genius, such as Galileo, achieves in his transition, then, is not only a new way of under- standing nature, but also and inseparably a new way of understanding the old science's way of understanding nature. It is because only from the standpoint of the new science can the inadequacy of the old science be characterized that the new science is taken to be more adequate than the old. It is from the standpoint of the new science that the continuities of narrative history are reestablished.

Kuhn has, of course, continuously modified his earlier formu- lations and to some degree his position. He has, in particular, pointed out forcefully to certain of his critics that it is they who have imputed to him the thesis that scientific revolutions are nonrational or irrational events, a conclusion he has never drawn himself. His own position is "that, if history or any other empirical discipline leads us to believe that the development of science depends essentially on behavior that we have previously thought to be irrational, then we should conclude not that science is irrational, but that our notion of rationality needs adjustment here and there."

Feyerabend however, beginning from the same premises as Kuhn, has drawn on his own behalf the very conclusion Kuhn so abhors. And surely if scientific revolutions were as Kuhn describes them, if there were nothing more to them than such features as the threefold incommensurability, Feyerabend would be in the right. Thus if Kuhn is to, as he says, "adjust" the notion of rationality, he will have to find the signs of rationality in some feature of scientific revolutions to which he has not yet attended. Are there such features? Certainly, but they belong precisely to the history of these episodes. It is more rational to accept one theory or paradigm and to reject its predecessor when the later theory or paradigm provides a standpoint from which the acceptance, the life story, and the rejection of the previous theory or paradigm can be recounted in more intelligible historical narrative than previously. An understanding of the concept of the superiority of one physical theory to another requires a prior understanding of the concept of the superiority of one historical narrative to another. The theory of scientific rationality has to be embedded in a philosophy of history.

What is carried over from one paradigm to another are epistemological ideals and a correlative understanding of what constitutes the progress of a single intellectual life. Just as Descartes's account of his own epistemological crisis was only possible by reason of Descartes's ability to recount his own history, indeed to live his life as a narrative about to be cast into a history—an ability that Descartes himself could not recognize without falsifying his own account of epistemological crises—so Kuhn and Feyerabend recount the history of epistemological crises as moments of almost total discontinuity without noticing the historical continuity that makes their own intelligible narratives possible. Something very like this position, which I have approached through a criticism of Kuhn, was reached by Lakatos in the final stages of his journey away from Popper's initial positions.

If Polanyi is the Burke of the philosophy of science and Feyerabend the Emerson, then Popper himself or at least his disciples inherit the role of J. S. Mill—as Feyerabend has already noticed. The truth is to be approached through the free clash of opinion. The logic of the moral sciences is to be replaced by *Logic der Forschung*. Where Burke sees reasoning only within the context of tradition and Feyerabend sees the tradition as merely repressive of the individual, Popper has rightly tried to make something of the notion of rational tradition. What hindered this attempt was the Popperian insistence on replacing the false methodology of induction by a new methodology. The history of Popper's own thought and of that of his most gifted followers was for quite a number of years the history of successive attempts to replace Popper's original falsificationism by some more adequate version, each of which, in turn, fell prey to counterexamples from the history of science. From one point of view the true heir of these attempts is Feyerabend; for it is he who has formulated the completely general thesis that all such attempts were doomed to failure. There is *no* set of rules as to how science *must* proceed and all attempts to discover such a set founder in their encounter with actual history of science. But when Lakatos had finally accepted this he moved on to new ground.

In 1968, while he was still a relatively conservative Popperian, Lakatos had written, "The appraisal is rather of a *series of theories* than of an isolated *theory*." He went on to develop this notion into that of a research program. The notion of a research program is, of course, oriented to the future, and there was therefore a tension between Lakatos's use of this notion and his recognition that it is only retrospectively that a series of theories can be appraised. In other words, what is appraised is always a history; for it is not just a series of theories that is appraised, but a series that stands in various complex relationships to each other through time, that is appraised. Indeed what we take to be a single theory is always "a growing developing entity, one which cannot be considered as a static structure."[5] Consider, for example, the kinetic theory of gases. If we read the scientific textbooks for any period we shall find presented an entirely ahistorical account of the theory. But if we read all the successive textbooks we shall learn not only that the kinetic theory of 1857 was not quite that of 1845 and that the kinetic theory of 1901 is neither that of 1857 nor that of 1965. Yet at each stage the theory bears the marks of its previous history, of a series of encounters with confirming or anomalous evidence, with other theories, with metaphysical points of view, and so on. The kinetic theory not merely has, but is a history, and to evaluate it is to evaluate how it has fared in this large variety of encounters. Which of these have been victories, which defeats, which compounds of victory and defeat, and which not classifiable under any of these headings? To evaluate a theory, just as to evaluate a series of theories, one of Lakatos's research programs, is precisely to write that history, that narrative of defeats and victories.

This is what Lakatos recognized in his paper on *History of Science and Its Rational Reconstructions.*[6] Methodologies are to be assessed by the extent to which they satisfy historiographical criteria; the best scientific methodology is that which can supply the best rational reconstruction of the history of science and for different episodes different methodologies may well be successful. But in talking not about history, but about rational reconstructions Lakatos has still not exorcised the ghosts of the older Popperian belief in methodology; for he was quite prepared to envisage the rational reconstruction as 'a caricature' of actual history. Yet it matters enormously that our histories should be true, just as it matters that our scientific theories make truth one of their goals.

Kuhn interestingly and perhaps oddly insists against Lakatos on truth in history (he accuses Lakatos of replacing genuine history by "Philosophy fabricating examples"), but yet denies any notion of truth to natural science other than that truth that attaches to solutions to puzzles and to concrete predictions. In particular, he wants to deny that a scientific theory can embody a true ontology, that it can provide a true representative of what is 'really there'. "There is, I think, no theory-independent way to reconstruct phrases like 'really there'; the notion of a match between the ontology of a theory and its 'real' counterpart in nature now seems to me illusive in principle."[7]

This is very odd; because science has certainly shown us decisively that some existence-claims are false just because the entities in question are *not* really there—whatever *any* theory may say. Epicurean atomism is not true, there are no humours, nothing with negative weight exists; phlogiston is one with the witches and the dragons. But other existence-claims have survived exceptionally well through a succession of particular theoretical positions: molecules, cells, electrons. Of course our beliefs about molecules, cells and electrons are by no means what they once were. But Kuhn would be put into a very curious position if he adduced this as a ground for denying that some existence-claims still have excellent warrant and others do not.

What, however, worries Kuhn is something else: "in some important respects, though by no means in all, Einstein's general theory of relativity is closer to Aristotle's mechanics than either of them is to Newton's."[8] He therefore concludes that the superiority of Einstein to Newton is in puzzle solving and not in an approach to a true ontology. But what an Einsteinian ontology enables us to understand is why *from the standpoint of an approach to truth* Newtonian mechanics is superior to Aristotelian. For Aristotelian mechanics as it lapsed into incoherence could never have led us to the special theory; construe them how you will, the Aristotelian problems about time will not yield the questions to which special relativity is the answer. A history that moved from Aristotelianism directly to relativistic physics is not an imaginable history.

What Kuhn's disregard for ontological truth neglects is the way in which the progress toward truth in different sciences is such that they have to converge. The easy reductionism of some positivist programs for science was misleading here, but the rejection of such a reductionism must not blind us to the necessary convergence of physics, chemistry and biology. Were it not for a concern for ontological truth, the nature of our demand for a coherent and convergent relationship between all the sciences would be unintelligible.

Kuhn's view may, of course, seem attractive simply because it seems consistent with a fallibilism that we have every reason to accept. *Perhaps* Einsteinian physics will one day be overthrown just as Newtonian was; perhaps, as Lakatos in his more colorfully rhetorical moments used to suggest, all our scientific beliefs are, always have been, and always will be false. But it seems to be a presupposition of the way in which we do natural science that fallibilism has to be made consistent with the regulative ideal of an approach to a true account of the fundamental order of things and not vice versa. If this is so, Kant is essentially right; the notion of an underlying order—the kind of order that we would expect if the ingenious, unmalicious god of Newton and Einstein had created the universe—is a regulative ideal of physics. We do not need to understand this notion quite as Kant did, and our antitheological beliefs may make us uncomfortable in adopting it. But perhaps discomfort at this point is a sign of philosophical progress.

I am suggesting, then, that the best account that can be given of why some scientific theories are superior to others presupposes the possibility of constructing an intelligible dramatic narrative that can claim historical truth and in which such theories are the subject of successive episodes. It is because and only because we can construct better and worse histories of this kind, histories that can be rationally compared with each other, that we can compare theories rationally too. Physics presupposes history and history of a kind that invokes just those concepts of tradition, intelligibility, and epistemological crisis for which I argued earlier. It is this that enables us to understand why Kuhn's account of scientific revolutions can, in fact, be rescued from the charges of irrationalism leveled by Lakatos and why Lakatos's final writings can be rescued from the charges of evading history leveled by Kuhn. Without this background, scientific revolutions become unintelligible episodes; indeed Kuhn becomes—what, in essence, Lakatos accused him of being—the Kafka of the history of science. Small wonder that he, in turn, felt that Lakatos was not an historian, but an historical novelist.

A final thesis can now be articulated. When the connection between narrative and tradition on the one hand, and theory and method on the other, is lost sight of, the philosophy of science is set insoluble problems. Any set of finite observations is compatible with any one out of an infinite set of generalizations. Any attempt to show the rationality of science, once and for all, by providing a rationally justifiable set of rules for linking observations and generalizations, breaks down. This holds, as the history of the Popperian school shows, for falsification as much as for any version of positivism. It holds, as the history of Carnap's work shows, no matter how much progress may be made on detailed, particular structures in scientific inference. It is only when theories are located in history, when we view the demands for justification in highly particular contexts of an historical kind, that we are freed from either dogmatism or capitulation to skepticism. It therefore turns out that the program that dominated the philosophy of science from the eighteenth century onwards, that of combining empiricism and natural science, was bound either at worst to break down in irrationalism or at best in a set of successively weakened empiricist programs whose driving force was a deep desire not to be forced into irrationalist conclusions. Hume's Disease is, however, incurable and ultimately fatal and even backgammon (or that type of analytical philosophy which is often the backgammon of the professional philosopher) cannot stave off its progress indefinitely. It is, after all, Vico, and neither Descartes nor Hume, who has turned out to be in the right in approaching the relationship between history and physics.

NOTES

1. Bruno Bettelheim, *The Uses of Enchantment* (New York: Alfred A. Knopf, 1976), 74–75.

2. Ibid., 47.

3. David Hume, *Treatise of Human Nature*, ed. L. A. Selby-Bigge (London: Oxford University Press, 1941), Bk. I, iv, vii, 267–69.

4. Letter to his sister Valli, in *I Am a Memory Come Alive*, ed. Nahum N. Glatzer (New York: Schocken Books, 1974), 235.

5. Richard M. Burian, "More than a Marriage of Convenience: On the Inextricability of History and Philosophy of Science," unpublished paper, 38.

6. I. Lakatos, "History of Science and Its Rational Reconstructions," in Boston Studies in the Philosophy of Science, vol. VIII, ed. Roger C. Buch and Robert S. Cohen (Dordrecht-Holland: D. Reidel Publishing Co., 1974).

7. Thomas S. Kuhn, *The Structure of Scientific Revolutions*, 2d ed. (Chicago: University of Chicago Press, 1970), 206.

8. Ibid., 206–7.

Chapter 12

Realism & Imagination in Ethics

SABINA LOVIBOND

I

According to Wittgenstein's conception of language, the basis of our proposed moral realism, mutual understanding presupposes the common acceptance of some 'totality of propositions'—the theoretical counterpart of a common way of acting. What we call 'rationality', too, turns out on this account to be a quality ascribed to individual persons just in so far as they are held to be capable of taking part in rule-governed forms of behavior—notably, the practice known as *reasoned argument*, with its characteristic rules of inference. Essential to the Wittgensteinian picture is the idea that people whose behavior is psychologically alien to us will to that extent fail to qualify as candidates for participation, along with ourselves, in a shared language-game: i.e. that in order to communicate with other people we need to be able to 'find our feet' with them (*PI* II p. 223).[1]

Now these alleged truths of reflection supply no information whatsoever as to the possibility of finding our feet with specific individuals or groups. They do not tell us at what point a cultural divergence becomes so wide as to make any attempt at understanding pointless; neither do they tell us what to do in any actual situation where we may find ourselves unable to achieve understanding. In such a situation, we cannot turn to the above-mentioned parts of Wittgenstein's philosophy either for authority to lynch anybody, or for authority to insist upon toleration. And the same seems to be true of other brands of historicism about moral and intellectual norms: such doctrines are equally well-qualified to accompany a tolerant, experimentalist cast of mind, or a defensive and authoritarian attachment to tradition.

We might make use of a pair of familiar terms, 'conservative' and 'liberal', to denote two contrasting positions that are available to the expressive theorist of language. (There is, of course, a further position which, following Feyerabend, we might designate as 'anarchist', but I shall not consider this option explicitly: my remarks about 'liberalism' may be understood to refer to it by extrapolation.)

The adherents of these different positions should, I believe, be seen as advocates of different *policies* toward deviant or *unsittlich* behavior. The liberal commends a policy of toleration—of keeping an open mind as to whether the anomalous way of acting can be brought into connection with established social practices; the conservative, by contrast, calls for a strict policing of *Sittlichkeit* and demands positive disciplinary measures against the author of any anomaly. The relevant discipline consists in a withdrawal of the recognition previously extended to that person as a serious participant in the language-game.[2]

The distinction between recognition and non-recognition of a given individual as a serious participant in the language-game may be understood as a variant upon the Kantian opposition between treating persons as ends and as means. That opposition has, in fact, been presented to modern readers (by P. F. Strawson in his British Academy lecture, 'Freedom and Resentment') in terms of a contrast between the so-called 'participant' and 'objective' attitudes toward persons. To adopt the 'objective' attitude, in Strawson's scheme, is to see another person not as an equal (a fellow-citizen in the Kantian 'kingdom of ends'), but as something to be 'managed or handled or cured or trained'—a phenomenon in the natural world, our interest in the latter being assumed to be motivated by a hankering after manipulative power.[3] The 'participant' attitude, on the other hand, accords to the other person a status that makes him an appropriate object of emotions such as "resentment, gratitude, forgiveness, anger, or the sort of love two adults can sometimes be said to feel, reciprocally, for each other."[4]

The position I have designated as 'liberal' is that of the person who forbears to respond to moral dissent (or deviancy, as we may call it if it has no rationale that we can understand) with an objectifying strategy whose effect is to restrict the dissident's possibilities of taking part in social activity—and thus (in the long term) to undermine his status as a rational person. (Cf. Bradley: "As members of the system we are real, and not otherwise.") Such a person will advocate a looser code of practice: refusing to take mere non-conformity as a ground for expelling anyone from the rational community, he will demand a more rigorous criterion (in Mill's case, for example, "harming others" physically, or at least in some fairly tangible way). The conservative, meanwhile, is prone to think that deviation from the main channel of the language-games is a sufficient ground for the objectification of the deviant—the progressive annulment of any previously existing "participant attitude" toward him.[5] That is to say, he is prone to assimilate the physiognomy of language-games as such to that of specific language-games, such as arithmetic, in which any deviation from the consensus constitutes an *error* and is to be treated accordingly.

We might express the difference between the conservative and the liberal by saying that each has his own distinctive view about the sort of behavior that is to be expected from a *rational person:* rational either *sans phrase*, or in relation to some specified region of discourse. Having said this, however, we must recall that 'rational' is a *word*, and a word—on the present conception of language—'has the meaning someone has given to it': words stand in need of our criteria, and in the case of rationality these criteria are grounded in our material acceptance or rejection of certain modes of thought and conduct.

Wittgenstein writes (*PI* II, 178): "My attitude towards him is an attitude towards a soul. I am not of the *opinion* that he has a soul." We might wish, on occasion, to echo this thought as follows: 'My attitude towards him is an attitude towards a person whose values and beliefs are worthy of consideration.' With regard to certain individuals whose behavior conflicts in some sense with the spirit of the existing form of life, the liberal will be prepared to say this, and the conservative will not; and their different attitudes will find expression in different behavior.

II

We shall get a better idea of the meaning of our own responses to moral anomalies if we follow up a suggestion contained in Strawson's description of the 'objective attitude'. That attitude, says Strawson, defines its object as something to be 'managed'. What does this tell us about the state of mind of the person who adopts it?

I maintain that the way we react when we become aware of a discrepancy between our own moral beliefs and those of other people should be seen as the expression of a distinctive policy on our part. Wittgenstein's challenge at *RFM* VII §11, whose purpose is to dispel our sense of *not having a choice* at a certain sort of conjuncture in mathematics, is surely no less applicable to the moral aspect of life: "But you can't allow a contradiction to stand!—*Why not?* . . . 'We take a number of steps, all legitimate—i.e. allowed by the rules— and suddenly a contradiction results. So the list of rules, as it is, is of no use, for the contradiction wrecks the whole game! *Why do you have it wreck the game?'* "

It happens not infrequently that because of the incompleteness of intellectual authority within the moral language-game 'contradiction' arises in the course of that game even though none of the players can be said to have broken the rules (the latter not being sufficiently determinate to allow us to say this). In other words, people may disagree about the instantiation of moral concepts (about what is permissible, or obligatory, or in bad taste, etc.) without it being possible to refer the dispute to any kind of arbitration that will command general assent. In these circumstances none of the disputants can be *authoritatively* identified as having violated the rules for the application of the concept; or, to put the same point in material terms, the use of the relevant word is not subject to the control of any single agency which could enforce a single, coherent practice in connection with it.

Now it is in this kind of situation that the policy of an individual or group toward moral contradiction is revealed. Once the stock of arguments on each side is exhausted, and rational debate is therefore at an end, we can *choose* either to 'let the contradiction stand', or to continue to treat it as a theoretical challenge—an anomaly that detracts in an unacceptable way from the intelligibility of the world, and for which, accordingly, an explanation must be found.

A view about what needs explaining is an evaluative view. This is especially obvious in the overtly moral or political sphere. For example, a student of sociology might think it was worth looking into the reason why it was considered acceptable, within some ethnic minority group, for women to be rather vague and offhand about the paternity of their various children. The same person, if he were fairly unsophisticated, might never take it into his head to ask why the indigenous population did not in general find this acceptable. If he did not think of asking the latter question, this would provide evidence of his own assent to certain practical norms concerning reproduction and the family. Another example: a student of psychology might think it was important to find out what constitutional or developmental factors cause people to become homosexual. This (in the absence of a parallel interest in the process by which heterosexuality is established) would show that he, the student, did not look upon homosexuality as something he himself might perfectly well go in for. Another: in economic theory, it is possible to treat military expenditure either as an aberration or as a *prima facie* rational use of resources. Thus a Marxist may seek to account for such expenditure, for example, in terms of the absorption of surplus; while a conservative may not recognize anything here that calls for a nontrivial explanation. (We need bombs, he may say, so we make them.) These two approaches display different evaluations of a given state of affairs in respect of rational intelligibility: one registers a source of mental discomfort where the other does not.

Nietzsche makes the following helpful remarks about the subjective significance of theory-building:

> I asked myself: What is it that the common people take for knowledge? What do they want when they want 'knowledge'? Nothing more than this: something strange is to be reduced to something *familiar*. And we philosophers—have we really meant *more* than this when we have spoken of knowledge? What is familiar means what we are used to so that we no longer marvel at it, our everyday, some rule in which we are struck, anything at all in which we feel at home. Look, isn't our need for knowledge precisely this need for the familiar, the will to uncover under everything strange, unusual and questionable something that no longer disturbs us? Is it not the *instinct of fear* that bids us to know?[6]

This passage recalls Wittgenstein's conception of the activity of thinking—of making judgments—as part of a continuing exercise in *finding one's way about* (cf. Z, 393). According to that conception, our attempt to understand the world (whether under its natural or under its human aspect) is an attempt to equip ourselves with a system of beliefs, and a corresponding system of behavior, such that we shall not come seriously unstuck either in our interaction with the physical environment or in our relations with other people. To succeed in this attempt would be to arrive at a world-view which was 'habitable' both in a cognitive and in a practical sense—our cognitive control of things being, of course, grounded (on a Wittgensteinian view) in our ability to control them practically.

I suggest that the strength of our compulsion to *explain* any discrepancies that may come to light between our own moral beliefs and those of others corresponds to the degree of insecurity, or fear, that we feel when confronted by such discrepancies. The different policies we can adopt in response to moral contradiction reflect the varying extent to which our cognitive control is threatened by the existence of the alternative view. Thus if the threat is severe, we may prefer not to 'let the contradiction stand', when reasoned argument fails us, but to switch to an objectifying treatment of the anomalous opinion that will enable us to consider it in terms of its causal origins.[7] If the threat is slight or negligible, on the other hand, we may not see fit to give the matter any more thought. For instance, a rationally irresoluble disagreement as to whether it is fun to ride on the big dipper is a contradiction of a kind we habitually allow to stand.

Sometimes our sense of insecurity in the face of moral differences is well-founded. To deny this would be to commit ourselves to a policy of acquiescence in any and every form of human barbarity.[8] At other times it merely betrays a closed mind and a bad conscience— as with the (fictional) immigration officer who says, "We call them integrated when they are indistinguishable from ourselves."[9] An ability to tell the first kind of case from the second is the goal of that department of moral and political theory that considers "how to realize in human nature the perfect unity of homogeneity and specification";[10] how to establish within society a system of "differentiation, meaningful to the people concerned, which at the same time does not set the partial communities against each other, but rather knits them together in a larger whole."[11]

Libertarian thinkers are sensitive to the workings of a mechanism that has been named the "segregation of dissent."[12] This 'segregation' is the badge of a community in which the dominant criteria of rationality—and especially of moral or political rationality—are such as to call into question the participant status of any person who expresses unorthodox or non-consensual opinions.[13] In this kind of community, deviation from the moral consensus will be treated as a sufficient ground for expulsion from the language-game. The deviant individual, simply on the basis of his deviation, will be held to have forfeited his right to be treated 'as a soul'. This is, of course, the situation represented by 'conservative' exponents of our expressivist moral realism as obtaining universally, in virtue of the essentially social nature of rule-governed practices in general; but I have argued that, so far from being a corollary of any such general (ahistorical) facts about language-use, it is the outcome of a distinctive response to moral dissent, which may or may not be displayed by a particular community at a particular time.

Those who believe in the 'segregation of dissent', as a historical phenomenon to be observed within existing societies, believe also that that phenomenon is a morbid one. They think that the disposition to apply 'intolerant' criteria of moral and political rationality—criteria whose effect is to banish dissenting individuals from the 'rational' community—is, in general, symptomatic of an attitude of mind that perceives dissent as a threat to the community's intellectual and practical security, and as requiring, therefore, to be 'managed'. Such an attitude is not necessarily irrational from the standpoint of the conservative, for the primary loyalty of the latter is to the 'solid fact of a world so far moralized'—and if he ever comes to have doubts about the 'strength of the moral organism against dissent', he will be acting rationally, *qua* conservative, in seeking to *stifle* dissent. In absolute terms, however, his position exhibits not only the irrationality (such as it may be) of the social order to which he is committed, but also that of repressing a variety of moral and political tendencies that are not, in fact, hostile to the cohesion of the community as a whole. This repression may be seen as indicative of a wrong approach to the problem of reconciling the social values of 'homogeneity and specification'.

The defense of an established way of life—regardless of the wisdom or unwisdom of such a policy in given historical circumstances—depends for its success, as expressive theorists have often noted, on the attitude of the community at large. It is assisted by the prevalence of an objectifying reaction to any item of human expression that differs from what people are used to: any attempt to extend an existing symbolic system, or to propose some unfamiliar kind of behavior as a new way of acting in accordance with the rules. Conversely, it is obstructed by any inclination to adopt a 'participant' attitude toward experimental or dissident thinking; i.e., to treat the dissenting views as possibly valuable or true, to compare them on merit with one's own. Materially speaking, these contrasting responses are expressed in terms of the extent to which the community's channels of communication, and its intellectually authoritative institutions, are made accessible to dissidents.

Those whose beliefs and values run counter to a consensus are obliged at every moment to resist the process of objectification. They cannot consent to become the target of a 'management' policy conceived and executed by the representatives of 'common sense'; for the aim of that policy will be precisely to forestall the process, whereby a recessive mode of rationality 'encompasses and cancels' the dominant one. Such people have to seek to remain 'inside' the rational community; to retain their status as serious participants in the language-game; to be talked *to* rather than *about*. They have to insist on their right to be seen as members of the 'party of humankind' rather than as exemplars of 'vice and disorder, its common enemy'. An awareness of this necessity is reflected in the concept of 'marginalization', meaning the condition of a (radical) political movement that is not assigned participant status in relation to the 'serious' or 'real' political life of the community. It is reflected, too, in the struggle to maintain public recognition of certain social tensions as being of a political character, and not to allow them to be classified as problems of 'law and order'.

III

A time-honored method employed by linguistic communities in controlling their dissident elements is that of 'divide and rule'. As far as theoretical ethics is concerned, this manifests itself in a refusal to recognize any middle course between, on one hand, submission to the dominant intellectual authorities; on the other, mere selfish individualism—an attitude of indifference to moral considerations.

Hume set up the opposition between motives traceable to self-love, and those flowing from 'some *universal* principle of the human frame'. Subsequent writers have continued to assume that failure to see the moral world 'objectively'—that is, as it is seen by the 'ideal' moral observer—indicates a moral sense distorted by straightforwardly egoistic bias. Thus Bradley writes of a moral universal that "wills itself in us against the actual or possible opposition of the *false private self*";[14] Kolnai alludes to the "anarchic *self-assertive* impulses of individuals and minority groups";[15] Iris Murdoch thinks that "in the moral life the enemy is the fat relentless ego," and that "moral philosophy is properly . . . the discussion of this ego and of the techniques (if any) for its defeat."[16] It seems, in fact, to be characteristic of objectivist moral philosophy to attribute any rejection of the demands of consensual morality to the dissidents' assertion of their own private claims at the expense of the common good.

There is an obvious ideological incentive to portray dissent as a peculiarity of isolated individuals. This story goes some way toward concealing the fact of internal strain within a form of life: tension between competing 'formulae', as Collingwood puts it which threaten to issue in the development of moral or political subsystems within the body of the larger 'moral organism'. Moral theories that incorporate the 'private/universal' opposition in its *a priori* form express a refusal to recognize the existence of such sub-systems; they represent the latter, at best, as shadowy entities, 'between being and not-being', devoid of any organic relation to a viable form of life.

Two distinct species of mystification can be seen at work here. In the first place, there is the reifying tendency that serves to obscure the theorist's (and the reader's) complicity in a form of life that happens to be antagonistic to moral experiment. The 'unreality' of a recessive moral formula is not a fact of nature, but a reflection of certain habits of thought and behavior which happen to prevail in the community at large. It is the moral commitment of the theorist, and of others like him, that ensures the truth of his claim that dissenting attitudes are unlikely ever to find expression in materially effective institutions; unlikely, therefore, to generate new sources of intellectual authority that would command widespread respect. And so it is this same commitment that lends plausibility to the suggestion that any person who disregards his *sittlich* obligations—who rejects, in other words, the moral demands grounded in the established form of life—thereby reveals himself as indifferent to moral considerations altogether. It makes that suggestion plausible, because it helps to maintain in the real world a state of affairs in which the one and only objective morality is, indeed, 'the' consensual one—all others having been chased from the scene; and to the extent that such a state of affairs obtains, it will be difficult or impossible to point to an *objective justification* for defying consensual morality in any respect.

Phenomena as diverse as the Dada and surrealist styles in art, the Baader-Meinhof style in politics, and assorted 'repulsive' styles in popular culture may all be understood as ironic responses to what is perceived as a too cohesive moral, political or aesthetic rationality. The exponents of these styles may be thought of as taking up the challenge that society, in their view, presents in due course to each of its members—a challenge relating to the consensual scheme of values, which is felt to be on offer only as a package: either you buy it, or you accept the status of a moral and intellectual outlaw, an 'unreal' person for social purposes. In these circumstances, to opt deliberately for outlaw status is merely to answer the question in the terms in which it was posed, even though the content of the answer may not be what was expected.[17]

The second mystificatory feature of the 'private/universal' polarity in ethical theory is that it involves a *historical* fabrication—a panoply of unsupported assertions about the actual configuration of intellectual authority within the community to which the theory is supposed to apply. We should not be too quick to concede the monopolistic claims sometimes made on behalf of 'our' consensual value-system. It is, in any case, far from clear how one would set about assessing the truth of such claims. The 'conservative', for example, tells us that recessive institutions are powerless to provide the material basis for a different, yet habitable, moral world-view, or to bring us by a non-standard route to the point of being able to participate rationally in moral and political discourse. But how would he know that? How would he, or indeed anyone else, *know* anything at all in this area? (Cf. Wittgenstein, *CV*, 45: "Go on, believe! It does no harm."[18])

At this point moral philosophy is engaged, not in the disinterested investigation of a certain historically specific sign-system, but rather in a propaganda war. For the philosopher happens to be particularly well-placed to convey to alienated members of his community, individually and severally, the idea that the blame for their condition lies with themselves; that their disaffection from consensual morality is, at bottom, merely a symptom of 'fat relentless egoism'. In propounding a holistic account of rationality, it can easily be suggested that 'we', the orthodox, form an organic unity in virtue of our possession of a common way of life; while 'they', the dissidents, are nothing but an aggregate of rootless individuals, lacking any shared practice that might offer competition to 'ours'. This message will tend to discredit any moves the dissidents might variously have been contemplating that would have tended, objectively, to bring them together in the service of that historical process whereby 'dialectical reason' progressively encompasses and cancels the dominant rationality. By telling the disaffected person that he is in a minority of one, the moral philosopher can help to ensure that he remains so.

There is, incidentally, nothing mysterious about the content of the 'historical fabrication' we have just been discussing. To say that a certain ethical theory is misleading because it denies, or glosses over, the existence of 'recessive' elements within a wider social practice—elements that are at variance with the general character of that practice—is just to say that the theory misleads us by denying the internal tensions of society itself. The degree of cohesion or fragmentation of a linguistic community in respect of its criteria of rationality may be read off directly from such phenomena as, for instance, the frequency with which discussion is abandoned in favor of confrontation. Mathematicians, Wittgenstein remarks, "don't come to blows" over whether a rule has been obeyed or not (*PI* I, 240): this is the kind of fact in which the absence of contradiction in mathematics—of rivalry between different intellectual authorities—is displayed. But there are other matters over which people do come to blows, either figuratively or literally; and that kind of occurrence in turn displays the extent to which, as a community, we fall short of having a unified rationality for the purposes of morals, politics, or whatever it may be. The latter type of fact is immanent in the former: the individuation of forms of life, and of the respective modes of rationality grounded in them,[19] is one more field in which "everything lies open to view" (*PI* I, 126).

IV

In the context of an expressivist view of language, a connection comes to light between the 'divide and rule' tendency we have just been considering, and the suggestion (which Iris Murdoch cites approvingly from Simone Weil) that as moral agents we have to seek to "control and curb imagination."[20] I will try in this section to demonstrate that connection.

The need to 'curb imagination' is presented as part of the more general program of putting the rumbustious 'Kantian man' under sedation: moral excellence, it is asserted, consists not so much in the exercise of an unconditioned personal will as in the ability to assess situations justly and without self-deception. Murdoch maintains that we need to think of our obligations as contextually determined: "A philosophy which leaves duty without a context and exalts the idea of freedom and power as a separate top level value ignores this task [sc. the task of coming to see the world as it is] and obscures the relation between virtue and reality."[21] Yet it seems that we exercise no control over the context of our duty, but must humbly accept it in all its violence; for virtue, in the Murdoch world, is typically displayed in gloomy surroundings. Hardship, oppression, even wartime atrocities provide the backdrop for her chosen examples of morally admirable behavior: witness her approval of the "virtuous peasant" and of "inarticulate, unselfish mothers of large families," not to mention the revelation that her personal vision of saintliness is a vision of unselfish behavior in a concentration camp.[22]

The same thought is to be found in Bradley. "Practical morality," he writes, "means singlemindedness, the having one idea; it means what in other spheres would be the greatest narrowness. Point out to a man of simple morals that the case has other sides than the one he instinctively fixes on, and he suspects you wish to corrupt him. And so you probably would if you went on. Apart from bad example, the readiest way to debauch the morality of anyone is, on the side of principle, to confuse them by forcing them to see in all moral and immoral acts other sides and points of view, which alter the character of each . . . ."[23]

This kind of talk may cause the reader to wonder how the concentration camp originally came to be built—and to suspect that what made such an aberration possible was, above all, the fact that the citizens at large were tied up with Strength through Joy, Winter Help, and other blamelessly inarticulate activities. A little more 'imagination' might have helped them to get the measure of events; but then, as Bradley observes, "The non-theoretical person, if he be not immoral, is at peace with reality."[24]

Here we find ourselves in an impasse, and it is natural to seek a way out by concluding that after all, one had better not insist too much on humility in ethical matters, or allow oneself to be cheaply consoled for the existence of concentration camps by the fact, however moving and impressive, of unselfish behavior on the part of some of their inmates. Our real need, we might argue, is for a world in which that kind of virtue would not be required. However, if the word 'imagination' means anything at all, it hardly seems open to dispute that the task of constructing such a world would make large demands on our imaginative powers—the very powers certain moral realists apparently want to bring under control. Why, then, are these writers so anxious that the ordinary person should take a 'narrow' view of things?

The temptation to answer this question in a cynical vein grows stronger when one places Bradley's rationale for 'narrowness' side by side with Richard Norman's account of rational value-change. Norman describes a process whereby new modes of behavior, together with the values they embody, are made generally intelligible by plotting their position relative to the habits and value-concepts already current in a linguistic community: using the familiar concepts, in other words, to advocate unfamiliar courses of action. In giving this kind of presentation to a new 'ethic', Norman suggests, we are "*ipso facto* providing possible reasons for adhering to it—not reasons which consist in deriving it from something else which is external to the ethic, but reasons which consist simply in showing what the ethic is."[25]

This is, of course, merely a special case of the process by which individuals (notably children learning their native language) are introduced to new moral concepts: for example, "the meaning of dishonest can be explained only by indicating its position within a whole nexus of ethical concepts . . . ."[26] The mechanism discussed by Norman diverges from the basic educational procedure only in so far as it implies that moral understanding—competence with moral language—is not a static condition, but a perpetually evolving one. Yet the latent power of this mechanism must not be underrated, for Norman tells us that it promises to accomplish a dialectical transition—within the framework of a common normative language—from liberal to socialist morality.

We seem to have located a possible tension within the type of realist doctrine constructed in this book. The problem is that by encouraging the imaginative exploration of social experience, geared to discovering novel moral aspects of situations and thus achieving a more adequate grasp of moral reality, the philosopher is sowing the seeds of a critical tendency he cannot undertake to control: the tendency toward a state of affairs in which the 'moral fabric' of the community is perpetually being demolished and rebuilt. For, as Bradley observes, when people begin to consider customary forms of behavior from unfamiliar points of view, their assessment of such behavior at a more abstract level of evaluation is liable to alter also. The implications of a change of perspective may therefore be far-reaching: it may become necessary, in order to restore coherence to one's total moral outlook, to qualify or even withdraw one's previous unreflective endorsement of some existing moral institution. In this way the initial, bland-looking imaginative exercise of "trying to see different sides of the case" may open a path to the more contentious project of applying one's imagination to the construction of alternative institutions—and that project, in turn, may come to be seen as involving a radical re-ordering of the material basis of the relevant language-games.

From the point of view of those who would like to insure against this risk, it makes sense to argue that imagination should be cultivated just to the degree required for competence in a simple form of moral discourse which is, as far as possible, free from the contagion of 'recessive formulae'. Thus with regard to 'collisions of duties'— situations in which one seems to detect objective reasons for pursuing each of a number of mutually incompatible courses of action—Bradley suggests that "these are avoided mostly by each man keeping to his own immediate duties, and not trying to see from the point of view of other stations than his own."[27] This is essentially in keeping with the views of Iris Murdoch, as illustrated by the passages cited above; and in both writers it seems safe to attribute the advocacy of an 'unimaginative' morality to a politically motivated sense of unease at the direction the moral language-game might take, if allowed full scope to unfold itself dialectically.

I spoke just now of a process of demolition and reconstruction of the 'moral fabric' of the community. In this connection, it is interesting to notice that contemporary radical movements do, in fact, make extensive use of a deliberately inculcated resistance to the forces that constitute Quine's 'pull toward objectivity' in the moral and political spheres: a conscious refusal, that is, to take up one's moral position on the spot designated by society as the standpoint of the 'ideal observer'. Quine himself mentions the way in which *artists* may seek to recall to consciousness the 'cues' that cause their expressive responses to sensory input to conform to those of other people.²⁸ This willful undoing of the socializing process involves an emancipation from *objectivity*—a (partial) reversal of that earlier emancipation from *subjectivity* which endowed us with our social identity. As such, it has a place in politics as well as in art; though politics can hardly rest with the mere deconstruction of the identity we have acquired, but must show us how to construct a new one, based on a different conception of publicly observable moral reality. (Nietzsche again: "We can destroy only as creators.")²⁹

V

At an earlier stage of this discussion we were concerned to develop a certain philosophical conception of what *objectivity* amounts to in moral and political discourse. That conception was one that I tried to show to be implicit in the later writings of Wittgenstein. I believe that it is the only account of objectivity that can support a plausible, and non-mystificatory, moral realism.

In the light of such an account, we can see moral and political *conflict* as arising out of tension between the partisans of a given mode of intellectual authority (and of the institutions that form its material basis), and those who seek to replace that mode of authority by another. We can think of it as a confrontation between rival habits of thought, each regulated by its own norms, and resting upon the material forces it can call in to enforce those norms.

Our proposed account of objectivity implies that any (non-disruptive) engagement in an existing language-game displays *complicity* with the social practice, which constitutes playing that game. Where the practice in question is one that we regard as sound (one that is acceptable to us on reflection), we shall find no fault with that complicity: critical thinking will not then have the effect of placing us outside the established 'ethical substance', or *Sittlichkeit*, but will leave us at liberty to make a descent from (philosophical) description of the language-game to (practical) participation in it. It will allow us to say, in the spirit of *OC*, 281: "People in general think like this; and *I* agree with them." On the other hand, if reflection leads us to condemn existing institutions, we shall, of course, regard any kind of complicity with them as *prima facie* irrational or wrong.

Even if no one within a particular community actually possesses this philosophical conception of moral and political conflict, outside spectators (e.g. historians) can still, where appropriate, describe the experience of that community in the terms it suggests—in terms of a struggle, that is, between those forces tending toward a 'breakdown of ethical substance', and those resisting such a tendency. These processes can, and often do, take place without any articulate plan of action on either side. For example, Wittgenstein's story of the tribe that develops a new way of making lists leaves it open whether, or to what extent, the behavior that initiated this change was prompted by a reformist *theory* of list-making.[30] However, if our philosophical considerations about objectivity are consciously accepted within a given community, it follows that any members of that community who subsequently set out to realize—or carry on trying to realize— an alternative form of social life will necessarily be conscious participants in the 'breakdown of ethical substance'. Their attempt to subvert established modes of intellectual authority (the 'solid fact of a world so far moralized') will take the form of an effort to *initiate* the kind of situation that also occurs spontaneously when intellectual authority gives out: a situation in which "the rule is explained by the value, not the value by the rule" (Z, 301). Such persons will express in their actions a disdain for the constituted authority-relations—as if the latter already enjoyed only a feeble, attenuated existence—and an implicit claim that it is their actions that now specify, in concrete terms, how the relevant social practice is to be carried forward. They will use Wittgenstein's "Who says what it is reasonable to believe in *this* situation?" (*OC*, 326) as a rhetorical question rather than an innocent one (an expression of defiance rather than of disorientation).

Now the idea of a calculated assault upon *Sittlichkeit* may prompt the objection that Wittgenstein's view of language makes our very identity as rational beings contingent upon our being bound together, as a community, by a shared system of beliefs and a shared way of life. This (the objection will run) implies that the project of dismantling our customary scheme of values, whether in the practical or in the theoretical sphere, will have an inherent tendency to cut off the branch on which it sits: to leave those who undertake it in a position of disengagement from *every* social formation that wields intellectual authority. To be in this position is to have lost the power to question or criticize anything at all, for in order that any part of my total world-view may be called into doubt, it is necessary that the rest— or much of the rest—should 'stand fast': "If I want the door to turn, the hinges must stay put" (*OC*, §343).

The objection is valid in respect of an *all-embracing* skepticism: it does indeed follow from our proposed holistic notion of rationality that one cannot doubt *everything*, on pain of what we might call 'cognitive collapse'. But it is misleading, once again, in so far as it suggests that there are only two possible stances one can adopt in relation to intellectual authority (in morals or elsewhere), namely an attitude either of total defiance or of total surrender. The effect of polarizing our options in this way is, of course, to make the price of deviancy appear so high that an unreserved incorporation into *Sittlichkeit* will appear inviting by comparison. However, this Manichean picture of the relation between 'inside' and 'outside' is best understood not as a candid philosophical record of subjective experience, but rather as an opportunistic abuse of the metaphysical idea that "our life consists in our being content to accept many things" (cf. *OC*, §344). It is, in fact, a matter of experiment how much we have to 'accept'—how far our 'agreement in judgments' with other members of our community can be dismantled by critical thinking before we begin to be in danger of losing the sense of our own identity, or of ceasing to be able to occupy the position of a subject of judgment.

This is equally true of individuals and of societies. At the individual level, it is evidently a matter of intersubjective variation how many 'unshakable convictions' one needs in one's life: 'needs', that is, in the sense of not otherwise being able to find things rationally surveyable. (This seems to be the sort of thing Wittgenstein is referring to at *OC*, 616: "Would it be *unthinkable* that I should stay in the saddle however much the facts bucked?") And at the collective level, too, we accept that different communities will vary with regard to the degree of fluidity that can be accommodated within their respective world-theories (and associated practices). We do not expect to find stability and instability present in the same proportions everywhere, or a single opinion everywhere as to how much of the total theory must 'stand fast' at any given moment if judgment or meaningful inquiry is to be possible. It is up to the community concerned to decide when *anomie* has gone too far—when people's behavior has begun to 'stammer' unacceptably. It will depend on 'what they want' in the way of intellectual and moral regimentation.

The ability, or will, to 'stay in the saddle' without the support of a ponderous array of 'certainties' (beliefs that 'lie apart from the route traveled by inquiry' (*OC*, §88) might be thought of as a moral dimension of personality. This theme is developed by Nietzsche; but it also occurs in non-philosophical literature, e.g. in Strindberg's Preface to *Miss Julie* (1888), where he expresses impatience with the 'man of character' as portrayed in bourgeois fiction and drama, and admiration for the type he describes as the "skilful navigator of life's river."[31] This is the ethical analogue of the transition from a foundational to a non-foundational theory of knowledge.[32] Empiricist moral philosophy, by contrast, shows a continued emphasis on moral *principles* and on *consistency*.

The quality of being able to renounce 'certainties' gracefully is, I think, a valuable one for ourselves. We could regard it as a distinctively modern form of *asceticism*. A person who displayed this ascetic quality in his relations with *Sittlichkeit* might be said to possess the same attitude to *culture* that the modern artist, according to Paul Klee, possesses to *nature*:

> [The artist] does not attach such intense importance to natural form as do so many realist critics, because, for him, these final forms are not the real stuff of the process of natural creation. For he places more value on the powers that do the forming than on the final forms themselves.
>
> He is, perhaps unintentionally, a philosopher, and if he does not, with the optimists, hold this world to be the best of all possible worlds, nor to be so bad that it is unfit to serve as a model, yet he says:
>
> 'In its present shape it is not the only possible world.'
>
> Thus he surveys with penetrating eye the finished forms which nature places before him.
>
> The deeper he looks, the more readily he can extend his view from the present to the past, the more deeply he is impressed by the one essential image of creation itself . . . rather than by the image of nature, the finished product.
>
> Then he permits himself the thought that the process of creation can today hardly be complete and he sees the act of world creation stretching from the past to the future.[33]

VI

"Words," writes Charles Taylor in expounding Herder, "do not just refer, they are also precipitates of an activity in which the human form of consciousness comes to be."[34] For Wittgenstein, too, language is a 'precipitate' of the shared activity of a certain species of embodied creatures, and it remains only to comment on the connection between this idea and another that we touched on some time ago: that of the natural limits to our capacity for making sense of the behavior of other intelligent beings.

The later thought of Wittgenstein could be characterized, in general terms, as an *anti-ascetic* philosophy—that is, one designed to remove misunderstandings (of the kind which give rise to traditional metaphysical constructions) by compelling our recognition of the bodily aspect of language. Accordingly, the 'form of life' within which we learn language, and hence acquire rational subjectivity, must ultimately be a form of *biological* life; and the beliefs and concerns of which we need to be able to find some counterpart in any community whose behavior we hope to interpret will necessarily be the beliefs, etc. of creatures with a certain physical constitution and a certain ecological location. But from this it follows that our acceptance of the idea that the 'limits of the world', in so far as we can talk about it, are determined by the limits of "that language which alone we understand" (cf. *T* 5.62) amounts to an acknowledgement that all we shall ever be able to say about the world will be said from a point of view that is essentially that of creatures thus constituted and located. And this, in turn, amounts to an acquiescence in what we might describe as a 'transcendental parochialism': a renunciation of the (ascetically motivated) impulse to escape from the conceptual scheme to which, as creatures with a certain kind of body and environment, we are transcendentally related.

'Parochialism' is a name we commonly give to the attitude of mind found in people who are satisfied with their own ways of going on, and have no curiosity about alternatives. This attitude expresses itself, in particular, in a disdain for critical challenge; and such disdain might be said to be just what is implicit in the dogmatic statements to which we are bound to resort in the Wittgensteinian situation where 'justification comes to an end'—statements such as Z, §309, "*This* is how we think. *This* is how we act. *This* is how we talk about it."

But the dogmatism of ordinary language appears in the context of Wittgenstein's philosophy not as a vice (in the way that ordinary, empirical dogmatism counts as a vice), but rather as something benign. To try to surmount it is, in effect, to revolt against one's membership of a community for whom, despite their unique achievement in constructing the institutions of rational discourse, 'the end of giving grounds is' (nevertheless) 'an ungrounded way of acting' (*OC* §110).

It is this fact of our insertion into the natural world which insures, for Wittgenstein, that the Socratic project of essentialist definition—of formulating rules such that anyone who had mastered them could reproduce the array of naturally acquired behavior that constitutes the correct use of a word—cannot be realized without residue. Because the use of language is interwoven with our wider physical life, no explanation of a word in terms of other words— and no justification of any aspect of social practice in terms of *reasons*, the offering and accepting of which is itself a social practice—could be successful if it were not for the fact that life encompasses the person to whom the explanation is given, as well as the one who gives it. Every such step toward representing our words and actions as part of a rational structure rests, ultimately, on an appeal to sub-linguistic consensus: "Adopt whatever model or scheme [of inter-pretation] you may," writes Wittgenstein (*BB*, 34), "it will have a bottom level, and there will be no such thing as an interpretation of that."

Compare the following anecdote from Collingwood's *Principles of Art*: "There is a story that Buddha once, at the climax of a philosophical discussion, broke into gesture-language as an Oxford philosopher may break into Greek [this was written in 1937!]: he took a flower in his hand, and looked at it; one of his disciples smiled, and the master said to him, 'You have understood me.' "[35] The present Wittgensteinian point could be expressed by saying that whenever we respond to another person's demand for something we do or say to be made intelligible to him, the exchange always ends—if it ends successfully—with an event analogous to the smile of *tacit* understanding in the Buddha story; though whether such an 'event' has, in fact, taken place, we shall ultimately judge by what the person in question *goes on to do* (cf. *PI* I, §180, and context).

Holding these considerations in reserve, however, something must now be said to redress the balance of emphasis as regards the 'dogmatic' theme in Wittgenstein's philosophy. What needs to be stressed is this: the fact that Wittgenstein identifies a form of dog-matism, or parochialism that is 'benign' (in the sense indicated above) does not mean that his conception of language cannot also accom-modate the more familiar idea of a *harmful* dogmatism. That con-ception, which claims to make our ordinary linguistic practice immune to philosophical criticism, must also place beyond criticism the habit of thought within which 'dogmatism' features as the name of some-thing bad—an undesirable quality whose incidence we record in the course of our (non-philosophical) thinking about human mental life. This quality might be labelled 'empirical dogmatism' (or 'empirical parochialism'), in contrast with the 'transcendental parochialism' to which, as I have suggested, Wittgenstein's reflections on language are meant to reconcile us.

The expressivist notion of rationality as grounded in a common form of life does nothing to commend any specific *policy* toward groups or individuals whose practices diverge from our own. That notion cannot, therefore, offer any justification for an attitude of hostility or contempt toward "what lies beyond our horizon," as Nietzsche puts it.[36] In so far as our expressivist considerations issue in the idea of a benign form of dogmatism, they relate not to the *historical* but to the *natural* 'limits of our language'. They are not concerned with the kind of intellectual limitation that can be imputed to an attitude or a policy—something we could change—but with the way in which our powers of 'making sense' are constrained, regardless of our own good or bad faith as interpreters, by our physical constitution and conditions of life. Accordingly, they do not supply any defense of the (empirical) dogmatism that may lead us, as mainstream exponents of a given language-game, to withhold participant status from any person in respect of that game. For this withholding will be an *act*, and as such will have a moral dimension; which means that philosophy, on the present view of that activity, cannot pronounce on it.

'Transcendental parochialism', as I have characterized it, is not an attitude or a policy—except in the purely negative sense that it consists in declining the attempt to transcend the human perspective. It is this attempt that Wittgenstein's philosophy is intended to discredit. For example, when we read (*BB*, 28) that "ordinary language is all right," the contrast is with a perfect language as conceived by certain formal logicians, free from vagueness of sense, etc.; in denying that we need such a language, Wittgenstein should not be taken to suggest that ordinary language (and the life in which it is grounded) is 'all right' as it happens, historically, to be, and that it would be a mistake to try to change anything. Wittgenstein in his capacity as a philosopher of language would not have presumed to offer an answer to this question.

I wish to suggest that it is the failure to distinguish empirical from transcendental parochialism that accounts for the proneness of holistic conceptions of rationality to distortion. The distortion I have in mind involves an appeal to the holistic ideas to sanction a specific practical policy—that of the moral conservative, whose notion of morality is largely or entirely *sittlich* in content and who consequently regards any deviation from established patterns of conduct as 'the very essence of immorality and pregnant with disaster'. This improper application of a doctrine that is neither ethical nor political, but metaphysical (in the wholesome sense of being about the relation of language to the world), results from omitting to *anchor* the dogmatism that follows upon the 'end of justification'. It results from allowing that dogmatism to float freely, so to speak, and to attach itself at random to any arbitrary historical configuration of social practices; whereas, by bringing it into connection with the embodied nature of speakers, we can insulate it from tendentious claims of philosophical authority for the specific corpus of moral institutions that happens to have been arrived at.[37]

The physicalist tendency of Wittgenstein's philosophy demands to be appreciated, for the powerful reason that if we slide over it carelessly we may thereby come to see Wittgenstein as a purveyor of the kind of activist doctrine that is essentially anti-rational, chauvinistic and violent in character. What we must understand, in order to avoid such an error, is that 'justification comes to an end' for Wittgenstein not because we get bored with it, but because rational discourse unfolds within a setting not chosen by ourselves. The steady perception of this fact could perhaps be equated with the condition described by Wittgenstein in the *Notebooks* (8 July 1916) as one of being "in agreement with the world," or "in agreement with that alien will on which I appear dependent"—the condition which is the goal of ethics, in so far as "ethics is transcendental" (*T* 6.421).

Failure to anchor the idea of legitimate, or benign, dogmatism to that of embodiment encourages a reading of Wittgenstein that would echo these words of the narrator in Anita Loos' book, *Gentlemen Prefer Blondes:* "I always think a lot of talk is depressing and worries your brains with things you never even think of when you are busy";[38] or, again, this passage in a speech by Margaret Thatcher to the Foreign Policy Association, New York: "Self-questioning is essential to the health of any society, but we have perhaps carried it too far . . . . The time has come when the West—and above all Europe and the US—must begin to substitute action for introspection. . . ."[39] That is to say, it can make Wittgenstein seem to lend his authority to a glorification of action at the expense of thought. But that is not what Wittgenstein has in mind when he says that "it is our acting which lies at the bottom of the language-game" (*OC,* §204). What he rejects is, rather, the kind of pseudo-thought typified by bad (transcendent) metaphysics, where language is 'like an engine idling'; and he rejects that kind of exercise in favor of *genuine* thought, which, as he conceives it, may belong to one of two kinds: it may refer to external reality (in which case the machine of language is performing its primary function), or else it may refer to *itself*—as in philosophy, the language-game which takes other language-games as its subject-matter, and which I compared to the action a machine would perform (if such a thing were possible) in servicing itself. What distinguishes these two legitimate uses of language, as recognized by Wittgenstein, from its illegitimate use is that in the former, but not in the latter, the machine is *doing something*: either its routine tasks, or a maintenance operation whose aim is to improve the machine's performance of those tasks.

It is not a consequence of Wittgenstein's views that in any particular case we are wrong to try to provide ourselves with an explicit account of our behavior as a community—whether that behavior relates to the use of a particular word (as in dictionary definition), or to the general conduct of our lives (as in the case of moral rules or principles). The mistake consists only in idealizing the results of this work—that is, in supposing that they encapsulate a kind of knowledge that could be possessed quite independently of our insertion into a material world. Thus the Socratic impulse to render articulate our grasp of abstract concepts, and to discourage reliance on a residue of sub-linguistic (i.e. purely practical) understanding, should not necessarily be seen as a symptom of the ascetic error discussed above. It may, rather, reflect legitimate resistance to the idea of a wholly *sittlich*, and therefore wholly static, relation between ourselves and the language-games we play. For the (reasoned) pursuit of change demands that we *intervene*, from time to time, in the practice that constitutes the approved use of certain sensitive terms: in particular, the 'essentially contested concepts' of moral and political discourse. Such change is one of the 'particular practical purposes' (cf. *PI* I, §132) that may motivate an attempt to draw artificially sharp boundaries (cf. *BB*, 19) around the concepts in question, and so to privilege a specific subset of the established uses of a word as against the rest; for our success in abolishing the unwelcome uses would imply success, also, in modifying the life of the community at large in accordance with our desires.[40]

It is perhaps worth observing that on the proposed expressivist account of language, the goal of our attempts to transcend *empirical* parochialism will actually be identified as a condition in which the boundaries of our conceptual scheme will have been pushed back, through critical reflection, to a *transcendental* limit. This point may be understood in the following way.

Our Wittgensteinian considerations clearly imply that the idea of a partial, or capricious, viewpoint makes sense only in relation to that of a universal, or public, viewpoint which belongs to some specific totality of persons. Thus, in the case of moral judgment, they imply that we cannot meaningfully speak of 'moral blindness' except in relation to the 'normal' moral vision of some historically existing community. If we consider a given local world-picture without reference to some wider one that transcends it, there will be no more scope for calling the picture 'parochial' than there is, according to Wittgenstein, for imagining the social practice of a community of mental defectives 'under the aspect of disorder' (Z §372): a succession of 'viewpoints', each arrived at by transcending the local peculiarities of the one before, should be seen as constituting a 'scale of forms' in which each level of understanding, until we go beyond it, represents the culmination of the series.

But now, it is important to notice that this thought can be counterposed: as long as we can form the concrete conception of a less arbitrary description of the world—as long as we can find other rational persons or communities, by reference to whose world-view new symptoms of (empirical) parochialism in our own world-view can be identified—there will still be ground to cover in order to emancipate ourselves from such parochialism. Only when we have exhausted the supply of dialectical material may we follow the Quinean course of 'acquiescing in our mother tongue and taking its words at face value'. For practical purposes, this means—in the words of a Marxist writer whose thought characteristically incorporates the Enlightenment ideal of a cosmopolitan rationality—that "Man knows objectively in so far as knowledge is real for the whole human race *historically* unified in a single unified cultural system. . . . There exists therefore a struggle for objectivity (to free oneself from partial and fallacious ideologies) and this struggle is the same as the struggle for the cultural unification of the human race."[41]

Acceptance of an expressivist view of language commits us, then, to interpret the idea of an "absolute conception of reality"[42] not in transcendent, but in immanent terms—not as a conception of reality from which all traces of human perspective would be excluded, but as one in which the individual or local perspectives of all human beings would be able to find harmonious expression. To arrive at an 'absolute conception of reality' in this immanent sense would be to attain to an intellectual condition in which the only form of parochialism of which we could be convicted would be the benign, transcendental kind. And the practical counterpart of that condition would be a form of life which was in agreement, as the Hegelian idiom would have it, with "universal reason."[43]

NOTES

1. The following abbreviations to works of Ludwig Wittgenstein apply:
BB: Blue and Brown Books
CV: Culture and Value
OC: On Certainty
PI: Philosophical Investigations
RFM: Remarks on the Foundations of Mathematics
T: Tractatus Logico-Philosophicus
Z: Zettel

2. Perhaps the force of the word 'serious' here can best be conveyed by way of an elaboration of the 'game' metaphor. Thus, a group of children playing may turn out on inspection to contain a hard core (the older children, say) whose moves are acknowledged as making a difference to the course of the game, while the younger ones run about on the fringes, imitating the others and calling out to them, but largely ignored by the core group. The members of this core group are the 'serious' players, in the sense I have in mind; the others, not.

3. Cf. Hobbes, Leviathan, 161: "I put for a generall inclination of all mankind, a perpetual and restlesse desire of power after power, that ceaseth only in Death."

4. P. F. Strawson, "Freedom and Resentment," in Freedom and Resentment and Other Essays (1974), 9. Strawson's position in this essay, of course, owes as much to Hume as to Kant, for his 'reactive attitudes' are directly descended from Hume's moral sentiments"

5. Cf. Patrick Devlin, The Enforcement of Morals (1965), 90: "Naturally he [the law-maker] will assume that the morals of his society are good and true; if he does not, he should not be playing an active part in government."

6. Nietzsche, The Gay Science, §355. Cf. John McDowell, 'Physicalism and Primitive Denotation: Field on Tarski', in Platts (ed.), Reference, Truth and Reality, (1979), 125–6: McDowell describes natural-scientific explanation as "a kind [of explanation] in which events are displayed as unsurprising because of the way the world works", while "intentional explanation makes an action unsurprising . . . as something which the agent can be understood to have seen some point in going in for" (emphasis added).

7. Platts (Ways of Meaning, 248) makes a bold (or maniacal?) claim for the primacy of this type of response: "The 'simple fact' of differences of moral judgement does not yet imply the falsity of moral realism. In moral

judgements, as in others, people can, and do, make mistakes. What realism requires is that their errors be *explicable*—in realistic terms."

8. Cf. R. G. Collingwood's reference to the "liberals, such as John Stuart Mill, who argued that people ought to be allowed to think whatever they liked because it didn't really matter what they thought" (*An Autobiography* (1939), 152).

9. Cf. *The Swissmakers (Die Schweizermacher)*, a recent film directed by Rolf Lyssy.

10. Bradley, *Ethical Studies*, 188.

11. Taylor, *Hegel and Modern Society*, 177.

12. Originally the title of an essay by E. P. Thompson (1961), reprinted in *Writing by Candlelight* (1980).

13. For a simple illustration of this tendency, cf. the following paragraph from *Radio Times* (10–16 May 1980), 39: "Defence has always been a world where decisions are taken in the darkest corridors of power. Public debate has been of little consequence. Any protest movement has invariably been tarnished with a fringe or leftish label. Yet today, in East Anglia, small groups of ordinary people are demanding the right to discuss openly just what military planning might mean for our future . . ."
The structural oposition between ordinary and leftish here makes at least as significant a contribution to the total meaning of the paragraph as the explicit statement that ordinary people as well as lefties are now concerned about the problem under discussion.

14. Bradley, *Ethical Studies*, p. 180 (emphasis added).

15. Kolnai, *Ethics, Value and Reality*, p. 162 (emphasis added).

16. Murdoch, *The Sovereignty of Good*, 52.

17. The concept of the 'outsider' has also, of course, had a large part to play within philosophy itself, especially in the existentialist tradition. To look no further afield, however, cf. Nietzsche on 'homelessness'; also Wittgenstein, Z 455, 'The philosopher is not a citizen of any community of ideas. That is what makes him into a philosopher.'

18. CV p. 60: "Who knows the laws according to which society develops? I am quite sure they are a closed book even to the cleverest of men. If you fight, you fight. If you hope, you hope."

19. Wittgenstein's philosophy has attracted a good deal of ill-judged criticism on this score. Thus Roger Trigg writes (in *Reason and Commitment* (1973). 72): 'Neither Wittgenstein nor any of those influenced by him have given any clear indication of how a form of life is to be identified . . . It [sc. the idea of a form of life] can only be confusing if applied to the area

of contemporary religion and morality in order to explain the fundamental disagreements which undoubtedly exist. We have only to ask whether religion, Christianity or a particular Christian denomination such as Catholicism should be regarded as a form of life. There is no clear way of answering such a question . . .'

There is also no *need* to answer it, for the attack is misdirected. The concept of a 'form of life' is no more suited to feature in *explanations* of the phenomenon of moral disagreement than e.g. that of 'sameness of sense' is suited to feature in *explanations* of the fact of inter-substitutability in opaque contexts (cf. McDowell, 'On the Sense and Reference of a Proper Name', 157). The urge to give epistemic priority to the first term in each pair is, a symptom of the 'disease of wanting to explain'.

20. Murdoch, *The Sovereignty of Good*, p. 40: 'As moral agents we have to try to see justly, to overcome prejudice, to avoid temptation, to control and curb imagination, to direct reflection.'

21. Ibid., 91.

22. Ibid., 74, 53, 73.

23. Bradley, *Ethical Studies*, 197n.

24. Ibid., 183.

25. Norman, *Reasons for Actions*, 170.

26. Ibid., 70. The same method of moral education, incidentally, is commended by Platts, who says that 'the procedure for understanding another's moral view is that of leaving oneself open to his efforts to draw our attention to the (distinctive) features [sc. of situations] he claims to detect'; also that 'discussion with others, like self-reflection, may prompt the attention that is needed, both to focus upon particular moral aspects of a given case that would otherwise have been overlooked and to see instantiations of novel moral concepts of which we previously had no grasp.' (*Ways of Meaning*, 251, 252)

27. Bradley, *Ethical Studies*, 198 n. 5.

28. Quine, *Word and Object*, 7–8.

29. Nietzsche, *The Gay Science*, 58.

30. Frazer's story about the King of Eyeo is equally opaque in this respect. Did *he* see himself as striking a historic blow against the tyranny of custom?

31. "The word 'character' has, over the years, frequently changed its meaning. Originally it meant the dominant feature in a person's psyche, and was synonymous with temperament. Then it became the middle-class euphemism for an automaton; so that an individual who had stopped devel-

oping, or who had molded himself to a fixed role in life—in other words, stopped growing—came to be called a 'character'—whereas the man who goes on developing, the skillful navigator of life's river, who does not sail with a fixed sheet but rides before the wind to luff again, was stigmatized as 'characterless' (in, of course, a derogatory sense) because he was too difficult to catch, classify and keep tabs on." (Strindberg, *The Father, Miss Julie and The Ghost Sonata*, trs. Michael Meyer (1976), 94)

32. It might be argued that the effect of that transition is merely to allow an older insight to rise to the surface. Cf. N. Machiavelli, *The Prince*, trs. W. K. Marriott (1908), ch. 25: "I believe also that he will be successful who directs his actions according to the spirit of the times, and that he whose actions do not accord with the times will not be successful . . . I conclude therefore that, fortune being changeful and mankind steadfast in their ways, so long as the two are in agreement men are successful, but unsuccessful when they fall out. For my part I consider that it is better to be adventurous than cautious . . ." (Why? ". . . because fortune is a woman, and if you wish to keep her under it is necessary to beat and ill-use her," etc.)

Machiavelli, as we know, was ahead of his time. It has been left to the writers of a much later period to "dismantle the edifice of our pride" (cf. Wittgenstein, CV, 26) in the matter of moral subjectivity.

33. Paul Klee, *On Modern Art* (1924), trs. Paul Findlay (1948) (1979 edn), 45.

34. Taylor, *Hegel*, 19.

35. Collingwood, *The Principles of Art*, 243.

36. Nietzsche, *The Gay Science*, §373: "Above all, one should not wish to divest existence of its *rich ambiguity*: that is a dictate of good taste, gentlemen, the taste of reverence for everything that lies beyond your horizon." It is this 'dictate' that informs Wittgenstein's words at OC, 645: "I can't be making a mistake,—but some day, rightly [N.B.] or wrongly, I may think I realize that I was not competent to judge."

37. I commend this thought to the attention of anyone who is inclined to believe in a link between repressive forms of sexuality and authoritarian politics—an idea, incidentally, which has long been familiar to conservatives, though the language in which they express it is sometimes a little quaint: thus Devlin, *The Enforcement of Morals*, 111: "A nation of debauchees would not in 1940 have responded satisfactorily to Winston Churchill's call to blood and toil and sweat and tears."

With reference to Wittgenstein, these remarks as always are by way of philosophical, not psychological commentary.

38. Anita Loos, *Gentlemen Prefer Blondes* (1925; Picador, 1974, 36).

39. *The Guardian* (19 December 1979). She went on to explain that 'action' means "modernizing our defences."

40. Thus we see that there is something true in Stevenson's theory of 'persuasive definitions' (cf. his paper of that name in *Mind* (1938), reprinted in *Facts and Values*, 32).

41. From Gramsci, *Prison Notebooks*, quoted in Alex Callinicos, *Althusser's Marxism* (1976), 24. See, however, above for the distinction between reductive and non-reductive conceptions of the linkage between truth, or objectivity, and consensus. I have tried to show that Wittgenstein's account of this linkage is of a non-reductive character.

42. For the transcendent interpretation, cf. Bernard Williams, *Descartes*, pp. 240ff. Here the 'absolute conception of reality', which Williams plausibly regards as "something presupposed by the possibility of knowledge," is introduced to us by way of a highly contentious process of extrapolation. The familiar and indispensable opposition of *being* and *seeming*, Williams points out, implies a contrast between "the world as it really is" and "the world as it seems to any observer in virtue of that observer's peculiarities." This contrast yields the thought that there can be "a conception of reality corrected for the special situation or other peculiarity of various observers." But now, by the ever more rigorous application of this notion of 'correction', we arrive at the idea of a conception of the world "as it is independently of the peculiarities of any observers": a conception, says Williams, "which, if we are not idealists, we need" (and an idealist, he warns, is "something that there is reason not to be").

According to this interpretation, then, the special characteristic of predicates that can feature in the 'absolute description of reality' is supposed to be their freedom from human-relativity. On the deeper values implicit in this ideal, compare Williams: "The Platonic presupposition that it is as pure rational intelligences that men have their real worth and purpose, and that although we find ourselves with bodies, we must recognize that fact as a limitation . . . is highly characteristic of Descartes's metaphysics . . ."

43. Cf. Taylor, *Hegel and Modern Society*, 92, 124.

Rationalistic Moral Theory Pro and Con: A Guide to Recent Literature

The literature for and against moral theory is rich but scattered and still inchoate. This essay organizes important parts of it according to the structure of the introduction. Quentin Skinner gives a shorter and broader review of many of the same issues in his introduction to *The Return of Grand Theory in the Human Sciences* (Cambridge: Cambridge University Press, 1985)—without, however, distinguishing theorists from grand anti-theorists. The present account is also narrower in limiting itself mainly to the literature of what is still called "analytic philosophy." Were it not so tightly focussed the list of anti-theorists could be extended with the names of Continental philosophers like Hans-Georg Gadamer, the list of theorists (albeit with qualifications) with Jürgen Habermas. Some of their representative works are cited at appropriate places below, along with references to examples of their Continental allies.

In addition to the anti-theoretical works reprinted here, important contributions include Alasdair MacIntyre's *After Virtue: A Study in Moral Theory* (Notre Dame, Indiana: University of Notre Dame Press, 2nd ed., 1984); Richard Rorty's *The Consequences of Pragmatism* (Minneapolis: University of Minnesota Press, 1982); Michael Sandel's *Liberalism and the Limits of Justice* (Cambridge: Cambridge University Press, 1982); Jeffrey L. Stout's *Ethics After Babel* (Boston: Beacon Press, 1988); and Michael Walzer's *Spheres of Justice: A Defense of Pluralism and Equality* (New York: Basic Books, 1983). MacIntyre has also edited a series of volumes with Stanley Hauerwas called *Revisions* (Notre Dame: University of Notre Dame Press). His introduction to Volume 3 (1983), "Moral Philosophy, What Next?," is especially useful. Among other shorter discussions, an outstanding piece is Cora Diamond's "Anything but Argument?" *Philosophical Investigations*, 5 (1982), 23-41.

Contemporary theoretical accounts include the utilitarianism of Richard Brandt's *A Theory of the Right and the Good* (Oxford: Clarendon Press, 1979); David Gauthier's contractarian assimilation of morality to advantage in *Morals by Agreement* (Oxford: Clarendon Press, 1986); Alan Gewirth's attempt to tie obligation to an inherent normative structure of agency in *Reason and Morality* (Chicago: University of Chicago Press, 1978); Thomas Nagel's Kantian inference of rational conditions on desire and action from the reality of other persons in *The Possibility of Altruism* (Oxford: Clarendon Press, 1970); R. M. Hare's derivation of a Kantian utilitarianism from the logical properties of moral words in *Freedom and Reason* (Oxford: Clarendon Press, 1963). J. L. Mackie's negative theory is developed in *Ethics: Inventing Right and Wrong* (Harmondsworth: Penguin, 1977).

If John Rawls is to be included in the company of theorists, it is because his *Theory of Justice* (Cambridge, Mass.: Harvard University Press, 1971) appears to claim that all rational persons will be led to the same principles of political judgment. The articulations of his views since then, however, are impressive testimony to the difficulties inherent in moral theory. Similar development from relatively abstract rationalism to increasing hermeneutical sensibility is evident in a succession of books from Ronald Dworkin: *Taking Rights Seriously, A Matter of Principle*, and *Laws's Empire* (all from Harvard in 1977, 1985, and 1986 respectively). In both Rawls and Dworkin, rationalistic stress upon principles has come to be moderated by claims made for customary judgments. Even Hare, in *Moral Thinking* (Oxford: Clarendon Press, 1981), has shifted in this direction, but he is properly included among the theorists because his influence lies there and because he was not among the initiators of the practice-view.

The relationship of moral principles to particular moral judgments defines one of the major issues before us. It was deeply questioned in a paper by W.S. Pritchard, "Does Moral Philosophy Rest On a Mistake?," *Mind*, 21 (1912); reprinted in his *Moral Obligation* (Oxford: Clarendon Press, 1949). A similar position is strongly asserted in Jonathan Dancy's, "Ethical Particularism and Morally Relevant Properties," *Mind*, 92 (1983), 530–547, which is "about the non-existence of moral principles. Its conclusion is a thorough particularism, according to which our ethical decisions are made case by case, without the comforting support or awkward demands of moral principles." A slightly more accommodating position is stated by Oakeshott, in *Rationalism in Politics*, p. 105, where he says we will always find principles but insists they are "merely abridgments" of the coherence exhibited by approvals and disapprovals. Hampshire goes much further in *Morality and Conflict*, p. 136, distinguishing two levels of morality, one defined by principles of justice and utility, the other defined by customs. However, he never ceases to stress "the particularity of the particular case," p. 8. So too does Nussbaum in "Flawed Crystals: James's *The Golden Bowl* and Literature as Moral Philosophy," *New Literary History*, 15 (1983), 25–50. This number of the journal is devoted to "Literature and/as Moral Philosophy" and contains several other articles of interest—including replies to Nussbaum and her reply to them. For a recent response to particularism, see Alan Gewirth, "Ethical Universalism and Particularism," *The Journal of Philosophy*, 85 (1988), 283–302.

The primacy of practices over principles is argued by D. Z. Phillips and H. O. Mounce in *Moral Practices* (London: Routledge & Kegan Paul, 1969). As Baier suggests in her contribution, similar issues are an emerging focus of controversy in "applied philosophy." See, for example, Barry Hoffmaster's argument for considering cases rather than applying principles, "Philosophical Ethics and Practical Ethics: Never the Twain Shall Meet," in *The Nature of Clinical Ethics*, ed. B. Hoffmaster, B. Freedman, and G. Fraser (Clifton, N.J.: Humana Press, 1988). This article makes extensive use of Noble's "Normative Ethical Theories." For related themes in literary criticism and legal philosophy see Stanley Fish's articles, "Consequences," in W.J.T. Mitchell, *Against Theory: Literary Studies and the New Pragmatism* (Chicago: University of Chicago Press, 1985), and "Dennis Martinez and the Uses of Theory," *Yale Law Journal*, 96 (1987), 1773–1800.

CONCEPTIONS OF MORAL THEORY

Williams characterizes the form of moral theory opposed by all of the works in this book in Chapter 5 of *Ethics and the Limits of Philosophy*. A succinct description of his target appears in the Preface to *Moral Luck: Philosophical Papers 1973–1980* (Cambridge: Cambridge University Press, 1981). His two characterizations of theory are not quite equivalent, a reflection of the still-developing formation of the anti-theoretical viewpoint and the diffuseness of the object of its criticism. Some of the important issues are interestingly discussed in Charles E. Larmore's *Patterns of Moral Complexity* (Cambridge: Cambridge University Press, 1987), which criticizes "Kantianism and utilitarianism" for "seeking a fully explicit decision procedure for settling moral questions" (ix).

A coherentist conception of moral theory is articulated in Nussbaum's *The Fragility of Goodness. Luck and Ethics in Greek Tragedy and Philosophy* (Cambridge: Cambridge University Press, 1986), pp. 10–11. She views this work as an articulation of Aristotelian "ethical theory" (p. 10), while Baier, in her contribution to this volume, insists that there is no "normative theory" in Aristotle (232). The points are consistent if a "moral theory" is any set of systematic claims about moral matters, whereas a "normative theory" claims the existence of rational standards capable of resolving moral questions definitively. MacIntyre also develops "something like" an Aristotelian account in *After Virtue.*

Some additional difficulties surrounding use of the word "theory" are evident in the development of Rawls's account of justice. As stated in *A Theory of Justice,* his views appear to represent a clear statement of the contractualism rejected by Williams. In more recent writings, however, Rawls appears to be increasingly inclined to interpret his view ethnocentrically. The tendency is especially evident in "Kantian Constructivism in Moral Philosophy: The Dewey Lectures 1980," *The Journal of Philosophy,* 77 (1980), and in "Justice as Fairness: Political not Metaphysical," *Philosophy and Public Affairs,* 14 (1985). It is easy to see this move as a natural development of the method of "reflective equilibrium" employed in *A Theory of Justice.* This method can be described in the words Nussbaum uses in her coherentist account, but it does not fit together easily with the rationalistic strains in Rawls's theory.

BASIC ARGUMENTS AGAINST RATIONALIST MORAL THEORY

The best contemporary statement of the rationalist view of moral language may still be Hare's *The Language of Morals* (Oxford: Clarendon Press, 1951). An effective attack on this conception was initiated by Philippa Foot in a series of articles, including "Moral Arguments," *Mind,* 67 (1958), and "Moral Beliefs," *Proceedings of the Aristotelian Society,* 59 (1958–59). Both articles are reprinted in her *Virtues and Vices* (Berkeley: University of California Press, 1978). Some similar views are developed by Iris Murdoch, *The Sovereignty of Good* (New York: Schocken Books, 1970). Another seminal critique of deontologial and consequentialist conceptions of morality was made by G.E.M. Anscombe, "Modern Moral Philosophy," *Philosophy,* 33 (1958). This article is reprinted in *Ethics, Religion and Politics,* volume 3 of her *Collected Papers* (Minneapolis: University of Minnesota Press 1981). A more recent treatment of related themes, discussed below in connection with "affective perception," is given in Nussbaum's *Fragility of Goodness.*

It may not be an accident that so many anti-theorists are women. A debate occurring in the literature of moral development suggests why this should be so. Lawrence Kohlberg clearly articulates Hare's view in "From Is to Ought: How to Commit the Naturalistic Fallacy and Get Away with It in the Study of Moral Philosophy," and other articles in his *Philosophy of Moral Development*, Vol. 1 of *Essays on Moral Development* (New York: Harper & Row, 1981). His claims include the assertion that from the psychologist's point of view the problem about virtues is that there aren't any. Carol Gilligan's *In Another Voice* (Cambridge, Mass.: Harvard University Press, 1982) replies by arguing that men and women perceive the moral domain in different ways and stressing the role of the virtues of personal relationships in a conception of morality more common among women. Gilligan's perspective is feminist, and feminist literature is a rich source of commentary on the inadequacies of supposedly male-oriented, rationalistic conceptions of morality. In this connection see Annette Baier's, "What Do Women Want in a Moral Theory?," *Nous*, 19 (1985), 53–63.

Many of the properties that differentiate virtues from principles are described in a number of Baier's recent articles, in particular "Theory and Reflective Practices" in *Postures of the Mind*. Some of the same themes are pursued in "Trust and Anti-trust," *Ethics*, 96 (1986) 231–60. Further reflections on the inadequacy of rationalism to virtue are found in Larmore's discussion of "the centrality of judgment" in *Patterns of Moral Complexity*. Also interesting in this connection is Ronald Beiner's *Political Judgment* (London: Methuen, 1983). The three arguments against rationalistic moral theory given in the introductory essay above are elaborated in Stanley G. Clarke, "Anti-Theory in Ethics," *American Philosophical Quarterly*, 24 (1987), 237–244.

THE HOLISTIC ALTERNATIVE TO THEORY

Quine's holistic alternative to empiricist theory was expressed in "Two Dogmas of Empiricism," *Philosophical Review*, (1951), reprinted with amendments in *From a Logical Point of View* (Cambridge, Mass.: Harvard University Press, 1953). He elaborates his views in *Word and Object* (Cambridge, Mass.: MIT Press, 1968). The project of dismantling foundationalist views of justification was also pursued by Morton White, *Towards Reunion in Philosophy* (Cambridge, Mass.: Harvard University Press, 1956), and by Nelson Goodman, *Fact, Fiction and Forecast* (Indianapolis: Bobbs-Merrill, 2nd ed., 1965). Coherentist moral theory also has correspondences to the non-formal, context-dependent views of scientific theory espoused by such writers as Thomas S. Kuhn in *The Structure of Scientific Revolutions* (Chicago: University of Chicago Press, 2nd ed., 1970), and Imre Lakatos in *The Methodology of Scientific Research Programs* (Cambridge: Cambridge University Press, 1978).

Rawls's use of the concept of reflective equilibrium as a moral expression of holistic or coherentist views was mentioned above. This moral application is developed by Norman Daniels in a series of articles including, "Wide Reflective Equilibrium and Theory Acceptance in Ethics," *The Journal of Philosophy*, 76 (1979), 256–82, and "Two Approaches to Theory Acceptance in Ethics," in D. Copp and D. Zimmerman, eds., *Morality, Reason and Truth* (Totowa, N.J.: Rowman and Allenheld, 1985). Among the criticisms of this conception resulting from tensions between the ethnocentric tendencies of reflection on existing bodies of belief and the rationalistic tendencies of contractualism are those developed in Noble's contribution to this collection. Objections are also raised by Williams in Chapter 6 of *Ethics and the Limits of Philosophy*. Rawls now appears to agree that the universalistic aspirations suggested by *A Theory of Justice* were unwarranted. The anti-theoretical position can be found in the book, but it becomes clearly stated only in "Kantian Constructivism in Moral Theory."

The scientific conception of knowledge which supports a great deal of anti-theory in ethics is developed by Williams in Chapter 8 of *Ethics and the Limits of Philosophy*, a version of which constitutes selection 3 above. Similar views are expressed by Taylor, "Understanding in Human Science," *Review of Metaphysics*, 34 (1980), 25–38. That anti-theory by no means rests exclusively on a scientistic separation of ethics from knowledge is evident from the account developed by Lovibond in *Realism and Imagination in Ethics* in the parts of the work which appear as the twelfth selection in this collection. Beginning from Wittgenstein's version of holism rather than Quine's, it ends with a form of moral realism rather than formal coherence. Wittgenstein's holism is expressed in many writings, notably *Philosophical Investigations* (Oxford: Basil Blackwell, 2nd ed., 1958) and *On Certainty* (Oxford: Basil Blackwell, 1969). See section 141 of the latter, where he observes that "light dawns gradually over the whole."

THE "EPISTEMOLOGIES" OF ANTI-THEORY

The term "epistemology" has to be used cautiously in discussions of anti-theory, since many opponents of normative theory extend their criticism to any theory of knowledge. The attack on epistemology is vigorously conducted by Rorty in *Philosophy and the Mirror of Nature* (Princeton: Princeton University Press, 1980). His conflation of scientific and moral inquiry is challenged by Williams, in the selection included here, and by Charles Taylor in "Understanding in Human Science," where he distinguishes between subject-related and absolute descriptions.

Gadamer's hermeneutical approach is also antagonistic to any conception of epistemology as a foundational inquiry aiming at subject-neutral facts capable in principle of resolving competing claims about the truth. In *Philosophical Hermeneutics* (Berkeley: University of California Press, 1976) he stresses the community of traditional expectations or historical prejudices as providing the "initial directedness of our whole ability to experience" (p. 9). His emphasis on prejudice is remarkably similar to the stress on presuppositions found in the pragmatist tradition, where, however, there is more interest in the prejudices of the species that are part of our biological makeup, the innate information-processing mechanism which appears to be partly constituted by a capacity for emotional response.

The cognitivist account of emotion is widely represented in philosophical and psychological literature. It is defended by Robert C. Solomon, *The Passions* (New York: Doubleday, 1976); William Lyons, *Emotion* (Cambridge: Cambridge University Press, 1980); R.S. Lazarus, "Thoughts on the Relations between Emotions and Cognition," in K.R. Scherer and P. Ekman, eds. *Approaches to Emotion* (Hillsdale, N.J.: Lawrence Erlbaum Associates, 1984). The contrary evidence includes arguments by Patricia Greenspan, "Emotions as Evaluations," *Pacific Philosophical Quarterly*, 62 (1981); R.B. Zajonc, "Feeling and Thinking: Preferences Need No Inferences," *American Psychologist*, 35 (1980). His experiments show that affective responses can occur without cognitive discriminations. For a wide-ranging discussion of this and other issues see Ronald de Sousa, *The Rationality of Emotion* (Cambridge, Mass.: MIT Press, 1987).

Hume's non-cognitivist account of emotion has its classical formulation in his *Treatise of Human Nature*, ed. L.A. Selby-Bigge (Oxford: Clarendon Press, 1960). Baier's appropriation of his view is developed in a number of articles, including "Master Passions," essay 17 of *Explaining Emotions* (Berkeley: University of California Press, 1980). The view of emotion as affective perception is central to Nussbaum's reading of Greek tragedy and modern fiction and to McDowell's discussion of reason and virtue. The concept has also been elaborated by us—by Simpson in *Reason over Passion: The Social Basis of Evaluation and Appraisal* (Waterloo, Ont.: Wilfrid Laurier

University Press, 1979) and by Clarke in "Emotions: Rationality without Cognitivism," *Dialogue*, 25 (1986), 663–674.

The issue of objectivity in moral judgment is developed in different ways in many recent works, including: Jonathan Lear, "Moral Objectivity," in S.C. Brown, ed., *Objectivity and Cultural Divergence* (Cambridge: Cambridge University Press, 1984); Thomas Nagel, *The View from Nowhere* (Oxford: Oxford University Press, 1986); the articles by Hare, Hurley, McDowell, and Williams in *Morality and Objectivity: A Tribute to J.L. Mackie*, ed. T. Honderich (London: Routledge & Kegan Paul, 1985); Alasdair MacIntyre, "Objectivity in Morality and Objectivity in Science," in *Morals, Science and Sociality*, ed. H.T. Engelhardt, Jr., and D. Callahan (Hastings Center, N.Y.: Institute of Social Ethics and the Life Sciences, 1978).

MORALITY WITHOUT THEORY

The anti-theorists to whom we ascribe an inherent conservatism are often called "communitarians," but this label masks some of the characteristics that deserve emphasis. For a brief critical outline of this movement one could look to Amy Gutmann, "Communitarian Critics of Liberalism," *Philosophy and Public Affairs*, 14 (1985), 308–322. Some similar views have been discussed under the headings of "moral pragmatism" and "moral contextualism"—the first by Jeffrey Stout in *Ethics after Babel*, the second by Don Herzog, *Without Foundations: Justification in Political Theory* (Ithaca: Cornell University Press, 1985). For another assertion of the conservatism of communitarianism see Joshua Cohen's review of Walzer, *Spheres of Justice, Journal of Philosophy*, 83 (1986), 457–468.

Macintyre describes the Burkean counterposition of tradition and reason in "Epistemological Crises, Dramatic Narrative and the Philosophy of Science." More general anti-philosophical tendencies of anti-theory in ethics are baldly stated by Rorty in "Postmodernist Bourgeois Liberalism," *Journal of Philosophy*, 80 (1983), 583–589. His message that intellectuals should not look to philosophy for a defense of their philosophical convictions is also stated in "From Logic to Language to Play," *Proceedings and Addresses of the American Philosophical Association*, 59 (1986), 747–753, and elaborated in "Solidarity or Objectivity?" A vigorous reply from the theoretical perspective is made by Ernest Sosa, "Serious Philosophy and Freedom of Spirit," *Journal of Philosophy*, 84 (1987), 707–726.

A number of the characteristic features of the conservative conception of morality are outlined in John Kekes's articles, "Moral

Conventionalism," *American Philosophical Quarterly*, 22 (1985), 37–46, and "Moral Intuition," *American Philosophical Quarterly*, 23 (1986), 83–93. They are also summarized in Evan Simpson, "Moral Conservatism," *Review of Politics*, 49 (1987), 29–58. Also useful in this connection are Andrew Lugg's critical survey of answers to the question, "Was Wittgenstein a Conservative Thinker?," *Southern Journal of Philosophy*, 23 (1985), 465–474; Charles Covell's *The Redefinition of Conservatism* (New York: St. Martin's Press, 1985); Roger Scruton's "The Significance of Common Culture," *Philosophy*, 54 (1979), 51–70. On internal realism see Hilary Putnam, *Reason, Truth and History* (Cambridge: Cambridge University Press, 1981), pp. 48–56.

The conception of the self that ties one's moral identity and capacity to social institutions and traditions is well articulated by MacIntyre throughout *After Virtue*; by Hampshire in Chapter 7 of *Morality and Conflict*; and by Sandel in his critique of the self conceived by deontological liberalism as "wholly without character, without moral depth," *Liberalism and the Limits of Justice*, p. 179. The limitations of social theory are strongly stated by Scruton in *The Meaning of Conservatism* (Harmondsworth: Penguin, 1980), pp. 36, 134, and explored in Charles Taylor's *Hegel* (Cambridge: Cambridge University Press, 1975), pp. 551–558. See also Dieter Misgeld, "The Limits of a Theory of Practice: How Pragmatic Can a Critical Theory Be?" in E. Simpson, ed., *Anti-Foundationalism and Practical Reasoning: Conversations between Hermeneutics and Analysis* (Edmonton: Academic Printing and Publishing, 1987).

The thesis that all goods are social goods is elaborated by Walzer in Chapter 1 of *Spheres of Justice*. The implication that goods are prior to rights and that rights have questionable support in human nature is most strongly asserted by MacIntyre in *After Virtue*, pp. 65–67. A contrary view is represented by Charles Fried, *Right and Wrong* (Cambridge, Mass.: Harvard University Press, 1978), and at least suggested by Ronald Dworkin in *Taking Rights Seriously*. MacIntyre's thesis that such philosophical defenses of rights reflect the disintegration of the self and moral concepts in modern society is criticized by J.B. Schneewind, "Moral Crisis and the History of Ethics," *Midwest Studies in Philosophy*, 8 (1983), 525-539), and by Jeffrey Stout, "Virtue among the Ruins: An Essay on MacIntyre," *Neue Zeitschrift für Systematische Theologie*, 26 (1984), 256–273. Some of the main issues are nicely developed by Cora Diamond, "Losing Your Concepts," *Ethics*, 98 (1988), 255–277, following a suggestion of Stanley Cavell in Part III of *The Claim of Reason* (Oxford: Clarendon Press, 1979).

Anti-utopian enthusiasm for moral contention is nicely stated by MacIntyre in *After Virtue*, pp. 160 and 206, and by Rorty in *Philosophy and the Mirror of Nature*, p. 377. Other good statements are found in Hampshire's *Morality and Conflict* and Walzer's *Spheres of Justice*, p. xv. Some of the logical features of inherently contestable concepts were described by W.B. Gallie, "Art as an Essentially Contested Concept," *The Philosophical Quarterly*, 6 (1956), 97–114.

REFLECTIVE PRACTICES

The validity of special obligations and the effects of Kantian and utilitarian moral theory upon them are explored by Christina Hoff Sommers, "Filial Morality," *Journal of Philosophy*, 83 (1986), 439–456. Among the conservatives who unwittingly endanger such obligations by conflating moral judgment with ideology is Roger Scruton in *The Meaning of Conservatism*. Rationalist moral philosophers who suppose that morality should exhibit the consistency of logical systems would benefit from Alfred Tarski's discussion of the inevitability of paradoxical statements in natural languages, in "The Concept of Truth in Formalized Languages," available in his *Logic, Semantics, Meta-Mathematics*, trans. J. H. Woodger (Oxford: Clarendon Press, 1956). The innocence of such statements has an obvious application to moral dilemmas.

The importance of discussion over solitary application of abstract principles in practical reasoning has been stressed by many writers. It figures in Gadamer's, *Truth and Method* (London: Sheed & Ward, 1975); in Paulo Freire, *Pedagogy of the Oppressed* (New York: Seabury Press, 1975); and in Jürgen Habermas's model of discourse leading to "generalizable interests" within communication communities in *Legitimation Crisis* (Boston: Beacon Press, 1975), pp. 107–108. In this and later works, Habermas discards the view of his predecessors in the "Frankfurt School" of critical theory that reflection and inquiry can have only negative results in modern society. See, for example, the pessimistic account of Max Horkheimer and Theodore Adorno, *Dialectic of Enlightenment* (New York: Herder and Herder, 1972).

An interpretation of the practical implications of Habermas's conception is given by Albrecht Wellmer, "Reason, Utopia, and the *Dialectic of Enlightenment*," in R. J. Bernstein, ed., *Habermas and Modernity* (Cambridge, Mass.: MIT Press, 1985). Rorty's objections to Habermas's grand theory are elaborated in the same volume in a paper called "Habermas and Lyotard on Modernity." Another critical account, useful for its observations about the criticism of ideologies, is Raymond Geuss's *The Idea of a Critical Theory* (Cambridge: Cambridge University Press, 1981). A reformulation of critical theory reflecting some of the main concerns of moral conservatism is given in Brian Fay, *Critical Social Science* (Ithaca: Cornell University Press, 1987).

There are many models of democratic institutions of discussion alternative both to Habermas and to the one sketched in the essay that begins this volume. One is suggested by Walzer in *Spheres of Justice* and *Interpretation and Social Criticism* (Cambridge, Mass.: Harvard University Press, 1987); another is described in somewhat more detail by John Burnheim, *Is Democracy Possible? The Alternative to Electoral Politics* (Berkeley: University of California Press, 1985). Still another is abstractly sketched by Roberto Mangabeira Unger, *The Critical Legal Studies Movement* (Cambridge, Mass.: Harvard University Press, 1986).

Index